Waterfront Regeneration

Waterfront regeneration and development represents a unique opportunity to spatially and visually alter cities worldwide. However, its multifaceted nature entails city-building with all its complexity, including the full range of organizations involved and how they interact. This book examines how more inclusive stakeholder involvement has been attempted in the nine cities that took part in the European Union-funded Waterfront Communities Project. It focuses on analysing the experience of creating new public realms through city-building activities. These public realms include negotiation arenas in which different discourses meet and are created – including those of planners, urban designers and architects, politicians, developers, landowners and community groups – as well as physical environments where the new city districts' public life can take place, drawing lessons for waterfront regeneration worldwide.

This book opens with an introduction to waterfront regeneration and then provides a framework for analysing and comparing waterfront redevelopments. Case study chapters highlight specific topics and issues, including landownership and control, decision-making in planning processes, the role of planners in public space planning, visions for waterfront living, citizen participation, design-based waterfront developments, a social approach to urban waterfront regeneration and successful place-making. Significant findings include the difficulty of integrating long-term 'sustainability' within plans and the realization that climate change adaptation needs to be explicitly integrated within regeneration planning. The transferable insights and ideas in this book are ideal for practising and student urban planners and designers working on developing plans for long-term sustainable waterfront regeneration anywhere in the world.

Dr Harry Smith is Senior Lecturer at the Centre for Environment and Human Settlements in the School of the Built Environment, Heriot-Watt University, Edinburgh, UK. With professional experience in architecture and urban planning in Europe, in recent years he has been involved in a number of research projects focusing on the production and management of the built environment. His research experience spans countries in Europe, Latin America and Africa.

Dr Maria Soledad Garcia Ferrari is Senior Lecturer at the School of Architecture in Edinburgh College of Art, UK. Professionally qualified in architecture and urbanism in Uruguay she has taught at Universidad de la Republica in Montevideo and worked as a research consultant for the Organization of American States on coastal growth in Latin American cities. Her main research focus is on current processes of urban development and regeneration in Europe and Latin America.

Waterfront Regeneration

Experiences in City-building

Edited by
Harry Smith and Maria Soledad Garcia Ferrari

London • New York

First published 2012
by Routledge
2 Park Square, Milton Park, Abingdon, Oxon OX14 4RN

Simultaneously published in the USA and Canada
by Routledge
711 Third Avenue, New York, NY 10017

Routledge is an imprint of the Taylor & Francis Group, an informa business

British Library Cataloguing in Publication Data
A catalogue record for this book is available from the British Library

Library of Congress Cataloging in Publication Data
Waterfront regeneration: experiences in city-building / edited by Harry Smith and Maria Soledad Garcia Ferrari.
p. cm.
Includes bibliographical references and index.
1. Waterfronts–North Sea Region–Case studies. 2. Communication in city planning–North Sea Region–Case studies. I. Smith, Harry (Harry C.) II. Garcia Ferrari, Maria Soledad. III. Title: Experiences in city-building.
NA9053.W38W36 2012
711'.42–dc23
2011034260

ISBN: 978-1-84407-673-4 (hbk)
ISBN: 978-0-203-13337-8 (ebk)

Typeset in Sabon
by Domex e-Data Pvt. Ltd. (India)

Printed and bound in Great Britain by the MPG Books Group

Contents

List of Figures and Tables

Figures

Tables

List of Contributors

Joakim Forsemalm has a PhD in ethnology and is a researcher at the Gothenburg Research Institute (GRI) at Gothenburg University, Sweden, and works as a consultant at Radar Architecture and Planning. Joakim's thesis, *Bodies, Bricks and Black Boxes* (2007), is concerned with the assembling of urban identity. Joakim conducts research on regional and local development from post-human perspectives and with ethnographic methods.

Kees Fortuin trained as a psychologist at the University of Utrecht, The Netherlands. After working as a researcher at the Verwey-Jonker Institute for 26 years, he started his own business in 2008 (Fortuin Sociale Gebiedsontwikkeling), specializing in 'social area development'. He has an interest in the interaction of social and physical development processes and, more generally, in social strategies for value creation. He has been a social supervisor in Schiedam, Zaanstad and Alkmaar. He contributes as a lecturer to the Masters in City Developer (Erasmus University, Technical University of Delft) and the Masters in Social Intervention (University of Utrecht). He is a member of the editorial board of the *Journal of Social Intervention* and of *Vitale Stad* (*Vital City*).

Derek Fraser is a senior lecturer at the School of Architecture, Edinburgh College of Art, and coordinator of the Diploma/Masters programme. He taught at the International Laboratory of Architecture and Urbanism (ILAUD) in Venice; the International Design Studio of Architecture and Urbanism (IDSAU) in ETSAB Barcelona; the IFHP Summer School, Helsinki; and the Amsterdam Academy of Architecture. Derek coordinates the staff/student exchange with the Rhode Island School of Design (RISD), USA. His teaching exchange with the Royal Danish Academy of Fine Arts in Copenhagen has helped to inform his research interests in modern Danish housing and urban design – built form typologies. He is a Fellow of the Higher Education Academy and an assessor for the UK annual Civic Trust Awards.

Maria Soledad Garcia Ferrari is a senior lecturer at the Edinburgh School of Architecture and Landscape Architecture, University of Edinburgh, UK. Professionally qualified in architecture and urbanism in Uruguay, her research focuses on current processes of urban development and regeneration in Europe and Latin America. Dr Garcia Ferrari taught in the Faculty of Architecture in Montevideo, the University of Seville, and has been invited speaker to the School of Architecture, San Pablo University, in Madrid. She is currently programme director for the BA/MA (Hons) Programme in Architecture in Edinburgh. While a research officer for the Royal Incorporation of Architects in Scotland, she worked on the development of the organization's research strategy and coordinated projects in architectural research.

Paul Jenkins is an architect and planner and has worked during the past 40 years across a wide range of built environment fields: architecture, construction, housing, planning and urban studies – in practice, policy-making, teaching/training and research. A major element of his work focuses on social and cultural issues and much of his work is in the global 'South', mainly sub-Saharan Africa, but also Brazil. His work in the 'North' (UK and Europe) includes architectural research development within academia and the profession, and research/knowledge development between these and other social partners. He currently teaches urban design and urban history.

Hans Kiib is an architect and professor in urban design at the Department of Architecture, Design and Media Technology, Aalborg University, Denmark, where he teaches and conducts research. His research is related to urban transformation and design, cultural planning, art and urbanism, and design methodology. Hans has produced a comprehensive range of articles and monographs in the field, including the following books: *Instant City@Roskilde Festival*, *Performative Urban Design*, *Architecture and Stages in the Experience City*, *Excite City.DK* and *Harbourscape*.

Freek de Meere is manager of the research group Citizenship, Safety and Social Vitality of the Verwey-Jonker Institute, The Netherlands. He specializes in the field of governance, especially on local social policies. He received his PhD in 1996 on a quantitative study on people's images of technology, risks and society at the Faculty of Social Sciences of the Erasmus University in Rotterdam. At the Vrije Universiteit in Amsterdam he was lecturer on governmental decision-making processes until 2003. His research at the Verwey-Jonker Institute is aimed at city improvement, local safety issues and civil society.

Solvejg Beyer Reigstad is an urban designer, educated at the Royal Academy of Fine Arts, School of Architecture in Copenhagen. Solvejg has worked with urban exhibitions at the Danish Centre for Architecture and was from 2007 to 2011 head of development in the Ørestad North Group, an association which worked with temporary and permanent urban projects, communication and networks in a new city district in Copenhagen. Solvejg has been centre coordinator at the Centre for Public Space Research, assisting Jan Gehl in his research, and was academic partner for Odense Municipality in the Waterfront Communities Project (Interreg IIIB). Solvejg is now working as project manager at Gehl Architects (www.gehlarchitects.dk).

Harry Smith is a senior lecturer and director of the Centre for Environment and Human Settlements at the Institute for Urban and Building Design, School of the Built Environment, Heriot-Watt University, Edinburgh, UK. With professional experience in architecture and urban planning in Europe, during recent years he has been involved in a number of research projects focusing on the production of the built environment, ranging from the relationships between state, market and civil society in urban development and housing processes to building and urban design issues, with a particular focus on participatory approaches. His research experience spans countries in Europe, Latin America and sub-Saharan Africa.

Knut Strömberg is emeritus professor in urban design and development at the Department of Architecture at Chalmers University of Technology in Gothenburg, Sweden. His research focuses on processes and tools for urban design and development. He is founder of Urban Laboratory Gothenburg, a platform for cooperation between academia, politics, business and civil society. He has been initiator and facilitator for several design and problem-structuring dialogues in the field of urban development. He has written (and cooperated in) a large number of books and articles, among them *New Urbanism and Beyond: Designing Cities for the Future* (ed T. Haas, Rizzoli, NY, 2008).

Preface

In a historical sense, waterfront regeneration as part of the rebuilding of cities is a timeless activity. The Greeks, Romans and Byzantines all engaged in harbour-building and waterfront renewal in response to changing political, economic and geological circumstances. In historic Ravenna, for example, its designation during the first century AD as a central strategic point for the Roman Imperial Fleet saw its fishing harbour regenerated into a major military port. The arrival of the Byzantines, and the city's designation as capital of the Western Roman Empire, saw the entire harbour moved to a more spacious location in the nearby town of Classe. Today, 2000 years later, Classe is landlocked by siltation of lagoons and Ravenna's harbour is miles away but still busy.

There is a significant difference, however, in current interest in waterfront regeneration, which is that the interest is now virtually global, with harbours from Baltimore to Singapore and from Hamburg to Sydney all engaged simultaneously in regeneration. This in itself is not surprising in that the challenge of waterfront regeneration is a response to processes of *globalization*. This is one of the first key themes of this valuable book, which unpacks the impact of globalization and links harbour regeneration to processes of city-building in that global context. The book argues that waterfront regeneration and development represents a unique opportunity to structurally and visually alter cities worldwide. The complexity of city-building includes the range of actors and organizations involved and how they interact, including involvement of local communities and the wider public in the city, both in the process and in benefiting from the resulting places developed.

A second theme of this book is assessment of regeneration processes within a sophisticated analytic framework which takes an *integrated* perspective on the process of place-making, recognizing that everything from decisions on strategic regional planning to decisions on detailed urban design will have a bearing on the quality of place created by regeneration. In regenerated waterfronts the nature of the *places* that have emerged – in social and cultural terms – is hotly debated. Key issues include how are these places created; who is involved in their creation; who benefits from the new waterfront; what should the state's involvement be; should all cities follow the development model based on attracting increasingly footloose investment; what is the appropriate balance between commercial and residential and between public and private space; and what makes some waterfronts more socially and culturally attractive? These are examples of the fascinating issues which the reader will confront in this book.

A third important theme is the book's linkage of *theory and practice*, a fundamental objective of modern social science. This brings us to the origin and inspiration for *Waterfront Regeneration: Experiences in City-Building*, which is in a research project called the Waterfront Communities Project (WCP), funded by the section of the European Commission focused on the North Sea. This highlights a great strength of both the project and book which is the grounding of theoretical analysis and an understanding of the value of the theoretical perspective in hard-headed practical experience of real waterfront regeneration. The WCP involved nine North Sea port cities, all engaged in physical, economic and social regeneration. In many ways the experience of these North Sea ports, many active since at least the time of the Hanseatic League, mirrors the experience of waterfront cities around the world, now or in the future. In the past, the North Sea's traditional harbours and ports were gateways to cities and towns and vibrant communities in their own right. Changes in cargo handling technology, the decline of the fishing industry and the consolidation of business in fewer larger ports have left smaller harbours with little economic activity and large amounts of disused former industrial land. Even large ports such as Hamburg find the cargo business moving away from the traditional town-side harbour. These factors have contributed to rising unemployment in traditional harbour areas and waterfront communities characterized by physical dereliction and social deprivation.

At the same time, increasing pressures on land use in the North Sea's urban areas during recent years has led many cities to rediscover their waterfronts, earmarking them for redevelopment. These areas offer potential for high-quality urban regeneration characterized by a vibrant mix of refurbished historic buildings and new developments. With new economic activity, employment and housing, and a lively mix of households, new waterfront neighbourhoods can contribute to any port city's overall development ideals.

It is not enough, however, simply to build new buildings or to refurbish old ones. Given the importance of waterfront areas, it is vital to create real communities and re-establish links between the waterfront and the wider urban fabric. This presents major challenges in planning, urban design, citizen participation and infrastructure. Regeneration therefore needs to be carried out to a clear programme to meet multiple social, economic and physical objectives within a sustainable framework. Part of the solution to the economic decline of older traditional businesses is to create new sources of employment in waterfront areas in the high-tech, knowledge-based industries of the 21st century. However, this brings with it the risk that regeneration is dominated by the interests of speculative property development, ignoring local residents' pressing need for socio-economic renewal and wider public benefit.

Another risk is superficial redevelopment aimed at providing housing for wealthy households and/or tourist facilities, while ignoring the need for the social inclusion of existing residents and neighbourhoods. This is a particular factor in areas seeing an influx of new residents from socially excluded groups, such as recent immigrant groups, and increases the need to make redevelopment socially and economically inclusive and therefore sustainable. This suggests that redevelopment must be done in a way that fosters not only quality urban design but also better citizen participation, so that citizens are part of the process rather than just the recipients of the results. Involving citizens means better decisions, better implementation and more positive attitudes to local government.

So for both the WCP and this book, the North Sea's port cities have been test beds for urban regeneration, leading-edge sustainability and quality in the built environment. A key aspect of the WCP and the knowledge base which informs this book has been practical linkage between cities and research organizations working to an 'action research' model. The first step in the process was the linkage of the lead partner, Edinburgh City Council, with its academic partner, Heriot-Watt University, with the partnership between city and research organization being mirrored in each of the nine port cities.

In the form of the action research model used here, city governments agreed a working relationship with a local research organization to undertake a collaborative effort in which groups of practitioners worked with researchers to better understand their own institutional environment and how best to tailor their responses to that environment to achieve organizational and policy objectives. In this context, cities and local research organizations work steadily to improve the quality of governance – as it unfolds. This means politicians and local government officers, citizen representatives and other players discussing their concerns over policies with the research team, thereby getting critical but constructive feedback at the time when it is most useful. It requires openness on the part of cities as well as a proactive, involved approach to research.

Action research in organizations is intended to produce direct results in terms of innovation in policy, planning and implementation. This newer approach to research can be contrasted with traditional methods of enquiry in the social sciences which require that the primary objective of research remains unaltered during the research process and that the research is neutral and dispassionate throughout the process. The action research approach, on the other hand:

- involves direct or indirect intervention by researchers in the process that they are studying, thus altering that process on an on-going basis;
- emphasizes constructive reflection on the day-to-day business of urban management and unlocks 'learning-by-doing' from that process;
- replaces the neutral observer with a multidisciplinary learning group;
- uses pluralistic evaluation characterized by concern for institutional functioning, monitoring of project implementation, subjective views of major constituent groups, and a variety of data sources brought to bear for evaluation; and
- always attempts to generate adaptable learning from urban management experiences.

This book arises from that partnership between port cities and the researcher-authors of the book's various chapters. This linkage generated real benefits in developing a knowledge base in which research organizations' systematically assessed practical experience and derived learning that can be reinterpreted in different contexts. At the end of the WCP project it was found that the academic partners in the project had generated a substantial body of academic learning – far more than could be incorporated within the final report of the project. This gave rise to the inspiration for this book, to capture that learning so that it can also inform waterfront regeneration processes around the world.

Professor Michael Carley (retired), Heriot-Watt University, Edinburgh 2011

Acknowledgements

The action-research this book draws on would not have been possible without the participation of the local authorities that took part as partners in the Waterfront Communities Project, which was funded by the European Union Interreg IIIB North Sea Programme: the Municipality of Aalborg and the Municipality of Odense in Denmark; Gateshead Council and Kingston-Upon-Hull City Council in England; TuTech Innovation GmbH (on behalf of the Free and Hanseatic City of Hamburg) in Germany; the Municipality of Schiedam in The Netherlands; Oslo City Council in Norway; City of Edinburgh Council in Scotland; and Gothenburg City Council in Sweden. This collaboration was led by the Project Management Office established by the City of Edinburgh Council, with support from Heriot-Watt University as the lead academic partner.

We would like to thank all the contributors to this book for their constructive comments on the analytical framework that is presented in Chapter 2, as well as for their engagement with this framework in their respective chapters.

We are also grateful to the School of the Built Environment at Heriot-Watt University, and to Edinburgh College of Art, for funding the editors' participation in waterfront and port city conferences in Hamburg (*The Fixity and Flow of Urban Waterfronts*, 2008) and Antwerp (*Port Cities: Make Way for the Economic Initiative*, 2011), which provided opportunities to test the ideas developed in this book with wider audiences, as well as to gather further information on current and future waterfront regeneration issues and challenges in practice.

Further thanks go to Edinburgh College of Art for funding the fieldwork that served as a basis for the research on Copenhagen's waterfront presented in Chapter 10, thus adding a further interesting experience to the case studies analysed in this book.

Finally, the ideas and cases presented in this book would not have emerged without the discussion forum generated in our academic environments and the participation, interest and enquiring minds of our students at Heriot-Watt University, Edinburgh College of Art and the University of Seville.

List of Acronyms and Abbreviations

ABP	Associated British Ports
AIVP	Association Internationale de Villes et Ports (International Association of Cities and Ports)
BID	business improvement district
CCTV	closed-circuit television
CMP	Copenhagen Malmø Port AB
CPH	Copenhagen (used in CPH City and Port Development)
EU	European Union
GHS	Gesellschaft für Hafen-und Standortentwicklung
IBA	Internationale Bauausstellung (International Building Exhibition)
ICE	Institution of Civil Engineers
IGS	International Garden Show
IT	information technology
NGO	non-governmental organization
NID	neighbourhood improvement district
NUAB	Northern Riverbank Development Corporation, Gothenburg
PPS	Project for Public Spaces
RIBA	Royal Incorporation of British Architects
TEU	twenty-foot equivalent unit
TIF	tax increment financing
UK	United Kingdom
ULG	Urban Laboratory Göteborg
URC	urban regeneration company
US	United States
WCP	Waterfront Communities Project

Part 1

Context and Key Issues for Waterfront Regeneration

1

Introduction

Sustainable Waterfront Regeneration Around the North Sea in a Global Context

Harry Smith and Maria Soledad Garcia Ferrari

The spread of waterfront regeneration since the 1960s

The phenomenon of urban waterfront regeneration and development has spread geographically since its origins in North America during the 1960s and 1970s, where initial transformations in industrial buildings, creation of public spaces and celebration of festival marketplaces in cities such as Baltimore, San Francisco and Boston provided examples of what could be achieved in waterfront areas close to the city centre that had become abandoned or rundown. Over the next few decades other cities around the world started to regenerate and develop their waterfronts, first trying to follow the models of the pioneering North American cities and later developing their own approaches. This was driven by the obsolescence and abandonment of vast industrial areas in cities which have been entering a 'post-industrial' phase, including areas of former port activity freed up by the industrialization and containerization of port activity, with waterfronts being described by Bruttomesso (2001, p.40) as 'an essential paradigm of the post-industrial city'.

Bruttomesso (2001) identifies three types of activity which waterfronts normally require:

- 'recomposition': giving a common unitary sense to the different parts, both physical and functional, of the waterfront;
- 'regeneration': revitalizing urban areas which can be of considerable size and often centrally located; and
- 'recovery': the restructuring and restoration of existing buildings and structures.

Typically, these are linked to initiatives aiming to 're-join' the city and the waterfront physically and functionally. Such responses have evolved during the four decades of waterfront development and regeneration experience. Bruttomesso (2001) identifies a 'globalization' of waterfront themes in the sense that certain 'models' of waterfront development based on successful cases have set precedents and been copied worldwide, with a concomitant international uniformization of organizational methods, spatial typologies and architectural forms.

Shaw (2001) distinguished three generations of post-industrial waterfront development, the first being the early North American experiences mentioned above which focused on creating retail and festival marketplaces. The second generation took place mostly during the 1980s and spread around the world – with examples including, again, Boston, Sydney, Toronto and Cape Town – though it was in Europe that the scaling up from the initial first generation projects was more evident, as well as the development of new organizational models based on public–private partnerships and the extensive use of private investment (Shaw, 2001). A paradigmatic European example of this generation is London Docklands, with others being Barcelona and Rotterdam. Shaw (2001) characterized the third generation as one in which the elements developed in the first two generations are accepted into the mainstream of development practice and used in a range of situations, from small to large cities. He cites Cardiff Bay, Liverpool, Salford Docks and Berlin's Wasserstadt as European examples of this generation, with Sydney, Perth, Vancouver and a large number of developments in Asia, including Shanghai, as worldwide examples.

Shaw (2001) argued that a fourth generation was emerging during the first decade of the new century. Ideas in planning and architecture, according to this author, typically go through a 30-year cycle from radical and experimental visions (first stage), through expansion and broader application of the ideas (second stage), then consolidation and standardization of the ideas (third stage), with radical review and new visions in the fourth stage (or first of a new cycle). Although Shaw could not at the time have any certainty over what would characterize the experience of this fourth generation of waterfront developments in practice, he identified the context of post-1990s worldwide economic recession as an important factor, leading to cities rethinking the use of resources. How cities throughout these four generations of waterfront developments have conceptualized the waterfront itself as a resource and how they have brought other resources to bear in their regeneration and development are key questions which help to understand both past experiences and future potential of waterfront regeneration.

Through these successive generations of waterfront regeneration, approaches to redevelopment have grown in complexity and breadth, from the focus on retail and the festival marketplace experience in the early North American examples to a greater mix of leisure and housing in later examples – a model that has been particularly developed in continental Europe (Falk, undated). This spread and evolution of waterfront regeneration have yielded a wealth of experience reflecting different contexts in different regions and in specific cities. Often, however, the products of what have been perceived to be successful models have been copied without learning from or understanding the processes involved in such cases (Falk, undated). This book addresses these questions through analysing the experience of 'fourth generation' developments in waterfront cities around the North Sea, exploring whether they provide the radical reviews and visions predicted by Shaw and looking at the links between 'globalization' (both in its widest sense and in the sense of international replication of waterfront development models) and local determinants.

A key characteristic of recent dynamics of waterfront regeneration has been the multifaceted nature of current processes, with gradual acknowledgement that in many cases it entails city-building with all its complexity. To quote Bruttomesso (2001, p.42):

> On observing the main waterfront projects in detail, it is clear that one of the essential elements is the co-presence of numerous activities which, combined in different percentages depending on the cases, give life to new "pieces" of city, sometimes marked by an interesting feature entailing complexity.

Indeed, such waterfront 'pieces of city' have often been used to test new approaches to urban development, and in some cases they have been given a larger role in re-launching the entire city of which they form part. This complexity includes not only the physical and functional realms, but also the range of actors and organizations involved and how they interact, an element which is of particular importance in the context of changing and fragmenting governance in which urban development increasingly takes place. However, while waterfront regeneration and development processes are often examples of public–private sector partnerships and of negotiations between different authorities such as municipalities and port authorities, criticism has been directed at the lack of opportunity for involving local communities and the wider public in the city, both in the process and in benefiting from the resulting places developed. Why is this so? What are the origins of the physical and institutional legacies which provide the context for waterfront regeneration? Understanding this requires taking a longer-term historical view, which explains how our cities came to have such large areas of brownfield land available around waterfronts and waterways.[1]

The development of waterfronts through the different waves of globalization

Globalization and cities

At the beginning of the 21st century, a milestone is perceived in how humans inhabit the planet in the fact that urban population has begun to outnumber rural population (United Nations, 2004). City-building is taking place at a faster rate than ever, both through the creation and expansion of new urban areas and through the restructuring and renewal of existing cities and towns, with waterfront development having a role in both types of process and being seen as an opportunity for growth in the city.

There is no generally accepted model of how fixed human settlements began, but rather various explanations among which the role of settlements as trade crossroads and/or markets is prominent (Rykwert, 2000). In the Eurasian continent, the first urban civilizations arose in river valleys, with a twofold link to water as a resource for established agriculture (the surpluses from which allowed urban 'non-productive' activities to develop) and as a means of transport for trade and travel. Later urban development connected to seas and oceans rather than river courses and used these bodies of water as resources in additional ways: as sources of food, as routes for trade and travel, as means to reach other lands for conquest and colonization and, more recently, as a leisure environment.

Such urban development connected to waterborne activities can be linked to what Robertson (2003) has described as the 'three waves of globalization'. Robertson argues that during the last 500 years there have been three periods during which technological change has facilitated a growth in global interconnectedness, from a 'Northern' point of view. During the first 'wave', from 1500 to 1800, there was worldwide expansion of Europe's mercantilism, spearheaded by Portugal and Spain during the 16th century and followed later by England, France and The Netherlands through the activities of their chartered companies, which brought together state patronage and private investor capital – an expansion that was made possible through the development of new sailing technology. The second wave was the imperialist expansion of the 19th century, led by Britain and France, but involving also other European countries, through which a worldwide trading system based on flows of raw materials and food from the colonies to the imperial powers and the export of manufactured goods by the latter was developed. The technology underpinning this phase was steam powered. Robertson (2003) identifies the third wave of globalization, in which we are now immersed, as having started in 1945 and being linked to the post-World War II world order in which financial expansion has been led by the US. This current wave has been made possible especially by the new information and communication technologies, as well as by the continued development of infrastructures and transport connections.

Castells (1996) explains that since World War II, rising internationalization in production patterns took place and emerging processes of de-industrialization and re-industrialization began to affect urban spaces. These dynamics, together with increasing mobility and exchange, characterize a new complex and dispersed form of economy, which needs centres for control of exchange and information. In parallel to these economic changes, urban reconstitution processes began to take place after World War II with the implementation of slum clearance programmes and rebuilding of the existing fabric in each affected country. During this period, and due to economic changes showing the decline of cities and urban regions as centres of production, processes of suburbanization and peri-urbanization can also be observed, producing simultaneously prosperous and declining urban regions. In addition, with the adoption of new technologies for their operation, industries such as railways, gas, electricity suppliers and port authorities began to be able to work with fewer employees and in smaller areas of land, releasing urban areas for other uses. In particular, changes in the transport industry with the use of new technologies such as containerization, larger ship sizes and the wider use of road transport left large railway marshalling yards empty (Malone, 1996).

It was not until the 1970s and 1980s, however, that these changes became more severe, with actions focused on the regeneration of urban economies and the adaptation of declining urban areas to new economic roles hosting service employment and centres for consumption (Couch et al, 2003). Essentially, during recent years, urban development shifted from being based primarily on social objectives to pursuing primarily economic objectives, and from nationally defined welfare objectives to international market competition. This focus on competition involves the redefinition of the image of the city, weaving specific place 'myths' which are created to remove the previous negative iconography associated with economic changes, such as the decline of industrial activities (Barke and Harrop, 1994), as an element of attracting new investment and socio-economic activities.

The economic restructuring of the 1970s and 1980s also generated a growth in sectoral unemployment where specific industries closed, leaving employees jobless. This had spatial and social consequences with the emergence of deprived urban areas and varying forms of social disruption – for example, crime, racism, social exclusion, poverty, etc. (Marshall, 2001). Additionally, a range of significant environmental problems emerged, such as polluted sites and air, contaminated rivers and watercourses, and abandoned and decaying historic buildings. These social, economic and environmental problems were identified by city authorities, and since the 1980s significant regeneration plans have been implemented. In this context the development of different 'mega-projects' took place in many cities in the world, and these projects are occasionally associated with specific events such as Olympic Games, world exhibitions or cultural events. Examples include the London Docklands, Barcelona's Olympic Marina, New York's Battery Park, Paris's La Defense or Sydney's Darling Harbour. The overall aim of these transformations has been the provision of a new identity for these cities away from previous industrial activities and responding to the needs of global 'place' competition (Moulaert et al, 2003).

In general, the objectives of these regeneration processes cover a wide range of issues, such as the improvement or replacement of housing stock; the provision of new amenities; the provision of public infrastructure and spaces; the improvement of transport systems; and upgrading of the general environment. While these objectives could reflect similarities with the reconstruction aims of the post-war period, there are significant differences in the processes of urban restructuring of the last 30 years. In particular, at the city level there has been an increase in the conception of urban places as spaces for *consumption* and not for *production*. Cities are currently less conceived as places where goods and services are produced for sale or transfer and more as places where people visit, eat out, take part in events and visit cultural centres (Couch et al, 2003) – especially in the global North.

Regeneration responds thus to a number of global needs, summarized as follows, which tend to be based on market interests. The first is *good connectivity*: a number of spaces that are not directly connected to the city can benefit from high speed communication routes becoming new large-scale centres for consumption (Urry, 1995). Thus, physical proximity is not a priority but good accessibility is. The second need is *image* which, according to Muxi (2004), could have two faces: *nostalgic* or *technological*. The former could be based on the restructuring of historical areas for new uses, generally commercial or leisure, which involves processes of 'commercialization of memories' (Muxi, 2004). The latter is based on hyper-technological urban developments generating intelligent iconic buildings, which are generally linked to 'star' architecture practitioners (Urry, 1995). And the third need is for *branding* and/ or *emblems*, which is the objective of the creation of theme areas such as research parks, universities, business parks or theme parks, with enough strength to generate urban concentration processes (Zukin, 1991). As a result of these three market dynamics taking place in urban spaces, it is not generally possible to find a unified conceptualization of the city as a totality; consequently, urban areas may become disconnected, with increasing social and spatial fragmentation (Soja, 2000).

Fundamentally, these dynamics of place competition show the need for generating highly competitive environments that aim to express innovation and technological progress in order to attract global capital. Waterfronts are, in this context, considered as opportunities for the city as a whole. The restructuring of these areas becomes the expression of present and future aims, and at the same time they are reconnections between the past of the city and its future through present actions (Marshall, 2001). The redevelopment of these areas generally expresses physical signs of a wealthy industrial past, the social and economic structures of which no longer exist – the physical structures often existing but no longer used. Simultaneously, these places express the emerging connections between the city and its water edge, which are conditioned by the needs and possibilities of contemporary economic and social activities. The competitive advantage of these areas and their potential to attract wealth is a key issue and needs to be expressed in the project of regeneration. Obsolete harbours are, in general, highly visible areas of the city and their redevelopment not only affects the recovered area, but most significantly can influence the image of the city as a totality by expressing new city aspirations and identities (Marshall, 2001).

Globalization and waterfronts

Returning to the first wave of globalization and focusing on the case of Europe, which was at the centre of the first two waves of 'Northern' globalization, de Vries (1984) found that the major contributors to urban growth during the 1500 to 1800 period were capital cities, port cities and cities which were both. Growth was more continuous in capital cities than in port cities, however, with the fortunes of the latter depending more on changes in world trade patterns and geopolitics. In broad terms, there was a shift in relative levels of activity from Southern to Northern Europe, and from the Mediterranean Sea to the Atlantic Ocean. Waterfronts were the focal points of social and economic life for the urban areas which grew up around them and were often also fully integrated within the urban fabric (a paradigmatic example being Amsterdam) – though in some cases this urban fabric was that of a town which was separate from the main city that later absorbed it (as, for example, in Edinburgh or Valencia).

During the second wave of globalization the rapid intensification of waterborne trade, the larger size of steam-driven shipping and the resulting volume of shipment, together with the direct connection of docks to hinterlands through rail, required the creation of massive and extensive infrastructures such as large extended docks, canals, railway depots, bridges, shipyards, etc. These large infrastructures occupied whole waterfront areas, which became specialized zones from which the public was excluded and which in many cases grew into the water through reclamation. Although these developments were strongly linked to rapid urban development and urbanization, first in Britain and then in the rest of the industrializing countries of the 19th century, they also happened in port enclaves in the colonies which were linked into the colonial world trading system.

During the third wave of globalization, technological changes such as containerization and the construction of even larger ships, as well as the move of industrial activities such as shipbuilding to newly industrializing countries, has shifted port activities further away from the core of cities to places which allowed spacious storage and handling areas on the land side and deep moorings on the waterside (Harms, 2003), usually to areas closer to open seas or to areas of land which were undeveloped. In addition, due to the worldwide market changes described above, in our post-industrial era, commercial activities of modern ports do not need direct social contact and direct proximity to their markets, which also contributes to the move of port activities to locations distant from a city's central areas.

The waterfronts which are being regenerated today are therefore generally those developed during the second wave of globalization that peaked at the end of the 19th century, and which have been rendered obsolete or unprofitable through the technological and macro-economic changes described. The redevelopment of waterfronts is not a new phenomenon, as a closer look at economic, social and technological change in more detail within the timeframe of each of these broad waves of globalization – with their linked forms of urban and waterfront development – reveals shorter cycles of development and transformation which have left as a legacy different forms of land development and built environment. For example, Harms (2003) applied Kondratieff's 'long wave' economic cycle model, together with Schumpeter's notion of technological development as an initial thrust for economic development cycles, to an analysis of the development of Hamburg from the early Industrial Revolution to the present. Harms identified five economic cycles, each linked successively to craft-produced machinery and steam engines; industrially produced steam engines; electro-motors; mass motorization and production; and microelectronics and biotechnology. Each of these created new physical infrastructures which grew in size and specialization, in the process increasingly separating port functions from the city. In Harms' current fifth cycle, containerization has finally separated port functions from the city of Hamburg, for the first time making a port area close to the city centre functionally redundant, thus releasing a large area of land for alternative development – in this case as a new urban quarter.

Thus, the structural changes brought about during the second half of the 20th century by a vast expansion of worldwide trade predicated on new markets, new forms of transport, new locations of production, new forms of capital growth, and new forms of management and political control have led to the resurgence of interest in waterfront *spaces*. However, although there are clear links between changing political economies and waterfront redevelopment, the nature of the *places* that have emerged – in social and cultural terms – has been hotly debated. Key issues include: how are these places created; who is involved in their creation; who benefits from the new waterfront; what should the state's involvement be; should all cities follow the development model based on attracting increasingly footloose investment; and what makes some waterfronts more socially and culturally attractive?

In waterfront cities around the world, these questions are being addressed (or not) within very different contexts, the nature of which is to a great extent the result of the position such cities had in the worldwide trading system that emerged and evolved during these three waves of globalization. This book looks at the response in a particular part of the world which was at the core of the first and second waves, in particular, and has remained so during the third wave of globalization – the North Sea – and examines these questions in detail.

Waterfront regeneration around the North Sea: Key features and challenges

Urban and economic development around the North Sea strongly exemplifies links between port and city development. During the late Middle Ages, the Hanseatic guilds of city merchants which emerged initially around the Baltic Sea spread to other port cities around the North Sea, establishing a strong network of trading routes based on linking mainly independent cities, as well as founding new cities (along the Baltic coast). The emergence of territorial states around the North Sea (as more widely in Western Europe) entered into conflict with this network of cities and eventually gained military and economic control of the trading routes. While Scandinavian countries did so in the Baltic, The Netherlands dominated the North Sea at the end of the Middle Ages. The Netherlands' colonial expansion during the first wave of globalization linked the North Sea into worldwide trading routes, mainly to the West Indies and South-East Asia, with English and French ports developing and engaging in these and new trade routes mainly during the second wave of globalization, linked to the Industrial Revolution. The North Sea became a world hub of international seaborne trade, with its relative share in worldwide shipping freight peaking during the post-World War II period. Discovery of North Sea oil during the 1960s spurred further growth of shipping in the region, as well as providing a new base for economic growth and related urban development which has benefited some countries and cities around the North Sea more than others. Although the share of world seaborne trade through the North Sea routes is decreasing in relative terms through the shift of the dominant global hub of trade towards the Pacific Rim, this remains one of the areas with the densest concentration of ships in the world, with three of its container ports (Rotterdam, Hamburg and Antwerp) being amongst the ten busiest in the world in terms of twenty-foot equivalent units (TEUs) in 2010.[2] The share of port activity in the economy of their related cities is, however, diminishing, with innovations such as containerization reducing the labour force required and the move of shipbuilding elsewhere. Labour forces in port cities around the North Sea have therefore relied on diversifying their areas of economic activity.

A common feature of the waterfront cities around the North Sea is that they are all located in countries which developed some form of welfare state based on social democratic systems in the post-1945 reconstruction and development period, though following different models (Scandinavian, German, Dutch, UK).[3] However, a revision of social democracy based on more neoliberal values and related policy-making has taken place over the last few decades. From the 1980s onwards, UK waterfront cities were managed in an increasingly neoliberal national policy environment, with some aspects of neoliberalism spreading later, to a lesser degree, to the countries on the southern and eastern shores of the North Sea. In these political economies, in general, local authorities have their own mechanisms to propose and approve local development. However, the role and financial support from national governments also influences the development of some waterfront areas. In summary, in socio-political terms, waterfront cities around the North Sea operate within governance systems which are still broadly based on the notion of safeguarding public interest, but in which the public sector is increasingly limited in scope for action and requiring leverage of private capital. The need for private investment and for increasing the role of local authorities to act with an entrepreneurial approach has led to the creation of 'arm's length' public companies to free decision-making from state-related bureaucratic procedures and to permit public–private partnerships to access private capital. The institutional frameworks at city level vis-à-vis waterfront regeneration vary, however, as the relationships between city and port authorities range from the situation of, for example, Hamburg, where both are in the hands of the government of Hamburg city-state (Harms, 2003), to that of Edinburgh, where the port authority is completely independent from local government.

The physical environments that such institutional frameworks must work with are predominantly the result of major infrastructural investments and urban/port expansions during the 19th and early 20th centuries. Historic trade (as well as fishing) routes were at the origins of many settlements around the North Sea, in some cases having been pivotal in defining the actual form of what is now the historic core, such as in the case of Amsterdam, where the city itself was part of the port, and its economy, based on windmills and sailing ships, to a great extent determined the city plan (de Haan, 2003). In many cities around the North Sea this resulted in the historic waterfront now being in a central location. However, the high intensity and large scale of construction of rail and dock infrastructure during the 19th century resulted in such centrally located port areas being physically separated from the inhabited city centres, a separation which was reinforced in many cases by the development of road systems during the mid 20th century. Building activity in these port areas included actual creation of new land through reclamation, as well as building a variety of infrastructures ranging from warehouses to cranes on this new or existing land, thus generating a built legacy which is both a challenge and an opportunity for regeneration and urban development. Heritage and urban identity are key aspects of these processes. In addition, rejoining the city and the waterfront is a key challenge that masterplanners and local authorities face when redeveloping these areas.

In summary, historic waterfronts in cities around the North Sea tend to be centrally located but often cut off from the city through infrastructural barriers, and can have a rich built heritage. Although some of the ports linked to these cities still have an important role in worldwide shipping, these have abandoned the more centrally located port sites, which no longer provide traditional port-related employment opportunities through traditional port activity. These areas are therefore available for development of new employment-generating activity more closely linked to the new areas of the economy which city strategies around the North Sea are pursuing, focused on the knowledge economy in a world system where production of primary, secondary and even tertiary goods has shifted (and continues to shift) elsewhere, and on the leisure society, including through tourism. This type of development is seen as being physically supported by the creation of new mixed-use quarters where living, working and leisure can be combined, often making use of built heritage to underpin tourism. City authorities are also engaging with the issue of balancing investment in economic development in these areas and addressing the equity issues being raised by increasing socio-economic disparities, which in some cases are linked to migrant populations which have settled in these waterfront cities, often from the ex-colonies that the cities' port activity thrived on during the second wave of globalization. In opening up cities to the water again, another challenge is the forms of use of outdoor spaces in a climate that is cold and wet during a considerable part of the year, and which can be extremely windy in cases where the waterfront is exposed to the open sea. In addition, environmental issues such as climate change and sea-level rise are increasingly requiring consideration.

The Waterfront Communities Project

This book is the result of a collaboration among academics who took part in the European Union-funded Waterfront Communities Project. Led by Edinburgh and involving ten partners in six countries (see Table 1.1), the project was created to examine how more inclusive involvement of the various stakeholders in the waterfront regeneration process and in the new cityscapes has been attempted in nine cities around the North Sea: Aalborg, Edinburgh, Gateshead, Göteborg, Hamburg, Hull, Odense, Oslo and Schiedam. The learning network established by these cities' local authorities, with support from local academic institutions, aimed to inspire, test and foster innovative solutions and sustainable spatial strategies for creating socially inclusive, economically productive and high-quality environments in restricted waterfront areas and their hinterlands. Recognizing the complexity of waterfront regeneration as described above, the network addressed a wide range of key themes (see Table 1.2) through an action-research approach, thus aiming to develop an integrated approach to waterfront regeneration by considering strategic planning, economic development, social participation and integration, and urban design in a coherent whole, which had long-term sustainable development as its goal.

Table 1.1 *Partners in the Waterfront Communities Project*

Country	Project partner
Denmark	City of Aalborg Council City of Odense Council
Germany	TuTech – City of Hamburg
Netherlands	City of Schiedam Council
Norway	Oslo City Council Waterfront Planning Office
Sweden	Gothenburg City Council
UK	Edinburgh City Council (lead partner) Heriot-Watt University, Edinburgh Kingston-upon-Hull City Council Gateshead and Newcastle city councils (led by Gateshead)

Table 1.2 *Waterfront Communities Project themes and lead partners*

	Themes	Lead city
Meeting strategic objectives and fostering organizational innovation	Integration of waterfront development with city and regional strategic objectives	Edinburgh
	Visioning processes as a means of developing consensus	Gothenburg
	Organizational innovation and social integration	Schiedam
	Citizen participation and governance	Hamburg
Setting standards for urban and social design quality	21st-century city living for Europe: mixed use with affordable housing	Gateshead
	Sustainable transport and the integration of waterfront in the urban fabric	Oslo
	Urban design quality and the public realm	Aalborg
	Harbour heritage and arts/culture as catalysts to redevelopment	Hamburg
	From now to then: bridging activities to maintain the physical heritage and the local economic structure	Odense

The project had the following objectives:

1   Develop a 'learning network' of participants in urban management and regeneration processes in port cities of the North Sea region, linking city governments, research partners, port managers and other stakeholders in a process of mutual learning and experimentation.
2   Develop a conceptual framework for integrating knowledge of key aspects of urban sustainable development and requirements of policy and action.

3   Bring together a database of good practice on waterfront redevelopment from around the world that would inform innovation in each partner city and in other cities in the North Sea region.[4]

4   Use action research to systematically test, monitor and evaluate good practice techniques. The database of good practice was used to select the most relevant techniques or methods for each city to apply to their own waterfront areas, in the context of the nine themes, of which partner cities decided to test one or more by applying the same methods or to test different techniques in different national and regional settings; thus the project covered a wide range of options. Each city considered strategic planning, economic development, social integration and urban design in a coherent whole. The academic partner and academic consultants helped the cities to force the pace of innovation through action research. The work done to test good practice techniques and methods was systematically monitored and evaluated throughout the course of the project.

5   Develop a best practice toolkit derived from the database of good practice, study visits and the testing carried out by the cities. The toolkit, published in March 2007, included guidelines for achieving successful waterfront areas in the context of each city's experience and focus-themes of the project. The toolkit reported on tools and methods which can be applied to the regeneration of waterfront areas. It was aimed to help project partners, developers, investors, professionals and the general public in the North Sea region and beyond to access key learning points from the Waterfront Community Project experience.[5]

The project began in April 2004 and ran until 2007, with partners leading on areas of particular interest to them and inputting information into other themes. Each partner also developed its own regional network to maximize the benefits of being involved in the project. Research activities were carried out in three main phases. Phase 1 (April to September 2004) involved setting up the project management, developing a research framework, appointing academic consultants in each partner city, and establishing a web-based communication strategy. Phase 2 (October 2004 to September 2006) was based on each city working on thematic subgroups (as above). Phase 3 (October 2006 to March 2007) focused on evaluating the final outcomes of the project and disseminating the findings through the project website and a 'toolkit' which was launched at the project's Final Symposium in March 2007 in Edinburgh. In parallel to the key activities in each phase, the project undertook a series of activities from research coordination to evaluation and dissemination of experiences. In addition, staff secondments between partner cities, study visits by partners to non-partner cities within the North Sea area and transnational meetings between project partners were organized.

The Waterfront Communities Project research generated a number of cross-cutting recommendations which drew on the various project themes. These are presented in the toolkit (Waterfront Communities Project, 2007) and cover a range of issues, including:

- the importance of developing strong but consensual views on the future direction for the city through visioning processes, as the quality of urban vision influences all aspects of waterfront regeneration;
- the need to develop long-range (30 to 40 years) sophisticated economic, social and environmental strategies in order to start making such visions operational;
- the critical nature of strong leadership by municipal and city-region authorities in order to balance commercial opportunities created by regeneration with a long-term flow of public benefits;
- the role of both leadership and organizational innovation to drive forward waterfront visions and strategies through new organizational forms within local government itself, partnerships of key stakeholders or 'special purpose vehicles';
- the achievement of social integration through participation which goes beyond 'mere consulting' and develops widespread support for challenging regeneration programmes;
- the need for public investment in integrated transport and infrastructure, seen as a key to unlocking economic and social benefits;
- landownership as a critical factor, and the mechanisms to address control over land when this is not publicly owned; and
- the potential of urban design to achieve a 'paradigm of urban complexity', creating the diversity of function and complexity of human interaction of the typical inner-city neighbourhood.

The project also resulted in recommendations about 'learning to learn', proposing the experience of the Waterfront Communities Project's action-research approach, which linked city governments and local research organizations as a powerful learning model. During the project, 'learning to learn' from both local success and failure, and from good practice around the world, was seen to have the potential to pay dividends in policy, regeneration practice changing organizational culture and job satisfaction for key players.

Learning more about waterfront regeneration

This book takes learning from the Waterfront Communities Project one step further, by providing the results of academic reflection on the above experiences. The close collaboration of academics with the project not only supported the action-research approach already described, but also made a rich vein of in-depth experience available for theoretical reflection. The focus in this book is on analysing the experience of creating new public realms through these cities' city-building activities, both as negotiation arenas where different discourses – including those of planners, urban designers and architects, politicians, developers, landowners and community groups – meet and are created, and as physical environments where the new city districts' public life can take place, drawing lessons for waterfront regeneration worldwide. Thus, its focus is on the interaction between place-making and city-building processes and resulting urban environments which support long-term social and economic sustainability. The next chapter sets out the theoretical framework that underpins this analysis.

Notes

1   Waterfront regeneration does not refer only to that taking place in coastal areas and seaports. Many examples of regeneration which are labelled as 'waterfront' are located on riverbanks, along canals, etc.

2   A widely used measure for ranking port activity is the 'twenty-foot equivalent unit' (TEU), against which containers and their number are measured (http://geography.about.com/cs/transportation/a/aa061603.htm, accessed 24 April 2011).

3   According to the Danish Royal Ministry of Foreign Affairs (2002), European countries can be divided into four welfare models: the Scandinavian; the Anglo-Saxon (liberal); the Central European (conservative) and the Southern European (subsidiary). The Scandinavian/universal model is based on the notion that benefits should be given to all citizens individually (e.g. married women have rights independent of their husbands). However, the largest share of the financial burden is still carried by the state and financed from general taxation. The Anglo-Saxon, on the contrary, is a needs-based model and benefits are given only to those in need. The Central European model is achievement-oriented based on participation in the labour market. The Southern European is also called the Catholic model and is based on other forms of contributions for social benefits beyond the state (e.g. church, family, community, etc.). This is an idealistic description of welfare models and, in practice, the concepts involved are not strictly applied.

4   This database can be accessed through the Waterfront Communities Project website and is available at www.seeit.co.uk/waterfrontcp/goodprac.cfm.

5   The toolkit can be accessed through the Waterfront Communities Project website and is available at www.waterfrontcommunitiesproject.org/toolkit.html.

2

Negotiating City-Building in Waterfront Communities Around the North Sea

An Analytical Framework

Harry Smith and Maria Soledad Garcia Ferrari

On developing an analytical framework for the study of waterfront regeneration

As explained in the previous chapter, this book builds on the experiences from a 'transnational' project which brought together urban planning and regeneration decision-makers, professionals and academics, bridging the gap between them through action-research. In the same vein, this book aims to be of use to practitioners, academics and students by putting forward an analytical framework based on an approach which believes in the necessity of analysis to understand the context in which interactions between structure and agency take place (Giddens, 1984).[1] Such understanding can aid academic investigation of specific cases, as well as students' learning; but in addition, importantly, it can aid reflection in practitioners, leading to changed action. In short, the analytical framework developed here is proposed as a tool to generate 'critical consciousness' within the field of waterfront regeneration.

In this book we apply this tool to exploring some key questions deriving from recent experiences in waterfront regeneration and development around the North Sea, connecting this to current theoretical debate. Key questions addressed are: to what extent does this experience reflect a new generation of waterfront regeneration practices? What changes in the production of the built environment underpin such practices? How do global and local processes interact in these practices? Does waterfront regeneration around the North Sea present particular characteristics which give it a distinctive identity?

What we know about waterfront regeneration

A substantial literature has emerged which documents, showcases and analyses waterfront regeneration and development processes around the world.[2] Several key books in this literature (Brutomesso, 1995; Hoyle, 1996; Malone, 1996; Marshall, 2001; Desfor et al, 2010) focus on the analysis of a range of specific cases and are based on conferences, reflecting the proliferation of such events. The stream of professional and academic conferences on waterfront regeneration and development continues, often in conference centres which are part of a waterfront regeneration project. Several organizations are key players in promoting such conferences at an international level, including Cities on Water (based in Italy), Association Internationale de Villes et Ports (AIVP, based in France) and the Waterfront Center (based in the US).

Compendiums of major international waterfront regeneration projects are provided by Breen and Rigby (1996, 1997), which include case studies from around the world organized around topics. This kind of information is increasingly available through online databases, including that developed as part of the Waterfront Communities Project.[3]

More in-depth analysis of waterfront regeneration tends to be focused around specific topics such as transport (Brutomesso, 1995; Hoyle, 1996) or particular places (Dovey, 2005). Wider analysis based on a defined theoretical framework or approach is provided, for example, by Malone (1996), who focuses on economic and political factors from a post-structuralist critical viewpoint that may be of more limited value to practitioners.

Waterfronts have also been used as case studies in key works on urban sociology, such as Harvey (1989), Castells (1996) and Soja (2000). Published analyses of waterfront experience based on explicit theoretical frameworks (from international perspectives as well as focused on specific places) tend to be found, however, in academic journals, which are not easily accessible to the wider non-academic public nor, indeed, to professionals, and again tend to focus on specific cases.

A general theme that emerges across the literature is that waterfront regeneration is a form of, and opportunity for, city-building. In some locations it is even identified as a 'leading force in the future of the development of the city' (Bruttomesso, 2001, p.41). Although the notion of 'city-building' has been criticized for implying that 'the city is only that which the built environment professions have physically constructed' (Landry, 2006, p.8), it is considered useful for the purposes of this book for two reasons. First, while 'city-making' (Landry, 2006) does perhaps better portray the vast array of processes through which urban areas are created and transformed, this book is addressed principally (though not exclusively) to readers who are engaged in the production of the built environment in a professional role. And, second, Landry's interpretation of the term 'building' is rather narrow as it does not appear to recognize the usages of this term to refer to activities and processes of 'social construction' that accompany not only the creation of built environments, but also city life in general – activities and processes such as 'building trust', 'building relationships', etc. In other languages, the more holistic interpretation of 'city-building' is perhaps more common, such as the Spanish language notion of '*construir ciudad*'.

Of course, if city-building is what it is about, ideas relevant to the understanding and practice of waterfront regeneration and development can be found not only in publications which are specifically about waterfronts. As argued in Chapter 1, waterfront regeneration and development as it is currently happening tends to be about the creation of 'pieces of city', with all the complexity in process and product which this entails. This understanding instantly makes large swathes of literature on urban development, land and market economics, urban sociology, planning, urban design and architecture relevant to the task – and the list could continue.

Such sources can provide partial answers to some of the questions posed at the beginning of this chapter; but a more focused approach on both physical and social aspects of the process of waterfront development and the negotiations that take place in city-building is needed to generate a more holistic understanding of the practice of 'building' these urban areas and therefore to contribute to decisions and actions of future practitioners. This is what we turn to next.

An analytical framework for the study and practice of waterfront regeneration

Waterfront regeneration and development as a socio-spatial process

Analyses of waterfront regeneration and development have been made from different perspectives, including those of geographers, physical planners, practitioners and critical theorists (Gordon, 1998). Based on such analyses, some authors have identified sets of factors which are seen as essential for waterfront regeneration, with different emphases, ranging from conceptual criteria to procedural steps or instrumental factors. Bruttomesso (2001), for example, identifies three key conceptual factors which significantly contribute to the attainment of urban complexity in waterfront regeneration:

1   assigning a plurality of functions to the area – in relation to both the regeneration area and its relationship with the rest of the city;
2   achieving a mix of activities within the redeveloped area; and
3   the co-presence of public and private functions, spaces and actors.

Between conceptual and procedural would be Eckstut's (1986) approach to solving complex urban design problems on the waterfront: think small; learn from what exists; integrate; and design streets, not buildings. A more procedural approach is Millspaugh's (2001) set of lessons, which can be seen as instrumental to the success of waterfront redevelopment: public–private partnership; a masterplan; a business plan; consensus and support from the community; and design controls.

The framework that is proposed in this book is not a 'recipe' for implementation of waterfront regeneration and redevelopment programmes and projects, but rather a conceptual framework which should enable both analysis and action based in relation to such processes. It is based on the premise that urban space is socially produced, and that the processes involved are part and parcel of the processes whereby society itself is produced and reproduced. Madanipour (1996) describes urban space as a 'socio-spatial entity' and sees urban design as a 'socio-spatial process'. Madanipour argues that those involved in the activity of urban design (and to this we would add activities of planning and architecture, as well as other activities that are related to urban place-making) need to understand the intersections between space production and everyday life, which is an 'intersection between systems and lifeworld, between structure and agency, between exchange value and use value' (Madanipour, 1996, p.218). And to understand these, in turn, 'we need to know about the political, economic and cultural processes that produce and use urban space' (Madanipour, 1996, p.218).

Indeed, in the field of urban studies, broad-based and cross-disciplinary theoretical approaches have developed in relation to the study of planning processes. Theoretical approaches to urban design, however, have been more focused on specific aspects and are more self-referential (Cuthbert, 2007), with little uptake from the wider development of urban studies, though some influential works on urban geography from a political economy perspective, for example, have used case studies examining the urban design of developments, including waterfronts (see, for example, Harvey, 1989, on Baltimore). In this book we put forward a conceptual framework which draws on approaches developed in sociology, geography and economics, proposing an institutionalist analysis combined with spatial political economy that may help to elucidate and understand planning, urban design and architectural design processes, as well as inform practice of these activities.

An institutionalist approach

Institutionalist analysis, or more appropriately 'new institutionalism', emerged as a theoretical and analytical approach within political science, economics and sociology during the 1980s. This does not constitute a unified body of thought because of its independent emergence in different disciplines and as a response to different schools of thought within these, thus resulting in historical, rational choice and sociological institutionalisms; but these different analytical approaches do share a purpose to 'elucidate the role that institutions play in the determination of social and political outcomes' (Hall and Taylor, 1996, p.936). In relation to economics, the institutionalist turn has also been linked to a renewal of political economy through the development of an institutionalist or new political economy which sees economics as inseparable from the political and social system within which it is embedded.

A central concept in this analytical approach is that of institutions. Jenkins and Smith (2001) propose a dual interpretation of 'institution' as a 'mental model' underpinning the structure of society, economics and politics; and as an 'organizational form'. As Jenkins and Smith (2001, p.21) argue: 'Mental models cannot become operational without organizations, just as organizations need to be underpinned by mental models.' For example, the development of cities' waterfronts during the 19th century as large-scale industrially related sites for production and trade was accompanied by organizational development in the form of port authorities, linked to the mental model of the waterfront as a workplace. The control of such large tracts of land by these public and semi-public authorities and companies was legitimized by this mental model. With economic obsolescence of this form of use of the land, the mental model has shifted to that of the waterfront as a mixed-use area, with accompanying organizational changes in the management of this change towards real estate development, which in turn promote the new mental model of urban quarter development in place of industrial and infrastructural development.

This conceptual approach is particularly linked to the historical and sociological strands of institutionalism, as analysis of the mutual interaction between 'mental model' and 'organization' helps to understand how organizations, their policy frameworks and their actions may evolve in time and explore the extent to which they are geographically specific (hence, historical institutionalism's concept of 'path dependency'), as well as to understand how this interaction is mediated not only by formal rules, procedures or norms, but also by symbol systems, cognitive scripts and moral templates which provide 'frames of meaning' guiding human action (Hall and Taylor, 1996).

Institutionalist approaches have been applied particularly in planning theory and in the analysis of planning experience – for example, in elucidating new mental models and organizational structures developed through and for the wider and deeper engagement of civil society in urban development (Carley et al, 2001); in studying innovation in governance capacity (Gonzalez and Healey, 2005); and in evolving more inclusionary approaches to integrated, place-focused public policy and governance (Healey, 1997, 1999, 2007). The application of such approaches in planning is becoming consolidated (see, for example, Verma, 2006); however, this is not the case in urban design, where theory has not attempted to 'link the material creation or "designing" of urban space and form to fundamental societal processes' (Cuthbert, 2007, p.177).

If urban planning and design are seen as part and parcel of the social production of space and, therefore, of urban form, or as socio-spatial processes (Madanipour, 1996), an understanding of the social milieu from which these emerge and in which they operate is necessary. New institutionalism offers a way to develop such an understanding which avoids the determinism of structuralism and the relativism of phenomenology (Carr, 1985).

Three types of relations in urban development

One of the sources of inspiration for the way in which 'new institutionalism' has been interpreted in planning (see Healey, 1999) is the 'middle way' between deterministic structuralism and relativism that Giddens (1984) offered through his theory of structuration. This theory focuses on the relations through which social practices are constituted and transformed, and is thus of relevance to the socio-spatial production of urban form. According to Giddens, human action takes place within the context of a pre-existing social structure, which is governed by a distinctive set of norms and/or laws; but reproduction of such sets of norms depends on human action, and therefore these structures are neither permanent nor inviolable. This theory sees 'structure' as 'rules and resources recursively implicated in social reproduction' (Giddens, 1984, p.xxxi), with institutions in social systems having 'structural' properties in the sense that they stabilize relationships across time and space. Drawing on Giddens's discussion of the nature of such 'rules and resources', Healey (2007) summarizes three relations which can provide a basis for analysis:

> Giddens identifies three relations through which specific actions are shaped by structuring forces, and through which structuring forces are themselves produced. The first relates to allocative structures (the way material resources – finance, land, human labour – are allocated; for example, public investment in infrastructure or land and property investment processes). The second relates to authoritative structures (the constitution of norms, values, regulatory procedures – for example, regulations over the use and development of land, or processes of environmental impact assessment). The third relates to systems of meaning (frames of reference, ideologies, rationalities, discourses).

> Healey, 2007, p.21

Allocative structures

What can an examination of these three types of relations tell us about waterfront regeneration and development? Let's start with *allocative structures*, focusing on the key resources of land, finance, human labour, materials and energy, as well as what may be termed 'institutional resources'.

The general context for waterfront regeneration that is described in the literature is generally one of land's use for industrial or transport activity ending and its value as a resource changing as a result. The value of this land as a site for both industrial/port activity and now urban development has largely been linked, as would be expected, to its location – in the first case because of being at the interface between land and water, facilitating mode transfer of goods and passengers between shipping and land-based transport; and in the case of regeneration and urban development because of its often fairly central location providing an opportunity for city expansion linking up with an expanse of water now seen as supporting amenity and leisure activities. This land has normally (since the 19th century) been under the control of a public or semi-public body, such as a local authority or a port authority, or of an industrial concern. The process now taking place is generally one of transfer of control of public-sector land to the private sector, and of increasing 'privatization' (sometimes in organizational *modus operandi* if not in ownership) of semi-public landowners, while access to the land is widened through the creation of new public and semi-public spaces. Key factors that are seen in this process as influencing the qualities of the resulting physical built fabric are how this land is parcelled up and transferred, and who controls what development takes place on the land and how it is used. For example, allocation of large areas of waterfront to large developers, to masterplan and development as a single concern are seen as conducive to different results compared to allocation based on small-scale plots going to different developers and designers. In addition, landownership influences the type of use – for example, ensuring public access to the water edge, if this is publicly owned, or applying planning policies which determine the use of the water to influence the use of adjacent land, if this is privately owned. The question emerges as to whether the types of land and landownership on regenerated and redeveloped waterfronts around the North Sea have features in common. And are these distinct from those elsewhere?

The state's capacity to allocate finance for development (or, rather, redevelopment) of this land is generally diminishing worldwide (at least in relative terms to private-sector capacity), with the private sector having growing financial leverage. The allocative structures emerging around the financing of waterfront regeneration tend to be based on public–private partnerships, with the public sector often financing decontamination, key infrastructure, public spaces and flagship developments, while the private sector invests in developments that will produce a clear financial return, such as residential and office buildings.

In this process the labour force involved in the activities carried out on the waterfront pre- and post-regeneration tends to change, with shipyard workers and stevedores being replaced by construction workers, and these in turn by office workers and service staff. This has implications for the relationship between the regenerated areas as a workplace and the location of workers' residences, and for the sense of belonging that workers may have. Dock workers traditionally often lived near the ports, concentrated in specific housing areas, while the new service economy in regenerated waterfronts is staffed by people who may live anywhere in the metropolitan or city region.

With regards to production of the built fabric, various forces are at work on the allocation of construction resources. Globalization is fostering increasing worldwide trade, making materials cheaper to source in emerging economies and countries on the periphery of the capitalist system, continuing the trend started through the colonial trade routes and intensifying this (Jenkins et al, 2007). As a result, the built fabric of regenerated waterfronts can incorporate a range of materials, from tropical timbers from Latin America to granite from China. An opposing force or structure is that driven by increasing environmental awareness and regulation, linked to the other two types of relation: authoritative structures and systems of meaning. This supports the valuing of the existing built fabric as a resource because of its embodied energy and the alternative it offers to the extraction of non-renewable materials (in addition to its symbolic value as heritage, which increasingly has an economic value attached). These are strongly contradictory forces. How are these affecting waterfront regeneration around the North Sea, an area which was at the core of the development of the colonial trade routes and which is bordered by countries that currently have some of the most stringent building regulations in the world (a result of the welfare state and later also driven by the European Union's normative structure)?

Energy is another resource that influences city development at macro and micro levels. As described in Chapter 1, technology based on the tapping of different sources of energy drove changes in forms of transport, which in turn spurred urban development around waterfronts. Energy sources have also underpinned urban development in more indirect ways, such as the discovery of oil in the North Sea, which has supported urban growth and different forms of waterfront development (including new industrial areas such as oil terminals and refineries). The exploitation and distribution of these sources of energy have been related to increasingly centralized organizational forms linked to complex distribution networks, as well as to a concomitant growing commodification of energy. Although this concentrated control of energy production continues in the development of some renewable forms of energy capture, such as offshore wind farms, a growing drive for decentralized energy production is emerging, with new developments increasingly being required to cover part of their energy needs from onsite sources. This is beginning to change the way in which urban developments are designed. Waterfront developments are a particularly interesting case in this respect because of the potential they have to use water and wind as sources of energy. To what extent is this potential being realized in waterfront developments around the North Sea? And how have national policies in the area which pursue high levels of renewable energy influenced these developments?

What could be termed 'institutional resources' are also a significant aspect of allocative structures. Processes of waterfront development often involve the creation of new organizations, which contribute to different aspects of the development process, such as information centres, support organizations, community organizations, etc. In addition, these processes occasionally generate the restructuring of existing organizations, such as municipal departments, in response to different development needs, preparing technical information, managing onsite work, etc. Allocation of resources for the operation of such organizations, as well as giving these organizations power to allocate resources are key elements in the implementation of waterfront regeneration.

To summarize, the above resources tend to be allocated by the state and the market in varying proportions and forms, while, generally, civil society has a very limited contribution, mostly because of the very limited control that it has over such resources.[4] Civil society does, however, have more scope to influence waterfront regeneration through its participation in authoritative structures and in the construction of systems of meaning.

Authoritative structures

Healey (2007) suggests that *authoritative structures* can include the constitution of norms, values and regulatory procedures. Such structures can take the form of organizational arrangements, including, for example, different levels of state organization, from local, national and regional through to transnational. Waterfront regeneration has taken place during a period in which the role of the state in many places has shifted from being a provider to being an enabler – a shift that is reflected at an international level in United Nations declarations and policies. This shift has taken the form, for example, of partnerships between state-sector organizations and private-sector companies, which have become a widespread norm for investment in infrastructure, and are also characteristic of key examples of waterfront redevelopment, such as London Docklands. A related phenomenon has been that of the creation of 'arm's length companies' to which the public sector has delegated powers and resources in order to 'free up' development processes from bureaucratic procedures. What models have been developed and implemented around the North Sea? Do these reflect worldwide trends?

These shifts in authoritative structures have been criticized for putting regeneration processes outside democratic control as they privatize some of the rights to allocate. However, the idea of increased democratic control – through participatory as well as representative democracy – has underpinned experimentation with 'citizen participation', albeit normally within already existing authoritative structures. In waterfront regeneration these initiatives raise issues related to 'who' participates, ranging from how to mediate between the interests of existing residents (often former workers in the defunct industrial or port activities) and those of incoming investors, to how to design participatory processes when there is no (or very little) resident population on the site, and thus the beneficiary population is arguably at city level. In this respect waterfronts around the North Sea offer a wealth of experience. Has this experience shown new ways of engagement between civil society and the state and market which have shifted the ways in which authoritative structures operate?

The above processes must still conform to regulatory procedures linked to planning which, because of how planning is defined in Europe, tends to be a state activity. The European Union is the relevant supranational organization that is increasingly influencing regulatory procedures relevant to developments – including waterfronts – around the North Sea (e.g. through environmental legislation). However, at national, regional and local levels there are also different traditions of regulation, a key example being the difference between the discretionary approach of the UK planning system and the more prescriptive planning systems in continental Europe.[5] To what extent does the diverse nature of these regulatory systems have an impact upon the processes and products of waterfront regeneration around the North Sea?

Systems of meaning

From an institutionalist perspective, such norms, rules and regulations and the organizations which implement them are based on *systems of meaning*, which they, in turn, influence. Healey (2007) lists frames of reference, ideology, rationalities and discourses as examples of such systems of meaning; Madanipour (1996) refers more simply to 'ideas'; and Landry (2006) refers to culture.

Such systems of meaning permeate actions related to city-building at many levels. City marketing, for example, relies on the generation of new narratives about cities in which urban planning and design have a strong role to play in how systems of meaning interplay with the political economy. In dealing with footloose capital, two options are available: to quickly adapt to market shifts; or to mastermind market shifts (Harvey, 1989). Both have been used through urban design by European cities in the last couple of decades, with cities in the older industrialized areas constantly changing approaches to meet market needs, as well as creating and managing markets through innovative design, and cities outside this old industrialized core (especially smaller cities) often being unable to quickly respond to market shifts and therefore attempting the longer-term strategy of producing innovations in design conducive to new market trends (Gospodini, 2002). Examples of the former include London and Paris, with the redevelopment of London Docklands being a market-led process (with all its pitfalls) and the Parisian large public projects being more state driven. An example of a smaller city on the European periphery is Bilbao, where the creation of new symbols through innovative design using 'starchitects' (Guggenheim Museum and other waterfront developments, Bilbao Airport, the distinctive metro system) has contributed to the paradigm of iconic architecture as a beacon for investment (Gospodini, 2002; Sklair, 2006).

In this context, 'urban design appears to be consciously "used" as a means of economic development of cities in the new competitive milieu' (Gospodini, 2002, p.59). In other words, in this phase of globalization, the quality of urban space is seen as a factor in attracting investment, and therefore affecting city competitiveness. Gospodini (2002) suggests that this reverses the historical relationship between the urban economy and urban design, with good-quality urban environments in the past having been made possible by economic growth, whereas they are now increasingly seen as enablers of economic growth – though this is arguable, as there has always been a two-way relationship. This is one way in which culture (if we see the urban design of a place as part of this) provides cities with a narrative about themselves (Landry, 2006).

This operates at the local level as well, with part of the task often faced by waterfront regeneration being that of transforming the way in which it is perceived by residents in the rest of the city it belongs to. This underpins a range of activities from marketing of the waterfront within the city (often by developers – i.e. the market), through citizen participation activities linked to planning projects (usually led by the local authority – i.e. the state), to awareness-raising activities such as design competitions, festivals and the location of information units within the area (often run by civil society organizations, including academia, professional bodies and neighbourhood associations). These can be the platform for new discourses around the use of the waterfront centred on notions such as re-linking city and water, making the waterfront accessible, and spreading the benefits to the wider surrounding communities, though the reality does not always match the rhetoric.

Such new physical and social discourses underpin both outward city marketing and inward awareness-raising, and they may originate from different sources, a typical one being the interface between planners and local politicians. In this context discourse can be seen as 'the policy language and metaphors mobilised in focusing, justifying and legitimating a policy programme or project' (Healey, 2007, p.22). But discourse does not take the form of words only. The actual designs of places and buildings can be interpreted as discourse through what they 'say' about the intentions of agencies promoting them. In the context of waterfront regeneration, what specific discourses have emerged around the North Sea and what do they tell us about the interplay between the local and global in this region?

A political economy perspective

Much of the recent institutionalist literature that has developed around planning has focused on the latter two types of relation – that is, authoritative structures and systems of meaning (and less on allocative structures). Some would argue that in the process a key means to understand the production of the built environment has been somewhat neglected: spatial political economy. This is a perspective with considerable explanatory power, particularly if we consider that 'rather than following function, form has increasingly been following finance' (Ellin, 1996, p.190). Ellin refers to the failure of postmodern urbanism to adequately consider the contemporary political economy, giving the example of False Creek, where a 'self-conscious attempt to build a postmodern landscape' failed because of the lack of consideration of political-economic constraints (Ellin, 1996, pp.156–157).

Political economy analysis has been applied to the study of waterfronts in geography (see, for example, Malone, 1996), and more application of this analysis has been advocated in both planning (McLoughlin, 1994) and urban design (Cuthbert, 2007). A fundamental critique of the political economy approach is the overriding importance it attaches to structure, which is seen to determine and dominate agency. However, new political economy approaches have developed, such as that known as the 'new international political economy', which look not only at how politics and economics influence each other, but also at how these are mediated by social (and cultural) institutions, and how the relations between all of these evolve historically, thus reflecting the preoccupation with the relations between structure and agency which has inspired new institutionalism, and going beyond structuralism to give scope to agency. This new political economy approach has been applied, for example, to the study of urbanization in the rapidly urbanizing world (Jenkins et al, 2007).

An institutionalist approach can therefore incorporate a political economy analysis within it and thus permit linkages between allocative structures, authoritative structures and systems of meaning. Although all three are linked to the political economy, the first two have particular instrumental relevance; however, issues of meaning also underpin allocative systems at a deeper level.

In summary

The above framework is proposed as a way of understanding the forces and relations that impinge upon the design of the built environment. If we take architectural design as an example, this social product reflects the relations we have described. The resources used in terms of land, materials, finance, labour and energy all affect the design, and the political economy surrounding the allocative structure of these can be 'read' in the building. The design conforms to a host of written (building codes, etc.) and unwritten (social norms) rules which are enforced by specific organizations and by social expectations – authoritative structures. In addition, its engagement with systems of meaning and its use in the creation of symbolic capital is probably the aspect that has, in fact, most exercised architectural critics since the 1980s, when Postmodernism increased architecture's self-consciousness about its symbolic power. This is very evident with waterfront design, whether in terms of buildings or urban form-making and the images used for these by designers.

Looking at the professional disciplines involved in the production of the built environment more widely, Ellin (1996, p.264) calls for a new sensibility which celebrates and incorporates difference, stating that 'for this to transpire in urban design, architects and planners must truly heed their own call for contextualism through a more sophisticated understanding of their place in history, of cultural differences, and of the larger political economy in which they currently work'. The framework proposed is offered to both analysts and practitioners as a means to further such understanding. The framework provides a way of interrogating urban development processes. It helps to identify and explore relevant questions in, for example, waterfront regeneration. Some of these are explored in the case studies which are analysed in this book.

The case studies

The framework presented here, including allocative and authoritative structures, as well as systems of meaning, is not applied in a mechanistic and systematic fashion in the case study chapters which are presented in Part II of the book. Rather, each of these chapters provides a specific focus on some of the issues outlined above, based either on a geographic approach ranging from a single city to comparisons across several, or on a thematic approach ranging from process to product. These chapters have been written mostly by local academics who accompanied the learning experience of the Waterfront Communities Project within each city, thus achieving in-depth insight into the action-research process as it happened, while also maintaining the necessary independence to provide additional in-depth critical reflection. These empirical experiences and specific analyses provide the basis for some theoretical reflection based on the application of the above analytical framework in the final chapter of the book, which takes an overview across all the case studies, applying the framework in a more systematic and holistic way. This allows conclusions to be drawn on the challenges faced by these North Sea cities and their relevance for other waterfront cities around the world, and on the institutional structures that respond to these, and, indeed, for other forms of complex 'city-building'.

Although the broader framework of concepts discussed above is embedded in the approach taken in the case study chapters, each of these draw particularly on parts of the framework which are more closely related to the issues that are examined. Thus, Chapter 3 has a particular focus on the influence of allocative structures, looking at different types of resources. In Chapter 3, Maria Soledad Garcia Ferrari and Harry Smith examine the role of physical and institutional resources in sustainable waterfront regeneration, with a specific focus on landownership, land-use control and leadership. This chapter provides a comparative analysis of how these issues have affected the development of the Edinburgh, Gateshead and Hull waterfronts, and contrasts these with the experience in the other participant cities in the Waterfront Communities Project. While highlighting the conflicts that can arise when landownership is fragmented or not under the direct control of a lead agency in regeneration, the chapter discusses the potential and limitations of various forms of shared decision-making over development that takes account of landownership structures and access to resources, as well as forms of focused intervention that can maximize impact, such as flagship developments.

Chapter 4, by Kees Fortuin and Freek de Meere, explores links between allocative and authoritative structures. It addresses the challenge faced by cities to strengthen their position among other cities by developing and managing their resources, with a focus on 'social and creative capital'. It argues that this is not an isolated and independent part of sustainable urban renewal, but has to be viewed in conjunction with spatial and physical resources, such as the housing stock and urban space. It describes the role, position and instruments of the figure of the 'social supervisor', which has been proposed and piloted in The Netherlands to facilitate the integration of the social context of urban regeneration within the design process. The practical issues encountered by the experience of putting in place social supervisors in Schiedam and Zaanstad are discussed. The chapter draws conclusions on constraints and challenges from these experiences, and proposes an approach to culture-led regeneration that gives *local* culture and identity a major role in city-building.

Chapters 5 and 6 explore the issues around the changes in authoritative structures related to different participatory processes that were established during the Waterfront Communities Project, as well as beyond this project.

In Chapter 5, Joakim Forsemalm and Knut Strömberg discuss knowledge and decision-making in planning processes, arguing that the traditional so-called rational approach to public planning, with its formal hierarchical and sectoral organizations and procedures, demonstrates weaknesses when it has to deal with non-standard issues that arise in waterfront city-building. There are no single decision-making bodies that have sole knowledge and competence to handle and take decisions on such complex issues. The chapter examines three different planning processes in the city of Gothenburg in which the clash between the rational approach and a variety of knowledge and agencies is clearly apparent. These dialogue processes developed at different stages of the planning process and with different mixes of participants, and were relatively easy to organize; but problems arose when the outcomes were to be included in the standard operational procedures for planning and decision-making in the municipality. The lessons from this contextually based in-depth case study provide points for reflection on similar processes elsewhere and on the social dimension of sustainable urban development.

In Chapter 6, Harry Smith and Maria Soledad Garcia Ferrari explore the challenges faced by wider stakeholder participation in waterfront regeneration, focusing on how the city of Hamburg has addressed three types of scenario. Here the highly successful HafenCity Hamburg project close to the city centre encountered a fairly common scenario in waterfront regeneration – that of a very limited amount of existing residents. The chapter looks at how the public development company that is regenerating this area tried to secure benefits for the 'public good' through strong controls on the design and management of developments. It then examines the 'Leap across the Elbe' framework plan, which covers three very different harbour development areas spanning north–south across the Elbe island, encompassing a variety of inhabited areas. The approach here was an international design workshop focused on drafting urban design scenarios for the International Building Exhibition IBA 2013 and involving expert and citizen groups, followed by a resulting public dialogue, and the creation of a citizens' and experts' forum and a board of trustees alongside the new development corporation. Finally, Chapter 6 takes a brief look at experiments being undertaken in Hamburg to deal with the long-term management and maintenance of regenerated areas, mainly through an adaptation of the Business Improvement District model, which may hold lessons for the sustainable management of waterfront areas.

Chapter 7 looks at how design-based processes have mediated between authoritative structures and the exploration of new systems of meaning. The starting point of Hans Kiib's chapter is Harbourscape Aalborg 2005, a workshop where three different design-based development methods were tested with the purpose of developing new concepts for the relationship between the city and its harbour, in addition to generating easily grasped images of a coherent harbour transformation. This experience is described and compared to earlier similar experiences in other North Sea waterfront cities: Hamburg's Bauforum (analysed in more detail in Chapter 6) and the Oslo Charrette. Analysis of these cases focusing on methodology, concept development and communication during the process provides the basis for the proposal of some principles in action-research. Those related to methodology, concepts and process will be of particular interest to researchers, and those on production of concepts, mutual understanding and quality of design will be useful for a variety of actors in the development process.

Systems of meaning are the focus for Chapters 8, 9 and 10, with Chapter 8 looking at process and Chapter 9 examining how this has translated into product – or place. Chapter 10 then examines the links between process and product.

In Chapter 8, Solvejg Beyer Reigstad examines the role of visions in creating a sustainable living waterfront, using the process undertaken to develop the Odense Waterfront as a case study. Odense is an interesting example of how the common waterfront regeneration challenge of large-scale existing physical structures and often a negative public image can be met in a way which ensures that people will be attracted to the new urban areas and, thus, contribute to their long-term social and economic sustainability. The chapter evaluates the method followed in Odense, which puts public life and development of visions upfront in the planning process. Odense invited public life into the area through holding events, creating public space and establishing a dialogue with stakeholders. These methods are analysed in a wider and more general perspective, including how planners can ensure that they plan a living city, and establishing comparisons with the waterfront project in Oslo, presented in Chapter 7.

Also focusing on the resulting quality of public space, in Chapter 9 Maria Soledad Garcia Ferrari, Paul Jenkins and Harry Smith try to capture what makes a great waterfront, and from this develop a longer-term basis for creating successful waterfront places. The key focus for the analysis is spatial, social and visual, with a view to understanding how some places are perceived as becoming successful in social and cultural terms, and how this relates to the visual and spatial environment. It takes three North Sea waterfronts (Gateshead, Malmö and Oslo) and explores the links between the regeneration process and the resulting quality of the public realm in each case. The chapter draws conclusions on the requirements for sustainable place-making at the macro- and micro-scale, including the importance of time in the creation of place, as well as providing some reflection on the physical characteristics of successful places.

The aim of Chapter 10, by Maria Soledad Garcia Ferrari and Derek Fraser, is to analyse design strategies and evaluate solutions proposed in the development of waterfronts, focusing on the Sluseholmen area located in Copenhagen's southern harbour. The chapter builds on the conceptual framework proposed in this book, understanding that urban change is the result of different forms of interaction between 'institutions' (as organizations and mental models) and 'actions' (such as for the allocation of resources, the constitution of norms and the definition of ideological frameworks). Its objective is thus to explore the connections between the design strategies adopted and the processes that the developments experienced, drawing on a series of semi-structured interviews which were carried out with key stakeholders in the process of development – planners, designers and developers.

In Chapter 11, Harry Smith and Maria Soledad Garcia Ferrari then provide an analysis of the findings from the above case studies and draw conclusions based on the analytical framework presented here, within the context of the challenges faced by waterfront cities around the North Sea in achieving sustainable city-building. Although at the regional level, the various cities studied in this book display great diversity in size in the relative strength and powers of stakeholders and in their legal and institutional frameworks, at the global level this is a fairly homogeneous region, with similar institutional structures and economic and social goals, which are a driver towards similarities in waterfront regeneration. Conclusions are drawn on the balance between these differences and similarities in terms of the physical environments that are being created on waterfronts around the North Sea. The overarching theme cutting across the case studies presented here is the forms of involvement of the various stakeholders in the regeneration process and the resulting quality (and qualities) of the public realm on the waterfront. Are these creating places that attract national and international investment towards the region, while at the same time providing attractive and sustainable new public spaces and opportunities for activities for local populations? Is this approach fundamentally relevant to any major 'city-building' project worldwide, and if so, why and how can it be translated into other contexts without a banal 'best practice' approach? Emerging questions around new challenges such as climate change and rapidly changing geo-politics are also explored. These conclusions are used to reflect on how the analytical framework developed in this book can help to understand and aid sustainable waterfront regeneration processes in other cities around the world.

Notes

1   Structure and agency are key concepts used in the social sciences. 'Structure' refers to the external factors which influence – or determine, according to some approaches – individual behaviour. These can range from cultural norms to organizational forms. 'Agency' refers to the capacity of individuals to act within a society. There has been a longstanding debate over the balance between the two, with, for example, structuralism considering structure to be

predominant in explaining actions, and phenomenology focusing on the power of individual agents to 'construct' the world. More recent approaches have explored the mutual interrelationship between the two, including Giddens (1984).

2   The International Centre Cities on Water has published an extensive bibliography of publications on waterfronts; see Città d'Acqua (2007).

3   The Waterfront Communities Project's database is available at www.seeit.co.uk/waterfrontcp/goodprac.cfm. Other useful databases include AIVP's online search facility (www.aivp.org/infos.html).

4   Labour is one resource which, during the last century, has structured itself through trade unions; but this type of civil society organization has seen its power retrench in recent decades, being faced with changes in regulatory systems (see authoritative structures) which have favoured markets over organized labour.

5   See Chapter 3 for a brief discussion of the different types of planning systems in Europe.

Part 2

Case Studies of Waterfront City-Building Processes Around the North Sea

3

Physical and Institutional Resources in Sustainable Waterfront Regeneration

Landownership, Land-Use Control and Leadership

Maria Soledad Garcia Ferrari and Harry Smith

Introduction

Chapter 2 introduced the concept of allocative structures as the relations which exist around the allocation of resources. An essential resource in urban development is land, which has both use value (i.e. as a material support for economic exploitation and development, as well as for inhabitation) and exchange value (i.e. as a commodity that can be traded for financial gain). The ways in which these values are realized are influenced by the allocative structures governing access to, and use and enjoyment of, the benefits attached to land. Such structures are formalized through diverse forms of land tenure, ranging from freehold ownership to state and community ownership[1] of land and different forms of rental, which tend to be conceptualized as 'bundles of rights'. Land is also related to authoritative structures, as the way in which it is used and developed is usually regulated by some form of planning system, which is state based in modern societies, and often based on customary socio-cultural practices in traditional societies.

The interaction between the allocative and authoritative structures related to land has an important impact upon city-building and urban form. A well-known historical example of this, focusing on the balance between private landownership and government power, is the comparison between the implementation of Nash's plans for Regent's Street in central London and that of Haussmann's *grand travaux* in Paris. Nash's proposals for grand street and avenue layouts had to be adapted in order to accommodate the interests of private landowners, as the power of the state was relatively weak in this regard. Haussmann, backed by a strong state-based authoritative structure, used expropriation in order to drive straight and wide boulevards through the existing built fabric of Paris – though the real-estate sector also benefited through this operation (Sica, 1980).

The built fabric of Edinburgh's city centre also provides a good illustration of the physical manifestation of land tenure in the built environment, displaying a variety of street layouts linked to property boundary patterns (see Figure 3.1). The 'fishbone' street pattern in the Old Town has its origins in the long narrow burgage plots set at right angles to the High Street on which only the frontages were developed initially, with densification later leading to development of the backlands and access through the narrow alleys (Stuart-Murray, 2005). The First New Town was designed and developed during the 18th century on an oblong area of land purchased by the Corporation of Edinburgh, which allowed a grand grid layout with large squares at each end. Subsequent New Town extensions during the late 18th and 19th centuries were developed by private landowners, with the boundaries of their landholdings being reflected in the urban layout, and street plans becoming more inward-looking around crescents and circuses (Youngson, 1966).

As seen in Chapter 2, waterfront areas have their own distinctive land tenure and control features. They are often areas which have been under control of public or semi-public bodies since the 19th century, and which during the late 20th century have been taken out of public control through the 'privatization' of the port authorities and other large landowners. Now, through their regeneration, property ownership (though not necessarily that of land) is being broken down into smaller units for sale, normally after the land has been redeveloped as new urban fabric. In addition, the public is gaining access to newly created public space. Some of this is happening on land that did

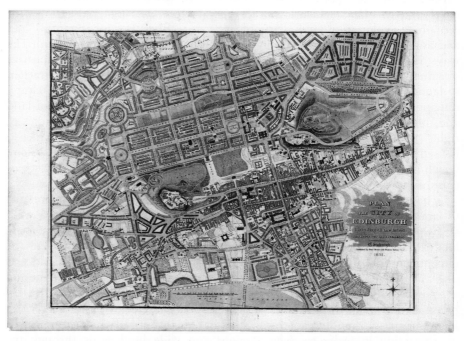

Figure 3.1 *Plan of the City of Edinburgh in 1831, including planned improvements, by John Wood and Thomas Brown*

Source: National Library of Scotland

not exist as such before it was originally developed as docks or for industrial use, as the waterfront is an area where land has often been created through reclamation (Desfor, 2008) – a process that is also part of current waterfront regeneration in some cases.

National and local specific characteristics of allocative structures around land therefore have a substantial bearing on how city-building activity linked to waterfront regeneration takes place, and on the physical results of this activity. Key issues that need to be understood include whether the regeneration is taking place on existing or new (reclaimed) land; who owns the land; who controls what happens on it; and how this control is exerted.

This chapter explores these issues in the case of waterfront cities around the North Sea. It first examines the approaches in the region to landownership and land-use control, including the role of leadership in such control. It then focuses on the specific characteristics of the approach in one national context – that of the UK. It examines in depth the cases of the three Waterfront Communities Project partner cities located in the UK: Edinburgh, Gateshead and Hull. Finally, it presents some conclusions on the consequences of different landownership and control regimes around the North Sea, and the importance of landownership and control in waterfront regeneration worldwide.

Allocative structures around land

Landownership can generally be divided into three types: private (held by individuals and companies or other legal entities); state land, which is under the ownership of a variety of state agencies, from national to local; and community, or 'third-sector', land (Home, 2009). All these forms of landownership are underpinned by the legislative, regulatory, registrational and administrative role of the state. Urban waterfronts undergoing regeneration tend to fall within the categories of state and private land. The rise and decline in state landownership that happened in Northern Europe and other parts of the world during the 20th century is reflected in similar trends in relation to port and waterfront areas, as seen above.

The relationship of these landowners to their land varies across different societies, depending upon their legal systems. Within Europe, the following 'legal families' are identifiable: those based on the Napoleonic Code (France, Belgium, Italy, Luxembourg, Portugal and Spain); the German system (Austria, Germany and Switzerland); common law countries (the constituent countries of the UK, as well as Ireland); the Nordic countries; and the Eastern European countries (formerly Socialist). Within these overall 'legal families' in Europe, there are further differences between countries (and within legal families) when it comes to land law (Schmid and Hertel, 2005). The continental land laws have their origins in a mixture of tribal/feudal law and Roman law, the latter being the basis for the codifications that took place during the 19th and 20th centuries, whereas the land law systems in the UK did not go through such codifications (though in Scotland there was a stronger influence of Roman law, and here the feudal system was only finally abolished in 2003).

Although not directly responsible for landownership, planning systems seek to define appropriate land use according to development objectives, and therefore affect land values and can have an impact upon landownership. Land-use planning can be defined as a specific form of government activity aiming to secure public interests in the development of land and property resources (Lloyd, 1994). Therefore, the approaches to land-use planning are closely linked to the aims of different political models, governance structures and institutional organizations in each country.

The 'legal families' described above also provide the institutional context for land-use planning, including the location of planning powers in government structures and the ways in which such powers are exercised (Newman and Thornley, 1996; Hague and Jenkins, 2005). Four categories of spatial planning have been identified in Western Europe (European Commission, 1997), of which two are particularly represented in the countries surrounding the North Sea:

- the comprehensive integrated approach, which is used in Germany, The Netherlands and Scandinavian countries – this is based on formal hierarchies of plans from national to local level, with extensive planning institutions and public-sector investment;
- the land-use management approach, which is used in the UK – this is locally managed following national guidelines, and is not closely linked to other forms of planning or government activity.[2]

In the case of The Netherlands, there is a long-established tradition of local governments acting as land agencies, preparing and supplying land for development, as well as a national spatial planning agency and national spatial plans (European Commission, 1999). In Scandinavia, the strong welfare tradition has been accompanied by a continuum of administration and planning instruments from national, through regional, to local level – with the latter having considerable independence – as well as integration of land-use planning with other areas of planning, such as economic (Newman and Thornley, 1996; Jensen and Richardson, 2004). However, the welfare model in Scandinavia has been affected by the recent influence of neoliberal policies, and decentralization has reduced the comparative power of the regional level (Baggesen Klitgaard, 2002; Bohme, 2002). In Germany, land-use planning and control falls within the responsibility of each municipality, and legally binding plans are prepared and established at this level. In the UK, though land use is managed locally, central government appears to have a stronger influence (e.g. through setting regional housing targets at the start of the plan-making process rather than as the result of considering economic, environmental and social factors) (Keenleyside et al, 2009). In addition, the German system shows a more complex distribution of responsibilities between federal and regional (*Landër*) levels, whereas in the UK the regional level for planning has had a varied history and overall has been generally weaker, as there has been no firmly established level of regional authority (Newman and Thornley, 2006).

The interaction between landownership, land-use control and leadership can be most clearly seen in the actual implementation of spatial planning. The European Commission (1997) again provides a clear indication of the forms of implementation of urban development that can be found around the North Sea, distinguishing three broad types:

1   a predominantly public-sector approach, such as the land assembly and servicing undertaken by local government following an approved plan that tends to be the norm in Denmark, The Netherlands and Sweden;

2   a mixed approach where the public sector may enable and promote development, coordinate land assembly, or engage in joint ventures and partnerships, as is the case in France and Belgium;

3   a predominantly private-sector led approach, such as the national schemes for specific areas requiring leverage of funding from the private sector that occur in the UK, particularly in urban regeneration.

In a global context, and from a governance perspective, in the North Sea region there are therefore two major actors – the state and the private sector – who tend to take the leadership in initiatives involving land use and management, often through partnerships between these. A much weaker role is played by civil society, unless facilitated by the state, or often as a response to both state and private-sector initiatives (see Carley et al, 2001). Generally, local authorities tend to be a major state player in regeneration initiatives in this region, with considerable powers and comparatively high levels of capacity to implement. Often these authorities have recourse to higher level sources of funding, which are essential for regeneration initiatives. In the case of waterfronts, it is very common to find other important state actors, such as port authorities and major infrastructure-related bodies (ministries related to public works, railway companies, etc.), due to the nature of activities and the development paths of such areas. National intervention is mostly related to creating the necessary regulatory frameworks, as well as to transferring landownership to new organizational structures and providing specific resources. The way in which these bodies interact with local government and the private sector has been affected by the privatization and semi-privatization of many of them as a result of the neoliberal trends that have prevailed since the 1980s.

These general characteristics do, however, encompass a wide diversity of regional and local-level conditions which give rise to a wide range of responses. Thus, in structure and agency terms, although at a world macro level, the North Sea region shares some important structural conditions, local paths of development have evolved (and continue to evolve) different sets of structural conditions offering varying scope for agency (Newman and Thornley, 2006). Questions that arise include: what influence do landownership patterns have on the scope for city-building on waterfronts? What scope do national planning regimes (policy and legislation) give for engaging with such landownership patterns in waterfront regeneration initiatives? How does leadership in waterfront regeneration emerge in these contexts?

Examples of allocative structures around land in the UK

As argued above, national contexts can provide part of the explanation of how allocative structures work (e.g. around land); but local specifics also have a part to play. In order to explore the scope for local variation in how an issue such as land may affect local city-building activities through waterfront regeneration, it is useful to compare the experiences of the three waterfront cities in the UK which took part in the Waterfront Communities Project. These share a common national cultural and legal context insofar as they are all within the UK, albeit there are differences in landownership legislation and land-use control legislation and policy between England (Gateshead and Hull) and Scotland (Edinburgh).

In both England and Scotland, land tenure in its current form has its origins in feudal systems (hence the use of the word 'tenure' in the English language), whereby property owners 'held' land within a hierarchical structure under the Crown rather than owning the land outright. This meant that 'feudal superiors' could enforce conditions on how the land could be used or developed. This system was only abolished in Scotland in 2003, but was abolished in England centuries earlier. Although the trend has been towards the spread of freehold land tenure (a form of tenure that suits the recent neoliberal push for enabling land and housing markets among others), the legacy of centuries of feudal landownership systems in England and Scotland is strong. Its major manifestation is the extreme concentration of landownership in a few hands. Another effect of the system was the ability of feudal superiors to impose conditions upon the development and use of land until very recently, this being of significance until land development rights were nationalized throughout the UK by means of the landmark Town and Country Planning Act 1947. The effects of this structure, however, can be seen in how Edinburgh, Gateshead and Hull have approached the regeneration of land on their waterfronts.

Divide and conquer: Landownership and master planning on the Edinburgh waterfront

Edinburgh, the capital city of Scotland, with a population of just under 0.5 million (approximately 700,000 within its urban region), is an example of a successful service-based and knowledge economy. In 2009 it was the second largest tourist attractor in the UK after London, home to the headquarters of major financial and banking companies, the fifth financial centre in Europe, and had four universities. Its economic success in the 1990s and 2000s led to population growth and increased demand for housing. Encircled by a tight green belt which is firmly embedded in the population's psyche, as well as in planning policy, the planning authorities sought to meet the rising housing demand through two approaches.

One approach was to 'export' new housing to neighbouring local authorities, where land was available. Although this gave access to cheaper land, it was criticized for turning localities on the periphery of Edinburgh into dormitory towns and shunting responsibility for service provision to neighbouring local authorities, while Edinburgh benefited from the inward investment from business. 'Leap-frogging' the green belt was also criticized on sustainability grounds for increasing commuting and using up greenfield land.

The other approach adopted by the Edinburgh planning authorities was to densify its existing built-up area, mainly through brownfield land redevelopment and regeneration. Within this approach, the largest areas for regeneration are around Edinburgh's two harbours:

- *Leith Docks* is Edinburgh's main harbour, with approximately 170ha available for redevelopment on docklands which protrude into the Firth of Forth. It is located in the old port town of Leith, which historically had developed separately from Edinburgh. Leith's trading activity goes back to the medieval Hanseatic, Baltic and North Sea trading routes. Dock activities started to move elsewhere in the estuary during the 1990s, freeing up the land for redevelopment. The centre of Leith already underwent regeneration during the 1980s and 1990s, with the docks becoming the 'new frontier' for regeneration in the 2000s.
- *Granton Harbour* was originally built during the 1830s as a deep water harbour at a time when Leith docks were still relatively undeveloped. Built for coal export, it later became home to a fishing fleet, as well as the location of the world's first ferry-train. Both commercial trading and fishing ended in the 1970s, and some of the area within the confines of the piers started to be filled in. The approximately 176ha of land identified for regeneration in the harbour's hinterland encompass a wide range of former uses – from former gas works to the UK's first car factory – and abut some of the most socially and economically deprived housing estates in the city.

The regeneration of these two areas is expected to provide 30,000 new homes over a 30-year period, together with a range of neighbourhood and city-level facilities, though notably without any major iconic or flagship buildings that might help to create an image for the waterfront at a national or international level. Although at some levels marketed as a single initiative (the Edinburgh Waterfront), the regeneration of these two areas has undergone very different processes, largely due to the different patterns of landownership and, linked to this, the ways in which leadership of the process has unfolded.

The regeneration of Granton was led by City of Edinburgh Council, which in 1999 commissioned a masterplan for the entire area. The masterplan envisaged an extension to the city based on perimeter blocks, with medium-rise high-density development enclosing well-defined public space and accommodating mixed use as well as housing. Ownership of the land covered by the masterplan, however, was divided among three major landowners, as well as a number of smaller landowners (see Figure 3.2). The major landowners – City of Edinburgh Council (via an arm's length company called Edinburgh Waterfront Ltd),[3] a national gas company and the port authority – subsequently commissioned more detailed masterplans for their respective landholdings, with little coordination among these. The disjunction of adjacent masterplans was compounded by the replacement of existing masterplans with new ones within each landholding, in some cases when the previous masterplan had already been partially implemented. The result was a fragmented emergence of new built environments and places, with connections between the cores of the three main landholdings being (provisionally at least) limited to new roads rather than continuous built fabric. In addition, competition among the developers of the different landholdings led to overprovision of two-bedroom apartments for a certain segment of the market, which quickly became saturated.

Figure 3.2 *Granton masterplan and approximate major landownership areas, Edinburgh*

Source: Redrawn by authors, based on City of Edinburgh Council masterplans and landownership information

Different dynamics were at work in Leith Docks. Regeneration of the built-up area of Leith had started during the 1980s and continued during the 1990s as a result of local authority initiatives, and support from the national government body then known as the Scottish Executive was manifested in the construction of its new headquarters by the port. Regeneration of the port facilities started later, in the first decade of the new century. Here a single powerful landowner – the port authority – initiated the regeneration of the docks with a flagship shopping centre and other developments, an approach that the local authority regarded as disjointed and piecemeal. The local planning authorities then put pressure on the port authority to produce a strategy for the development of the whole area. The Leith Docks Development Framework was prepared by consultants who were commissioned by the port authority and was approved in 2005 by the local authority. This framework divided the land into six zones for phased development. These were further subdivided into sites, which would be subject to specific planning permission, each containing a number of development parcels. These zones were identified as areas for subsequent, more specific masterplans, which would conform to a series of principles outlined in the development framework. Principles included the use of perimeter blocks giving shape to well-defined public space, the creation of view corridors linking the city with the water, and good connections to public transport, among others (see Figure 3.3). The approach taken by this single landowner in its development planning was hierarchical and structured, setting parameters which were intended to foster consistent development of the area over an extended period of time.

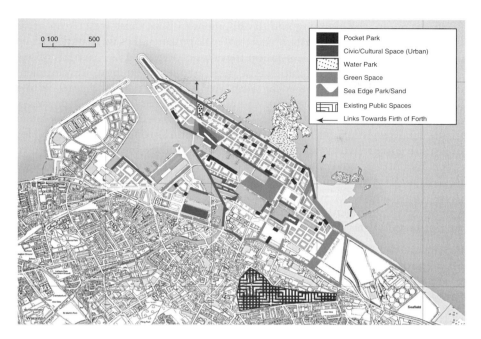

Figure 3.3 *Proposed hierarchy of public space in the Leith Docks Development Framework, Edinburgh, 2005*

Source: LDDF, 2005, Figure 1.10

In 2011, the City of Edinburgh Council published for consultation a draft Waterfront and Leith Area Development Framework, covering both the waterfront areas described above and attempting to chart a way for their development as places that are integrated with the existing urban areas. This was in response, to a large extent, to what the Foreword to the document described as 'the inability of all those with an interest in the waterfront to look in a meaningful way beyond the "red line" boundaries that define land ownership or the extent of planning applications' (City of Edinburgh Council, 2011). This initiative to provide an overarching vision for the Edinburgh waterfront deliberately avoided establishing a clearly defined boundary and focused on integration and connectivity. Whether this approach will be successful in overcoming the limitations imposed by fragmented landownership and lack of direct control over the land by the planning authority remains to be seen.

The dramatically negative impact of the 2008 recession upon the development of the Edinburgh waterfront brought about the search for new ways to reinvigorate the process. Interestingly, these included the proposal by the local authority to use tax increment financing (TIF), where finance for the implementation of key infrastructure is obtained on the basis of expected increases in tax revenue once the development is completed. This shows, to a limited extent, some approximation to the public-sector led approach to development taken by other countries around the North Sea (see previous section), though still retaining a requirement to lever in private-sector funding.

Summing up, the planning and development of both these waterfront areas illustrates the fact that, although private development rights were nationalized in the UK with the planning legislation that was enacted in 1947, actual control of the land through ownership has a huge impact upon how development unfolds. In both cases, the local authority tried to take the lead in the development of the waterfront: in the case of Granton through a proactive master planning role that was, to some extent, undermined by subsequent private landowner actions; and in the case of Leith through reactive demands for a more comprehensive approach and strategy. Although the latter has led to a (not uncontested) overall strategy, it remains to be seen how the balance of decision-making between planning authority and large landowner plays out in its implementation, as well as to what extent alternative views of how to develop this waterfront may impinge upon the results. The importance of the issue of landownership is further illustrated in the following case.

The land of dreams: Gateshead Quays

Respectively located on the north and south banks of the River Tyne, in north-east England, Newcastle and Gateshead form a large urban area with a population of 500,000 – of which 196,000 reside in Gateshead. Industrial decline in the conurbation during the second half of the 20th century has led to a legacy of underused, unused and vacant industrial land, particularly in Gateshead's central core, close to the dense urban centre of Newcastle. Following in the steps of regeneration initiatives in Newcastle, including along the north bank of the Tyne, Gateshead set about 'reinventing itself', creating cultural attractions and venues in particular locations as key drivers to spearhead the wider regeneration of these areas, including along its fluvial waterfront (see also Chapter 9).

Much of this culture-based regeneration has been located in the area now known as Gateshead Quays, on the south bank of the Tyne. This shoreline was the location of the original settlement going back to Roman times. Medieval development around narrow alleys gave way to tenement and factory development during the 18th century and to overcrowding and poor living conditions in the 19th century. Much of the densely packed historic fabric, built up to and even overhanging the riverbank, was destroyed in a great fire in 1854. This provided an opportunity to build a new quay, but it lacked facilities to compete with Newcastle's on the opposite bank and did not prosper in the long run, falling into disrepair during the 1970s and 1980s as industrial decline set in (Histon, 2006). In addition, new river crossings built during the 19th and 20th centuries linked to major railway and road infrastructures tended to be made at the higher levels of the deep ravine that the River Tyne forms at this point, thus making Gateshead Quays less accessible in relative terms.

During the mid 1990s, Gateshead Council started the process of regenerating East Gateshead, covering an area of 162ha of brownfield land, low-quality residential properties, industrial premises and the athletics stadium. This included the Gateshead Quays area, identified as a location for arts-led urban regeneration.

Initial regeneration of the area was based on the creation of three iconic landmarks and visitor attractors, plus one residential development (see Figure 3.4).

The flagship buildings were all the result of council-led seizure of funding opportunities and forging of partnerships, using land and properties that were available to the council. With national lottery funding for the arts, a 1950s disused grain silo was converted into BALTIC, the largest contemporary art gallery in the UK outside London, and one of the largest temporary art spaces in Europe. Funding from the Millennium Commission[4] was used to provide a pedestrian link between Gateshead Quays and the already successfully regenerated north bank of the River Tyne in Newcastle: the Gateshead Millennium Bridge – the world's first tilting bridge. Both these structures opened to the public in 2002. Finally, national lottery arts funding again enabled the construction of the state-of-the-art concert hall, The Sage Gateshead, which in 2004 provided a home to the North Music Trust in what was being transformed from an area of dereliction into an arts quarter.

Council-led development of these facilities encouraged investment from house-builders, with a well-known private-sector house-builder providing seven new apartment blocks on the land adjoining BALTIC by 2004, and a further mixed-use development of the area between BALTIC and The Sage Gateshead being planned in a second phase.

To a certain extent, due to the initial conditions on the site, the existing private landowners and businesses did not have a shared vision for the area's

Figure 3.4 *Aerial view of Gateshead Quays, showing BALTIC and the Millennium Bridge (left) and the Sage Gateshead (right): Gateshead town centre is top right*

Source: RMJM

development. Gateshead Council took the lead in transforming the area as identified in its wider regeneration strategy, making opportunistic use of funding available and land under its control. This succeeded in putting the area on the map (see Chapter 9). The lack of an initial overall masterplan was addressed later in the process. For example, a public realm strategy for Gateshead Quays (as well as for the wider Gateshead Central Area) was developed in 2003, and tight control was exerted over design quality levels in subsequent proposals presented by the private sector, such as those for the mixed-use development between BALTIC and The Sage Gateshead. Eventually, in 2010, a draft masterplan was issued for consultation, with a view to guiding completion of the regeneration of Gateshead Quays. This masterplan, finalized in December 2010, added a proposed International Conference and Exhibition Centre to be located within the area intended for mixed use, on land owned by the local authority.

However, where the council-led initiative found obstacles was on land belonging to other parties. In the central part of Gateshead Quays, Crown-owned land on the river's edge has so far thwarted development of a meaningful water's edge adjacent to the new public space in front of BALTIC. To the east of BALTIC, private ownership of industries backing onto the river has also caused a similar problem by making it difficult to extend public access to the riverside. Land to the south of the Sage is also the property of various businesses and occupiers. In the phasing of development proposed in the 2010 masterplan, these areas of land have not been given any fixed time period for development given the uncertainties surrounding them, as they are not within the control of the local authority. For example, the land south of the Sage requires prior site assembly (see Figure 3.5). In addition, issues of landownership even impinged

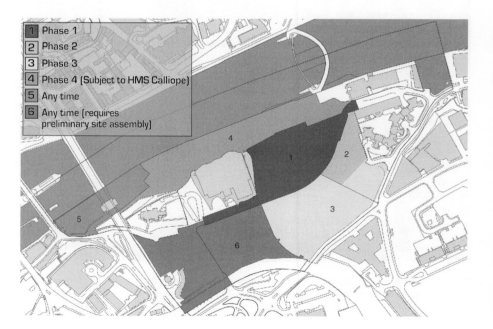

Figure 3.5 *Map from 2010 Gateshead Quays masterplan showing phasing and landownership*

Source: RMJM

upon the design of the developments that have been completed. For example, the design brief for the Gateshead Millennium Bridge required that no structure was to be built on the actual quayside on either side of the river (Johnson and Curran, 2003).

In conclusion, the factors leading to the success of this regeneration scheme include investment by the public sector in land assembly, land reclamation and public realm improvements, which resulted in increased land values and stronger investor confidence. However, although in the short term, imaginative use of council-controlled land has radically transformed the area, in the long term full development of the area has been (at least temporarily) limited by issues of landownership and control, as well as by the economic climate.

Land assembly: Hull Citybuild

Kingston-upon-Hull, located on the central east coast of England, has a population of 0.25 million within the city's tightly drawn administrative boundaries. Drawing higher income residents back into the city from its wider travel-to-work area (encompassing 420,000 people) as a way of addressing its acute levels of socio-economic deprivation is one of the city's strategic objectives – which underpin its on-going regeneration drive. Although it has moved away from the urban centre, Hull's port still plays a major role in the increasingly diversified economy of the city. Its fastest growing industry is tourism, and it is also a major sub-regional retail centre and has a university. The urban dynamics in Hull are the opposite of those in Edinburgh, with the issue here being how to stem population and socio-economic decline and draw in residents, rather than how to respond to economic growth and population influx.

Hull's development on the confluence of the River Hull and the Humber Estuary was closely linked to fishing and dock activity from its origins in the 12th century. From the 18th century onwards, 'town docks' developed, linked to intensive urban growth and the development of the fishing industry. The Old Town and Town Docks, which run throughout the city centre, declined from the 1930s to the 1960s. Docks outside the city centre have also eventually been affected by decline, with the main port activities now being concentrated in the eastern docks and new deep-water terminals on the River Humber. The central location of the first docks to decline led to early regeneration, with Queens Dock being closed in 1930 and filled in to create Queens Gardens. The regeneration of other central docks started in the 1970s and has been extended to the less central waterfront areas.

Given the close link between this city's development and its waterfront activities, port areas have been threaded through the city centre since its origins. This had led to the existence of large areas of brownfield land and underutilized sites in the city centre, as well as disconnection between key sites, thus affecting its attractiveness (GENECON, 2008).

The major waterfront landowner is Associated British Ports (ABP), the ex-privatized operator that runs the Port of Hull and controls over 50 per cent of the Humber waterfront within the city boundary. In addition, ABP has considerable powers to develop this land without applying for permission from the local authority, except in the case of significant developments. However, other waterfront land is in a variety of hands, therefore requiring engagement with a range of stakeholders when implementing regeneration.

Waterfront regeneration in Hull city centre is taking place as part of a masterplanned approach which identifies five strategic development areas – three of these being on the actual waterfront (see Figure 3.6). This masterplan was initially implemented by Hull Citybuild, an urban regeneration company (URC) that was created in 2002 by Hull City Council, the regional development agency (Yorkshire Forward) and the national regeneration agency English Partnerships. Its governing board included representatives from both the public and private sectors. Hull Citybuild assembled land into development opportunities which were made available to the private sector, including both land owned by the partners in this arm's length company and that owned by other organizations and individuals. The latter was acquired through agreement, when possible; but compulsory purchase was also used. In addition, Hull Citybuild sometimes funded site clearance, land remediation and site preparation works. It could also invest in infrastructure servicing sites or providing access to these. In 2008, Hull Citybuild was superseded by Hull Forward, the economic development company for Hull, which seeks to further develop Hull Citybuild's activities and transform Hull into a global economic player.

During its lifetime, Hull Citybuild delivered two of the strategic development areas in the masterplan:

- *Humber Quays Phase 1* – a high-quality office development and new residential development, set in high-quality public realm, which helped to address the outflow of office use in the city and unlocked the potential of the waterfront through the creation of a new business quarter on it (see Figure 3.7);

Figure 3.6 *Hull city centre masterplan strategic development areas*

Source: Hull City Council

Figure 3.7 *One Humber Quays*

Source: Hull City Council

• *St Stephen's* – a major city centre shopping and leisure development, together with a transport interchange, which have contributed to boosting Hull's attractiveness as a retail centre (GENECON, 2008).

In addition, Hull Citybuild made progress on the other strategic development areas, securing private-sector partners and/or public funding for most of these. The local authority supported Hull Citybuild's activities with its land-use planning and land assembly powers. Thus, the regeneration company was able to take the lead in the regeneration process with the backing of government powers, but without having to comply with the bureaucratic processes which accountability demands of the public sector. It avoided the discontinuities that political cycles and events can entail, and it succeeded in persuading both public-sector agencies and private-sector investors to participate in development activities. However, the ease and speed of action that this type of company was endowed with through its political independence was gained at the expense of democratic control of its actions, even though it was dealing with public land and funds.

The case of Hull is also illustrative of a further issue around land on the waterfront – its impermanence. The fact that much of Hull's waterfront area, and even of its city centre given its prior use as docks, is on reclaimed land next to a floodplain means that the city is very flat and has to be constantly drained by pumps. This made it an ideal case for a study undertaken by the Institution of Civil Engineers (ICE) and the Royal Incorporation of British Architects' (RIBA) think-tank Building Futures, in 2009, which looked at possible development scenarios for two waterfront cities in the UK in 100 years' time, taking into account sea-level rise projections (Building Futures RIBA and ICE, 2009). In a 'retreat' scenario, Hull was seen as giving up land to the sea, with the old city being protected and becoming an island linked to other communities by bridges. A 'defend' scenario sees large investments being put into building sea defences around 90 per cent of the city. In an 'attack' scenario, a network of static platforms and floating structures is created protruding into the estuary, converting recycled marine infrastructure such as obsolete oil rigs and using houseboats to provide for a mix of uses. All three scenarios require the intervention of allocative structures around land, whether in managing retreat and the associated losses, organizing the financing of sea defences around areas of land, or advancing into areas which are under the ownership of the Crown.[5] The issues raised by climate change are returned to in the concluding chapter.

The variety of approaches to land around the North Sea

The examples of waterfront regeneration seen in the previous sections illustrate the variety of landownership patterns that can be encountered within the UK, ranging from fragmented to concentrated in one powerful landowner, as well as the physical patterns of land available for regeneration and redevelopment, ranging from single large areas concentrated around a major port on a prominent and well-linked site (Leith), through well located but relatively disconnected sites (Gateshead Quays), to discontinuous patchworks of smaller plots scattered throughout a city centre (Hull). The planning system in the UK, though in principle bestowed with strong regulatory powers and with considerable decision-making authority located at municipal level, has had a limited role and success in driving the redevelopment of the areas discussed above. Although land development rights are legally state controlled in the UK, the degree to which this control is exerted is related to the pattern and form of landownership. Thus, planning instruments such as masterplanning have not been used with similar success, or in similar ways, across these examples. In Edinburgh, the council-initiated overall masterplan for Granton did not succeed in fully coordinating the subsequent masterplans developed by the separate major landowners, while the success of the port company's overall masterplan (or 'development framework') for Leith Docks remains to be seen. In Gateshead, initial regeneration of Gateshead Quay was successful in the absence of a masterplan or equivalent planning instrument, while in Hull the city centre masterplan provided the framework for Hull Citybuild's engagement with land assembly and development.

In fact, in these three examples, the forms that leadership in regeneration took have been as important as the landownership patterns and the planning regime in terms of determining the process. The case of Edinburgh shows limited and contested leadership, with the regeneration of Granton lacking in a single or even shared leadership following the initial intervention of the local authority via the commissioning of an area-wide masterplan, and that of Leith depending almost entirely upon the will of its powerful landowner: Leith Ports. The regeneration of Gateshead Quays illustrates how much can be achieved through strong and resourceful leadership from the council even in the face of non-comprehensive control over land and without strong planning instruments in place. That of Hull shows the potential that a partnership approach has – through a shared special purpose vehicle such as an urban regeneration company, in pulling together the resources (including land) of the public and private sectors, and leading on the implementation of an agreed masterplan.

This variety in circumstances and approaches regarding land and leadership becomes even wider if we look at experience beyond the UK, around the North Sea.

For example, public landownership in Hamburg's HafenCity (see Chapter 6), Germany, allowed a comprehensive masterplan to be prepared for the area, as well as very stringent and detailed control of how this land was developed. Land parcels designated for residential development are put out to competitive tender usually on the basis of a fixed price, the choice of successful bid being based on the quality of the proposal. The arm's length company established by the authorities to develop the area – HafenCity Hamburg GmbH – has remained in dialogue with the investors and builders throughout the process, with a phased handover system in place to ensure best quality in results and process. If the parcel developers fail in their obligations, the land can be repossessed (HafenCity Hamburg, 2008).

At the other extreme, a major challenge to the regeneration of Östra Kvillebäcken in Gothenburg, Sweden, was the fragmented nature of landownership, mostly in the hands of small businesses which were reluctant to move in order to allow the implementation of district improvements, including the introduction of a connecting road. Taking this regeneration initiative forward necessitated a visioning process to build consensus, led by the local authority. However, as is seen in Chapter 5, this process did not succeed, and it was eventually abandoned in favour of the purchase of small landholdings by the local authority in order to increase its power in negotiations with the larger landowners in the area.

Yet another different example was the redevelopment of the Oslo waterfront, where an Oslo Waterfront Planning Office was established to carry forward the implementation of the regeneration of 225ha of land along the fjord, divided into 13 areas. Redevelopment of the area of Bjørvika in order to build the Norwegian National Opera and Ballet right at the water's edge, as well as public realm, entailed rerouting the existing fjord-front motorway via an undersea tunnel, thus reconnecting the city with the water. The Oslo Waterfront Planning Office took a leading role in liaising between the local authority and other government bodies, landowners, developers and professionals.

Conclusions

The illustrative examples of allocative and authoritative structures around land in waterfront regeneration – and their relationship to leadership in such initiatives – from experience around the North Sea provide some insights to issues that are relevant to this type of activity worldwide. They highlight the importance of landownership and control, as well as its physical and environmental characteristics, in city-building in general, including in waterfront regeneration.

Land availability is therefore seen to be defined not only by physical constraints but also by socio-cultural norms and state regulation, such as land-use planning, as well as by economic conditions. It may be determined by circumstances on the actual waterfront, such as obsolescence of previous uses or increase in land through reclamation, as well as by circumstances elsewhere, such as, for example, constraints on outward city expansion through green belts and similar mechanisms.

Landownership forms and patterns range from private to public, from single to multiple, and from smallholding to large holding – the combination of these affecting the development process. As waterfront regeneration often takes place in old port areas, single landownership under a port authority or a company (shipbuilding, etc.) is quite common; but there are also situations where landownership is shared across several stakeholders, thus requiring not only land-use planning but also coordination of actions across different properties.

The variety of landownership patterns thus raises the issue of *land-use control* (i.e. the powers that are exerted over how land is used and the location of such powers). In the context of the North Sea, such power tends to be seen as residing formally (or legally) mostly in the municipality; but the examples seen in this chapter suggest that such formal power is often contested by the *de facto* power that landownership confers in practice (a factor that needs to be taken into account when planning any waterfront regeneration initiative).

In addition, the process of *land development and redevelopment* can take various forms, largely related to how land is assembled and made available for development. The examples in this chapter range from large development units taken forward by a single developer, whether this is a company or a partnership, to parcelling into smaller units for development by a diversity of developers. In the North Sea context, a common feature appears to be that whatever the final mechanism for land development or redevelopment is, small landowners tend to get taken out of the process, with land being consolidated into medium and large development units at least in the initial stages of the regeneration process.

Finally, long-term *land management* appears to be addressed to a very limited extent in the examples seen in this chapter. For example, the obligations imposed upon subsequent landowners/tenants by landlords in the historical development of land in the UK have been superseded by extensive municipal responsibility for the public realm, as is the case mostly around the rest of the North Sea. However, both through trends in privatization of urban space and through active experimentation with alternative forms of shared responsibility over urban space, including the public realm (as, for example, in 'business improvement districts'), new forms of land management are emerging. This is increasingly opening up opportunities for the involvement of wider sectors of society in the management of city-building and city management processes, including on the waterfront.

Notes

1   For example, the Land Reform Act 2003 in Scotland allows community organizations to buy land when it comes to be sold.
2   The other two categories, which are not strongly represented in the countries which participated in the Waterfront Communities Project, are the regional economic planning

approach (to some extent used by Germany in the eastern Länder) and the more physical 'urbanism' tradition (European Commission, 1997). For a summary of the implications of these four categories for the spatial planning systems in some of the countries around the North Sea, see Hague and Jenkins (2005).

3   The City of Edinburgh Council ceded the land to Waterfront Edinburgh Ltd, a company established by the local authority in partnership with the regional development agency. This arm's length company then commissioned the masterplans and coordinated development of the part of Granton under its direct control.

4   The Millennium Commission was an independent organization established in the UK in 1993 to distribute National Lottery funds to projects that were successfully designated as millennium projects. The commission ceased to exist in 2006.

5   In the UK, virtually all the seabed out to a distance of 12 nautical miles belongs to the Crown Estate.

4

Urban Vitality
Social Supervision in Schiedam, The Netherlands

Kees Fortuin and Freek de Meere

Introduction

The buzz of the city

> This report attempts to explain what creates the buzz and how a city can retain it, without overheating or losing momentum. Our core argument is that the buzz comes from the spirit, or soul, of a place. It is soul – that indefinable X factor – which gives a city its character and makes it a special place to live in or to visit.

This is a quote from the study *Northern Soul: Culture, Creativity and Quality of Place in Newcastle and Gateshead* by Anna Minton (2003). In this study, Minton claims that a city's buzz comes from its soul or spirit, and not its physical form. In The Netherlands, the discovery of culture and creativity as sources of vitality for cities has also been made only recently, mainly in the slipstream of Richard Florida's *The Rise of the Creative Class* (2002).

As long ago as 1961, the sentence Jane Jacobs chose to open her famous book *The Death and Life of Great American Cities* was: 'This book is an attack on current city planning and rebuilding.' Jacobs's opinion of the urban planning of the time was that it was too physically oriented and there was too little concern for the social form and meaning of the urban and the economic environment. Forty years on, her thinking reverberates in the three pillars – social, economic, physical – of Dutch urban renewal. Until recently, the economic aspect received by far the least attention. In fact, the debate in The Netherlands was about the difficult relationship between physical and social approaches, more than anything else. One explanation for this one-sidedness may be the fact that urban renewal was very much a matter of housing policy instead of urban revitalization. Of course, waterfront development would require a more integrative approach, and in turn it may be expected that it drives the thinking in this more integrative direction.

What fascinated Jane Jacobs was not the sum total of the physical, social and economic aspects of the city; it was its vitality. Major cities certainly have the density of social interaction and activity that we associate with vitality, dynamism and innovation. This interaction does not always have to be 'fun', refined or harmonious. On the contrary, creative cities, cities that go through a 'Golden Age' 'are almost certainly uncomfortable, unstable cities, cities in some kind of basic collective self-examination, cities in the course of kicking over the traces' (Hall, 2002, p.34). A creative city is one with problems that it has no choice but to deal with, which means being innovative. The innovators often come from outside, often being migrants who in the face of the hostility of marginalization they encounter have no other option than developing a perspective on their own. And as these cities under pressure typically are not the centres of culture, finance and power of their time, but more or less the outsiders among them, it can be said that innovation springs from the outsiders in cities who themselves are outsiders (Hall, 2002, p.35). A planned government-guided innovation would not appear to be the most promising approach: 'it seems likely that bottom-up, small-scale, networked innovation will always be necessary for really fundamental economic change' (Hall, 2002, p.36). In other words, a vital city emerges in and through the society itself; it is not created in a blueprint manner by the government.

The urban task is therefore not served by an exclusively physical approach, which, besides underestimating the complexity of the task, would also fail to deal with the dynamism of today's world. While the bricks stay the same, life develops at a rapid pace, constantly taking on new forms. It is inconceivable to create a new physical form or start a new urban renewal for every single change in social circumstances. The necessary flexibility will have to be achieved in a different way, which is why we – the authors – are making a case for emphasizing the social contribution to urban renewal. This aspect must not be forgotten in the *fuzziness* of urban development. We have accordingly developed the position of social supervisor. We explore in this chapter what a social supervisor might contribute to the urban development processes. We start by introducing the Schiedam project.

Social supervision in Schieveste, Schiedam

Schiedam is part of the metropolitan area of Rotterdam. It is a small city on the north bank of the River Maas, on the west side of Rotterdam. Traditionally the Genever distilleries and the shipping industries were prominent; but today the economy is mixed. In the process of the breakdown of industry, the confidence of the city has been damaged. Any area development would have to help overcome this lack of confidence, and precisely this lack of confidence would be the main obstacle. It is in this waterfront community, with its declined shipping industry and with Rotterdam, the second largest harbour in the world, as its neighbour, that the Schieveste project started. The Schieveste development, a brownfield site, will include offices, retail, residential, recreation, leisure and other activities. The site currently sits between a main railway line and a motorway connecting Schiedam with Rotterdam and the rest of The Netherlands to the east, and The Hague to the west. The site has excellent transport connections but poor environmental quality, with traffic noise and air pollution. The site is adjacent to Schiedam's main railway station and is about 1km from the city centre. The main focus of redevelopment will be a multipurpose shopping centre. Within this context, new jobs, housing and facilities will be created, including a regional education centre to improve the educational attainment of the local work force, which faces high levels of unemployment.

As a key area of innovation within the development framework, social integration is being fostered by piloting a new concept of 'social supervision', in parallel with attention to two related initiatives: floor management and location management (defined below). The Schieveste project engaged a social supervisor from the outset (i.e. in late 2000). This person liaised closely with the urban development supervisor in laying the basis for the masterplan. In Schiedam, social supervision focused on sustainable social integration through the development of a viable social structure and the mental adoption of Schieveste by the Schiedammers.

Dealing with urban complexity

Social supervision is not simply a matter of developing social activities and projects. The combined effect of social and physical interventions is more complex than just the sum of both effects. Some of the complexities involved are discussed in this section.

Cities (and, for that matter, countries and neighbourhoods) manage and develop whatever resources they have. Examples of resources are local identity, social and cultural capital, administrative networks, economic factors, the quality of the body of public servants, the housing stock, and so on. Cities use these resources, but at the same time develop them in order to improve their position in the midst of other cities. In the process, social, physical and economic developments interact, with the involvement not only of the government or professional organizations, but also of individuals in society. 'The city' in this connection is therefore not a monolith, but a network of mutually influencing developments, comprising countless actors, both inside and outside the city's administrative boundaries. It would be naive to think that a single actor – for the sake of argument, the city council – is able to 'save' the city on its own. It would be equally naive to think that a single strategy, whether physical, social, cultural or economic – could do so.

As an example, let's consider Florida's (2002, 2004) focus on creative class. Florida claims that the creative class is specifically decisive in the development of successful cities, and discards *social capital* as well as *human capital* as explanations. This claim has been contested (e.g. by Hoyman and Farici, 2009). It has also been argued that his theory is circular (Peck, 2005). For a former industrial and shipbuilding community such as Schiedam, this circularity would present an insurmountable problem: in order to have a sizeable creative class, you would already have to have a sizeable creative class.

However, on a practical level it is also possible to depict a plausible scenario in which social, human and creative capital approaches each play a part in a positive dynamic within the urban community. Cities such as Schiedam would be well advised to develop a substantial *civil society* and work on socially inclusive policies (i.e. *social capital*). Using the resources within civil society and in their social networks, individuals with initiative and better education will thrive and start to work on a fine-grained urban structure of services and business activity (i.e. *human capital*). The cultural vanguards whose time has yet to arrive should certainly be counted among these individuals, such as skaters, squatters and rappers. They can develop their talents in a poor neighbourhood at little expense, while the creative class dominates the gentrified, more expensive neighbourhoods. These cultural vanguards could then develop into the cultural elite of the future, which at a certain point will start to attract the creative class (i.e. *creative capital*) from elsewhere. You will then have a cultural strategy that emerges from the interplay between the city's social, human and creative capital.

From a social point of view, the challenge of urban renewal is further enhanced by the different levels of analysis and intervention involved. Whereas city planners, architects and other actors in the physical sector are used to working with the interaction of different scales or different levels at a time, for social actors in The Netherlands – community workers, social workers, educational and neighbourhood services – this is quite new. They also lack the elaborate professional infrastructure (e.g. organizations, education, funds and awards) to develop the necessary qualifications and expertise. And, finally, they do not have the position in the project organizations around area development. A community worker will not meet project developers, investors, architects and city planners and have discussions with them on a regular basis, so there is essentially no channel for communication about the social challenges involved in particular area developments. Of course, there are exceptions, an excellent one being Roombeek, a neighbourhood in Enschede that was ruined in a huge explosion of a fireworks depot. The reconstruction relied heavily on intensive participation of the residents, who also had to deal with the trauma they experienced. The community worker – a social entrepreneur with an excellent reputation – played a major part in the success; but still in the eyes of the public it is the city planner involved who 'reconstructed' Roombeek.

A social supervisor thus has to face different challenges at a time. The first is the development of the city as a whole and of the way in which the city can utilize and develop its resources. In the case of Schiedam, the development of Schieveste would not only have to be a success in itself, but would also have to boost the confidence of the city. A successful development does not do this if a sense of ownership and pride in the accomplishment are lacking. Participation and involvement of Schiedam at large would thus be a major goal. Second is the interaction of social actors and institutions with other involved disciplines and sectors. As noted above, this involves having a better position in the process. But the development of a shared conceptual framework and a set of established methods and instruments to link the social with other perspectives are also necessary. It should be noted that the challenge is not purely the development of a social framework for area development. The focus is on the interplay. Social professionals are players in an orchestra, just as all the other players, and they have to work on how they play as a team, not just on their individual qualities. Finally, there is the strength and quality of social interventions. Working with residents has its relevance for the city as a whole because the residents are its most important resource. But this also requires its own quality standards, and there is still much to be gained.

Each action must generally be seen simultaneously in the light of all three levels. An action may have maximum effect on a given level, but still be below standard if it is counterproductive on other levels. For example, maximum effort can be put into resident participation in the context of the development of Schieveste (the third level); but unless this participation leads to changes in the way in which the physical sector works (the second level), it will produce frustration, which on the first level may contribute to a negative atmosphere in the city.

Addressing three levels simultaneously is certain to make the urban renewal task more complex. But it will also considerably enlarge the perspective for actual renewal, for increasing the city's dynamism and, thus, the efficiency of urban renewal as a policy instrument.

A social supervisor

The idea of social supervision is an analogy of the position of a prominent city planner or architect as supervisor in area development. Such a supervisor often produces the vision and the masterplan, and is responsible for the quality and consistency of the masterplan in terms of the contributions of different designers, developers and professionals working in the area. Likewise, the social supervisor judges the quality and consistency of contributions to the area development, but from a social perspective.

The concept developed out of a growing number of projects in which a better fit between physical and social contributions was sought. In 1999, the city council of Rotterdam prepared a market analysis to study the possibilities for further development of de Wilhelminapier, part of the Kop van Zuid waterfront development in Rotterdam. One of the participants was TRS, a project developer. TRS had the ambition to make a contribution in which social and economic aspects would be as prominent as physical features. For the social aspect, they contacted the Verwey-Jonker Institute. The social vision that Kees Fortuin and Jan Willem Duyvendak, who worked for the Verwey-Jonker Institute at the time, made was one of the main reasons that Rotterdam City Council chose the TRS plan. When Schiedam subsequently initiated the Schieveste project, the process manager, Ben Westerdijk, asked Kees Fortuin if he was interested in being the social counterpart of the supervisor, and suggested the name 'social supervisor' for the function.

At the start of the Schieveste project, the idea that you can formulate 'social images' for an area in development was new in terms of social policy. The sector tends, rather, to see itself as the implementer of the visions that emerge from physical thinking, or as a kind of a 'lubricant' for the physical process. A social supervisor can compensate for this submissive role and, if possible, turn it into a leading one.

The following section addresses the task that cities actually always have, which is to strengthen their position among other cities by developing and managing their resources. In this situation, the resource that is of concern to the social supervisor is 'social and creative capital'. This is not an isolated and independent part of urban renewal, but has to be viewed in conjunction with spatial and physical resources, such as the housing stock and the urban space. Next, this chapter outlines the role, position and instruments of a social supervisor. This is followed by a discussion of practical experiences in Schiedam. Finally, after a brief review of the further development of the figure of the social supervisor in Alkmaar, conclusions are drawn on the constraints and tasks for the future.

What does a social supervisor do?

Tasks

A social supervisor facilitates integrating the design process within the social context. Architects, urban developers and their clients often try to harmonize the design with the surroundings and history of the site concerned. The social supervisor has the same task, but focuses on the social aspects. Some of the important topics that he or she gathers information on are the local social history, the local culture (in particular, culture with a small 'c'), the identity, and the use and potential of the area. The social supervisor uses the knowledge gained as input to the design process, developing strategies for creating social impressions, and monitors the social quality of the area to be developed. In more concrete terms, the above comes down to the following points:

- It is expected that a social supervisor develop 'social impressions' that are compatible with the area or project. The impression of an area emerges from how it is perceived, which is always related to the things that happen there. An impression materializes from what people experience, not only visually, but also emotionally: people experience pleasant or unpleasant things in a given area. Furthermore, the impression is never 'finished' and constantly changes. Different people develop different impressions. History and past experiences are also important. A shopkeeper who has had to endure nuisance from the same source for years will have little faith in initiatives to alleviate the problem. In this way, the past can act as a brake; but positive effects are equally likely to act as a flywheel.
- It is expected that a social supervisor develop strategies for turning desirable impressions into reality, as well as organizational concepts for securing the desired social climate and ensuring that it 'bends' to suit changing circumstances. Because social impressions are rooted in events, and events never cease, a certain amount of managing what happens is necessary. This management does not stop when the development in the area is complete, but has to continue afterwards. The task is therefore far broader than one of organizing public participation within a specific development process. What is needed is a continuous development of social structure based on events and activities. Organization is necessary not only to guarantee continuity of this kind, but also to build and extend the social impressions, structure and social quality from a professional perspective. It is essential not to follow a one-sided technical or commercial approach, but to utilize all social opportunities.

- It is expected that a social supervisor monitor the social and the *overall* quality of the area or project to be developed. We are not saying that the social view should predominate; other experts from other sectors also monitor overall quality. The social supervisor is the champion of social quality in the development process. He or she protects the project against poorly judged moves and identifies opportunities for achieving favourable social effects during the development process. The important thing is not to protect institutional interests, or an unbalanced social orientation just as a counterpart of an unbalanced physical orientation. The urban renewal task can only reach fruition from the perspective of the development of the city as a whole. The social supervisor therefore argues the case for the social viewpoint from a sectoral, but integral, perspective.

Position

Social supervisors' main role is in the design and planning process, and less so in their execution. Their contribution is on a programme level to the extent to which they forge an inspiring vision that mobilizes local society and all stakeholders. They must make the necessary difference with persuasiveness and information gathered in the contact between the various parties.

Figure 4.1 *Schiedam inner city*

Source: Kees Fortuin and Freek de Meere

Social supervisors contribute to – and are not owners of – the masterplan, which is the basis for the chosen development direction. Their recommendations are oriented towards administration and programme management. They need a budget for consultancy and can issue instructions as needed for deploying people, resources and competencies by the local authority and the project management office. It goes without saying that these people, resources and competencies have to be present and available, which sets requirements on an administrative level. The ambition must actually exist on an administrative level for making a real social achievement. Because the social supervision concept is still under construction, some pioneering work is called for, which makes it important to have good relations with social implementers. Social supervisors will preferably seek partnership with local social organizations (not only welfare organizations, but also those in education, sport and culture, as well as the police), not to mention commercial partners outside the municipality.

Social quality

In terms of the social quality to be advocated, the social supervisor has three guiding concepts. It is important to strike a proper balance between these three because a one-sided emphasis could destroy the innovative capacity of the area.

Social vitality

Social vitality is concerned with the dynamism in the area in a social and economic sense. Vitality is more than the harmonious vision of liveliness, animation, freedom and growth. Vitality does not stop conflicts, friction, irritations and disasters from happening, but does mean that 'the area' can cope with them far better. From a physical and spatial viewpoint, the opportunities for change and adaptation are modest. In practice, the main ways in which an area adapts to changes will be through social and economic processes.

Personal safety

A society will ultimately have to produce its own safety, however necessary the professional 'safety-makers' may be. It is well known that the quality of social relationships is the most important determinant of a perception of safety. Urban renewal, therefore, demands a public that has an attachment to the space and that will take the space under its protection. Social activities ensure social structure and, therefore, safety. They provide an environment for creating the social networks that offer safety through an ability to intervene if necessary. This is true as early as the construction phase. For example, children make the physical space their own in an extremely intense way. From the viewpoint of physical safety, it is perhaps understandable that children should be kept away from building sites; but from the viewpoint of attachment, and therefore personal safety, to do so would be counterproductive and a missed opportunity. This is almost practically impossible unless under very controlled conditions; but it is necessary to make this kind of participation possible.

Social sustainability

An area is created with the aim of sustainability. However, thinking about social sustainability starts with a consideration of impermanence. An area that stays fixed when it is surrounded by turbulent social developments is like a rudderless and helpless dinghy at the mercy of a violent current: it is unable to manoeuvre. Social sustainability is served well if it is adaptive with respect to developments in the environment. It also has to provide for reflection and monitoring because it is essential to anticipate changes. Management (in a broad sense, including management of social activities) will have to be sufficiently flexible to respond rapidly to new situations. Proper integration within urban and regional networks is important for being able to generate and mobilize resources quickly.

Two leading principles

Continuity versus discontinuity

A physical approach often involves discontinuity. It is often the case that an undeveloped area is filled with new buildings, or existing buildings are replaced by something new. In creating more differentiated housing, a discontinuity is also introduced (e.g. by bringing people with higher incomes into the neighbourhood). In a social approach, it is actually continuity that you try to use by building upon the opportunities of the existing society, and seeking out the history and identity of the area and the existing social structures, qualities and opportunities. While doing so, you try to set a process in motion towards a more vital society. In the spirit of Jane Jacobs, we might perhaps say that a city has to pull itself out of the quagmire mainly by its own hair. Its citizens live in the city and nowhere else. If they are enterprising, they will devote their efforts to the city. They are part of a social structure that *exists* as opposed to being a fantasy. A social supervisor therefore builds upon what already exists in order to develop a more vital urban area. The fact is that continuity exists in social life. A city in a social sense is not changed fundamentally just by altering the built environment.

The development strategy: Activity takes precedence over structure

The development strategy in the social approach is fundamentally different from the physical one. In the latter, a physical structure is first developed and built before being taken into use. Only then do the activities begin: structure therefore takes precedence over activity. The opposite is true in the social approach: a social structure cannot emerge on the basis of a preconceived final picture. It develops through a pattern of social activities: activity therefore takes precedence over structure.

A social structure develops in use. This use leads to a history of the area, social impressions and attachment on the part of the users. They may be positive or negative, but together they form the building blocks that you have to work with. The social supervisor must therefore devise a development strategy in which the social impression is created through activity. The

Figures 4.2a and 4.2b *Activity changes space: a skating rink on the station forecourt*

Source: Kees Fortuin and Freek de Meere

impression is like a plant that you care for. You do not know what the plant will look like exactly, and you only have limited control. The centre of the 'creative activity' is actually not the designer, but society. The point of a social approach is therefore to stimulate activities that are always the starting point of a growing number of other activities (see also the section on 'Budget' below). Attachment and long-term commitment ultimately arise only in a long chain of events that is never really broken.

Experiences in Schieveste

Introduction

The independent appointment of the social supervisor in the Schieveste project was advantageous in that he was outspoken in terms of the participation of local residents in the development project. We will briefly describe some of the work of the social supervisor on a practical level. However, there were also several concerns. We will set out the most important ones at the end of this section, together with the limitations that a social supervisor has to work with.

Location and floor management

A high point in the Schieveste project development was reached with the publication of the Schieveste masterplan. The masterplan is evidence of vision and ambition, not only to provide Schieveste with an attractive appearance in terms of spatial quality and economic potential, but also from a social perspective, making the location vital, sustainable and safe, and reflecting local culture, history and identity. In addition, neighbourhood support for the Schieveste project was strong at this early phase, and a great number of activities involving the community in all its guises were organized. The initial organization was an unofficial conglomerate of activities, cooperating partners and sources of funding. The challenge was to develop the existing organization into a more formalized area management organization that was sensitive to the commercial aspects of development but did not lose sight of social elements and the sense of community.

A location management instrument was devised in order to retain and, where possible, strengthen this initial character of Schieveste. Location management was defined as the instrument that is available jointly to the market and government for retaining and strengthening Schieveste's long-term liveability, quality and property value. While the social supervisor helped to organize the overall strategic approach to community participation, the 'location manager' was available on a day-to-day basis to promote local activities and events that improve the social cohesion of the area. For Schieveste, these included:

- a temporary winter skating rink onsite to mark the launch of Schieveste from a local residents' point of view;

Figure 4.3 *Children filling in a questionnaire*

Source: Kees Fortuin and Freek de Meere

Figure 4.4 *Residents presenting their vision*

Source: Kees Fortuin and Freek de Meere

- a formal lunch on the construction site for local residents in order to give them a first-hand view of redevelopment;
- a variety of briefings for the community, including special briefings for children;
- 'a platform of prominent Schiedammers' who championed activities during the development of Schieveste – as a result, the development would carry their 'mark of support', building positive consensus around the development;
- a major information meeting on redeveloping an urban entertainment centre at Schieveste.

These activities were aimed at establishing an organic link between the Schiedam community and Schieveste, and initiated by the social supervisor. For instance, the temporary ice rink was created on the railway station forecourt that was due to be transformed so that the residents and users could continue to perceive it as 'theirs'. But the timing was essential. The possible displacement of drugs-related nuisance was anticipated in good time when a more stringent approach in Spangen in Rotterdam was introduced. Schiedam was able to ensure that the station forecourt did not become the new drugs hot-spot.

After this, the 'floor manager' post was introduced as a way of promoting a positive social climate. The manager was based in a small cabin on site where he held weekly surgeries. He could also be reached on his mobile telephone. The manager was present in Schieveste since the start of the first phase of the project, in May 2005, as the 'eyes and ears' of the everyday experience in the area. On the level of the 'high street', the manager acts as an important link between the area's existing social relationships and those to be developed. He builds relationships with people who are to play an important role and engages passers-by in conversation in order to get feedback on the area from their perspective. It is essential that the manager's information on the social situation in the area is incorporated within the project's organizational decisions. He links detailed knowledge of the people on the ground with the competencies of the project organization. Among the subjects that may come up is the location of seating, rerouting a cycle path, policing requirements or organizing an activity. The floor manager's input should reflect the viewpoint of residents and other users of the centre, sharing a similar professional approach to the social supervisor, but with actual authority on an operational level. Key lessons from this experience are the need to develop a business plan for the 'floor management' and to locate the manager within the area renewal organization. Floor management will be incorporated within the permanent organization for location management that will be paid for by Schieveste customers. However, it remains to be seen whether all the work had satisfactory results. The ice rink was moved and the municipality cut back on security sharply. This is evidence that initial success offers no guarantee whatsoever of quality and continuity.

Some concerns

The idea behind the concept of social supervisor is that a social contribution to urban renewal will be most effective if it is present from the outset and has a 'champion' within the development process. This idea was tested in real life in Schieveste. Of course, practical problems did arise. For example, the social supervisor's role should be made clear to all involved over and over again, as many will be completely unfamiliar with the role and its rationale. However, in the process of looking for proof of concept, the three most important concerns were about organizational issues, the capacities of a social supervisor and the instruments that he or she can use.

First, people within the local organizational structure continually asked how the social supervisor is located within the organization. Because the supervisor has an unclear local role, their opinions can also be ignored as coming from 'someone outside the structure'. The lesson here is that the social supervisor needs to work hard to establish links not only with the community, but to 'build bridges' with local government officers, politicians and representatives of the development company. This is essential if the views of the social supervisor are to be taken seriously and to influence the development process.

Second, in the case of Schieveste, the social supervisor came from a background of research and policy analysis, and there were concerns that his use of language was overcomplicated for an audience unfamiliar with community development expertise. Both problems were addressed by open discussion of key issues and how to improve on-going processes of social supervision. This process of continuous improvement is the essence of an action-research approach. While the process was sometimes difficult, it created a better fit between academic thinking/working and practice.

Third, a key aspect of social supervision is open and honest review of on-going activities in the project as it affects social participants. Schiedam tackled this by both using academic partners for critical but constructive review, and hosting a mini-symposium which reviewed the project from a variety of viewpoints, including those of local residents and workers. Their views, brought together in a video, were not always comfortable for project officers. But they did result in recommendations (e.g. 'link Schieveste with elderly and disabled people'), 'points of attention' and seven priorities for action.

Working on limitations

The experiences in Schieveste and those in other cities (e.g. Inverdan in Zaanstad) (Fortuin and de Meere, 2004) led the social supervisor to describe five essential points upon which to reflect.

Involvement from the outset

If the social supervisor becomes involved in the process at a late stage, he or she could easily interfere with the status quo that has developed already. This disruption might sometimes have a positive effect, but in this scenario we would expect the social supervisor to be seen as a risk factor for continuity. Furthermore, many assumptions are set down in an early planning stage, and they become more firmly embedded as the project proceeds. A social supervisor who enters too late will no longer be able to exercise much influence. The social viewpoint will then be limited to 'refining' a masterplan that was initially worked out from a physical viewpoint. Anything else will be considered to be pushing back the train to stations that were passed long ago.

Positioning and continuity

Although much of a social supervisor's advice is given informally and sometimes also publicly to keep away from administration and politics, we actually urge continuous interaction. Keeping a distance has great benefits for designers and implementers, but if you are working on the future of the city, you have to have an understanding with the elected administration. Because social development never ends, the interaction with the administration will need to have a permanent character. However, the social supervisor should ensure cover against the vicissitudes of politics. No positioning whatsoever can, or should be able to, protect the social supervisor against the field of conflicting forces that naturally surrounds urban renewal.

Chemistry and momentum

The social supervisor has to deal with various counterparts. In Zaanstad (Fortuin and de Meere, 2004), a counterpart within the municipal social sector proved fruitful. Without such a counterpart, the communication gap with the generally far more physically and technically oriented project organization could rapidly become too great. However, it is also necessary to build on 'chemistry and momentum' within the project. A team that inspires each other also generates new ideas and attracts outside interest. The resources may then expand steadily after the start. It is not uncommon in urban renewal to work in this way: starting with a small team that is inspired and functions as a unity, and then growing in quality and the number of people involved in activities.

Budget

In Schieveste, the social supervisor worked with a marginal budget. This is understandable in view of the lack of any tradition with social supervision. At the same time, other parties in the social sector are normally tightly controlled so that, even if resources were to exist, there is little enthusiasm for partnership. The supervisor then suggested developing a 'living money strategy'. Every activity that was organized had to give rise to a multitude of new activities. And every budget used preferably linked the programme with other policy programmes and financial resources. In this way, social activities could act as *multipliers* for both the activities themselves and for the budget. It cannot be stressed enough that funding and the search for it contribute to the development of the project. For example, developing activities and finding the necessary funding is a training context for local talents, and this creates precisely the desired vitality.

Routines and reflection

Something that is hard to organize in the on-going process of urban renewal is reflection, both in the government and in the commercial world. Although the task is extremely complex, the integration of physical and social approaches still cannot be taken for granted. A condition for developing social supervision is the documentation of experiences, reflection, research and exchange of knowledge, not only at the higher levels, but down to the very lowest level. After all, the complexity of the process makes it very sensitive to 'initial conditions' and details.

Experiences in Overstad, Alkmaar

One project that enabled us to take the concept of social supervision one step further was the development of Overstad in Alkmaar. Alkmaar has a finely grained old inner city that is surrounded by water, which is an obstacle to its growth. Next to the centre, on the other side of the North Holland Channel, lies a business district, Overstad, which will be restructured as a second part of the city centre. The land is owned by 42 different parties, which makes it complicated to develop. Alkmaar has contracted a social supervisor. He is independent and has been commissioned directly by the city council. Quality is considered a public interest, so the commission should come from the public sector. As quality entails a certain degree of subjectivity, it is preferred that the supervisor is an independent professional of considerable standing. The city planner/supervisor is Adriaan Geuze and the social supervisor is Kees Fortuin.

New in Alkmaar is the fact that the municipality set out a tender to select a private-sector party with whom to form a public–private partnership. The social supervisor was part of the selection committee, and social criteria played a substantial part in assessing the proposals. As a consequence, a partner was selected with an enthusiastic attitude towards social aspects of area development. It was a consortium in which a major housing corporation participated, so it brought with it a lot of expertise in participation and co-creation practices. The municipality and the consortium thus both participate in a public–private partnership (Nieuw Overstad BV). Besides Nieuw Overstad, independent projects taken forward by individual owners are still possible as long as they fit within the masterplan. However, every plan is subjected to the same quality assessment by the supervisors.

The process is moving strongly in the direction of an organic development, as are the underlying concepts. This means existing qualities are preserved and taken as a departure point for further development instead of moving them all aside and replacing them by completely new buildings and sites. Although a business district is normally considered a low standard environment, the existing entrepreneurship is a definite quality and high value is placed on the participation of local entrepreneurs. Furthermore, a growth perspective – as opposed to a 'building perspective' – has been adopted, and reciprocal relationships with the urban environment are encouraged. The transition phase of Overstad is part and parcel of the on-going 'historical development' of the city.

At the time of writing, a social and cultural area vision has been completed, as well as a study of the 'cultural biography' of Overstad, resulting in a cultural atlas. At the moment, a 'social quality plan' is being written, which is a framework for assessing the social quality of development plans. It specifies the social requirements that project developers will have to meet. For instance, they are required to develop a vision on participation and processes of 'mental adoption' by the public. Participation plans are being worked out and a start has been made with forming an organization for area management in which residents, businesses, visitors and other stakeholders take an active part.

Good opportunities are being created for establishing businesses and creative industry. On the other hand, more traditional developments are also being planned and it is expected that building activities will soon start.

Conclusions

Our experiences in Schiedam and Alkmaar suggest that social supervision is a promising concept, still in the making, but definitely able to add value to urban renewal. The added value manifests itself in four areas.

First, the social supervisor puts social interventions in a better position to contribute. The single most important success factor is a good understanding and rapport between project manager, social supervisor and city planner/supervisor. It is also essential to have enterprising organizations that respond alertly to the opportunities offered, including social entrepreneurs who work on a commercial basis. The basis for financing these activities in Alkmaar lies – apart from limited initial investments by the local government – in the obligation for developers to comply with the social quality plan, deliver a vision on the social processes involved and contribute to the necessary measures.

Second, social supervision also leads to a broader interpretation of social policy, in which it acts as a productive factor and a contributor to value creation. In particular, the attention to culture and local identity offers opportunities for a social policy that is not limited to 'compensation for deficiencies'. The focus is broader than the individual having to make up lost ground, integrate or develop a new perspective. Social processes are seen as productive factors in the creation of the city of the future. Their relevance grows because the city and the developing area mutually influence each other – the area development driving the ambition and dynamics of the city, and the city developing its quality and vitality. Social processes are relevant to current issues such as globalization, the network society, the risk society, innovation, increasing mobility, integration, ethnic and cultural tensions, and perceptions of safety. This offers new perspectives for the social sector, which in The Netherlands is in great need of new inspiration.

Third, social contribution has a clear added value compared with other disciplines involved. It counters the tendency of many developers to start building as soon as possible because they, too, have to think of the social climate that they leave behind when the building activity has stopped. Conversely, the authors believe it will enable the social sector to link up with the complex and dynamic issues that are so important for the future of the cities.

And, fourth, in both practical examples, it would appear that more is possible in the city than was thought. Social supervision is able to help develop the strength and pride of the city. Alkmaar shows that the dynamic within the development continues to grow, creating chances for many more urban actors than in a traditional approach. It may even contribute to financial sustainability because, until now, the developments in Alkmaar seem to have suffered relatively little from the current economic crisis.

All of these activities have given us a better insight into the 'symbolic factor' (local culture and identity) of Overstad and in the ways to turn them into productive forces that stimulate area development. With hindsight, the project in Schiedam could have made better use of this symbolic factor. Schiedam is definitely a waterfront community. The collapse of shipbuilding activities, in particular, has left its mark on the local community. It should be noted that Schiedam Oost, the neighbourhood closest to Schieveste, was built specifically for the workers of a large shipyard.

In contrast, in Overstad, research into the roots of the area and the involvement of people with a history in Overstad make it possible to relate to the identity and the drives of stakeholders in the area, thus creating more momentum for the transformation.

Looking back, we come to the conclusion that social supervision is a focused intervention that brings the ideal of a vital city nearer. It is not social contribution by itself, however, that creates this result. It is the complex process of area development in which the social aspect is but one of many aspects. In this sense, the vision of Jane Jacobs presented at the beginning of this chapter is not lost.

5

On Dialogues and Municipal Learning in City-Building
Examples from Waterfront Development in Gothenburg

Joakim Forsemalm and Knut Strömberg

Introduction

Gothenburg is the second largest city in Sweden and has the largest port in Scandinavia. Until the middle of the 1970s, Gothenburg was also one of the world's leading shipbuilding harbours when the global shipbuilding crisis, in a very short time, completely changed the world map of shipbuilding. The shipyards, which were all located on the northern riverside, were closed down and numerous people became unemployed. After some unsuccessful attempts to re-engineer the vast areas for other industrial activities, the brownfield sites were cleaned up, and these huge areas have, since then, during a 30-year period, gradually been redeveloped with the official goal of creating a *good mixed city* with high-quality housing, knowledge-based activities and high-quality leisure areas as a new mental model for urban development. The focus from the city has been on attracting business (e.g. through an information technology (IT) and design cluster with a local TV/radio station) and establishing a science park located close to a new campus for the two city universities in the old industrial buildings. From an economic point of view, the conversion is considered very successful. From an architectural and planning point of view, it has good spatial standards; but the area has been criticized for being dead and lacking urbanity.

However, it is not only the areas close to the riverside that have been affected by the closure of the shipyards. Subcontractors and suppliers of services for the industry have also been affected and have left other areas in the vicinity of the waterfronts. Once the upgrading of the waterfront areas began, gentrification processes became imminent. This is what is feared by many for the development of the southern riverside, close to the historical city centre, after the heavy car traffic along the river has been led underground in a tunnel and left key areas open for new developments and a reconnection of the city centre with the water.

Figure 5.1 *Location of the three case study waterfront regeneration areas in Gothenburg: Södra Älvstranden (1), Långgatorna (2) and Östra Kvillebäcken (3)*

Source: Knut Strömberg, based on map from Gothenburg City Planning Office

During the last few decades, the development of Western cities has come to be increasingly characterized by political goals such as integration, participation and sustainability, often without being concrete or made operational. In order to achieve such broad and sweeping goals, the existing procedures and tools of the planning system are not enough; rather, cooperation with many actors outside of the domains of city planning authorities is required. The transition from 'government' to 'governance' – the process of moving decision-making from hierarchical, rigid and formal organizations to network-based and consensus-driven processes – has been questioned as to whether such cooperation is just paying 'lip-service', whether the participatory models are alibis for decision-making happening behind closed doors, or whether the openness to different kinds of dialogues make any real impression on the outcome of the decision-making processes. This was widely discussed in the media and by researchers in Gothenburg during the first decade of the 2000s.

During the mid 2000s, many Swedish municipalities conducted public dialogues with citizens and various constellations of actors affected by or affecting different municipal decisions (Cars and Strömberg, 2005). Unfortunately, the dialogue projects conducted have largely been carried out without the results being properly documented and analysed. There are important questions that need answers: do we get better cities through dialogue or other participatory models? Are these approaches more efficient as planning methods? Does participation become a value in itself (Strömberg, 2001; Strömberg and Kain, 2005)? How are participants' viewpoints in these processes taken care of? How are (abstract) political objectives integrated within everyday planning practice? Does the organizational structure of planning need to change and perhaps be endowed with new competences to meet the increased amount of 'politics' in complex planning issues?

This chapter examines three examples of how different forms of dialogue and participatory models have been used for different areas affected by waterfront development during different phases of the planning process (see Figure 5.1). The *Södra Älvstranden* case describes a public dialogue in a visionary phase of the planning process before programming and detailed planning. In the district of *Långgatorna*, the process was in the phase of developing a programme for the restoration of an existing area at the time of writing. The third, *Östra Kvillebäcken*, is in a former mixed area that has been used for small-scale industry, business and housing and was in a state of transition. The cases studied have the same organizational base or point of departure: the municipal planning office.

Dialog Södra Älvstranden

Transforming old industrial areas: Northern Älvstranden

The global shipbuilding crisis during the mid 1970s drove the four shipyards in Gothenburg into bankruptcy and left an enormous redundant area in the heart of the city. A large re-engineering process was initiated, and to be able to handle all material resources needed for investments in infrastructure, decontamination of land, etc., a drastic change in the allocative structures was implemented (Healey, 2007, p.21, citing Giddens, 1984): a publicly owned development company, NUAB Ltd, was established. All planning and building proposals in Sweden have to pass the municipal planning office and be accepted by the building permission committee (Strömberg, 2008). NUAB Ltd was, however, commissioned to coordinate and develop the area under the strategic leadership of the city's leading politicians on the company's board. This implies a change in the authoritative structure (Giddens, 1984; Healey, 2007) since the redevelopment was planned and tested politically before it went through the standard planning procedures.

The company is run, as politically decided, without any subsidies. It invests in infrastructure and develops activities, buildings and houses in close cooperation with actors who consider establishing in the area. This gives a strong economic incentive to NUAB, which owns the land, leads and monitors construction, and also gets the profit when the products are sold. The profit is reinvested in infrastructure and in developing new projects. The key working instruments for the company are networking, close cooperation and design dialogues with potential actors (Öhrström, 2005). The transformation is not only an urban planning endeavour, but a social-spatial process (Mandanipour, 1996) with an interactive play between the existing infrastructure, land, financial capital, potential locators and other actors. This also constitutes a new mental model (Jenkins and Smith, 2001) for the former industrial areas – a 'city of knowledge' is to be established. The new organizational form for implementing the new approach is called the Northern Riverside Model.

The public interest in the development of the northern riverside has so far been low and citizens have not taken part in participatory processes for developing the area beyond what is regulated by the Housing and Building Act. One explanation for the low interest is that the area is situated on the socially 'wrong' side of the river and is composed of mainly old industrial areas.

Reclaiming the waterfront: Southern Älvstranden

Quite another situation, concerning public interest, emerged when a lively debate on what should happen on the opposite southern side of the river, Södra Älvstranden, started after a decision was taken to construct a car tunnel to redirect traffic away from the waterfront. This part of the riverside is in the vicinity of the historical city centre; but the connection between the river and the city has been cut off for 30 years by a heavily loaded road along the riverside (see Figures 5.2 and 5.3). The opportunity to reconnect the city with the water called for a new mental model, from a heavy loaded transportation artery to an attractive part of the city centre as 'a living room for all citizens'. The great public interest also gave the municipality opportunity for testing a new institutional model, based on the experiences from the northern riverside, to coordinate the redevelopment (Jenkins and Smith, 2001).

Figure 5.2 *Södra Älvstranden from the south-west before the opening of the tunnel*

Source: Stadsbyggnadskontoret, 2006

The public debate became extra lively when a political decision changed the authoritative structure (Healey, 2007) for the development by giving NUAB Ltd the assignment to also develop the southern riverside, due to its demonstrated good ability to develop the old shipyards area. The first important step was to change the allocative structure. The ownership of all publicly owned land in the area was transferred to the development company in order to give it the ability to do the same trick as on the other side of the river: to develop the area; enhance the quality by planning, organizing, making investments and then selling off; capitalizing on the improved quality; and 'harvesting' the gain to put into further investments in the area. The requirement of self-financing was the same as in the northern riverside. The problem is that there is not so much land to develop on the southern side as on the other side, and the investments have to provide higher profit margins. Reacting to these events, citizens then noted the development on the northern riverside and put forward opinions such as: 'no more exclusive housing for the rich', 'the area belongs to all citizens', 'no more dead office areas', 'reclaim the riverside for pedestrian and cyclists', 'no more cars', etc.

The political parties became involved in an unproductive fight concerning where to put the tramline; after a citizens' referendum and a lively public debate, the city council decided to initiate a public dialogue where citizens were to be given the opportunity to put forward their visions, wishes and opinions on how to develop the area before the ordinary planning process started.

Testing new ways of public participation

The *Dialog Södra Älvstranden* was carried out in a first phase during spring 2005. The process had two steps, followed by an evaluation of the input from

Figure 5.3 *Södra Älvstranden traffic situation before the opening of the tunnel*

Source: Stadsbyggnadskontoret, 2006

citizens and its transformation into a formal document – a planning programme – to guide the subsequent detailed plans following the Planning and Building Act. The evaluation document and the planning programme were presented in a public exhibition for public consultation before political decision-making. By early 2011, no detailed plan had yet been decided upon. Public interest had cooled.

The expectations for the *Dialog* among many citizens were high. Others felt that this was just paying lip service – the dialogue would not make any difference. The goal for the dialogue was to find out what the area meant to the citizens and what wishes and visions existed or could be developed for the urban life in the area. This can be seen as building a new system of meaning for Södra Älvstranden (Schön and Rhein, 1994). The commission to develop the organization of the dialogue was given to NUAB in cooperation with Urban Laboratory Göteborg (ULG) – a platform for cooperation between academia, the city and different actors interested in the urban development of Gothenburg. Politicians were asked to keep away from party politics until the voice of the citizens had been heard in order to avoid political deadlocks.

Step 1: All citizens invited

The first step of the *Dialog* was to invite all citizens, and public interest was great. The dialogue took place in two arenas: one in the City Museum, with continuously updated exhibitions, seminars, lectures and debates; and one being virtual on www.alvstaden.se, where people could send messages, questions and proposals, and also download former plans, pictures and other material. The museum also organized 'city walk and talk tours'. The creativity was great and more than 1000 written proposals were registered and catalogued in the museum.

The first phase of the dialogue process was managed by a steering group from different departments in the city administration, academia and non-governmental organizations (NGOs). The group worked on a day-to-day basis in order to be adaptable and to find ways of handling upcoming situations. This part was a full-scale experiment and a continuous learning process for the management, without any experiences of the same magnitude to draw on.

Already in this phase of the public dialogue it was possible to identify differing perspectives within the steering group on what kind of process was going on. One understanding was that it was a process to get as many practically implementable ideas as possible for the future planning of the area. Another was that this was a democratic experiment in generating the

Figure 5.4 Dialog Södra Älvstranden *logotype*

Source: Gothenbug City Museum

commitment and engagement of citizens in the future life of the city. The differing opinions in the steering group were managed through compromises.

The number of proposals was overwhelming and the dialogue process was taken into a second step to address the views of citizens. Here again different views on the meaning of the dialogue became visible within the steering group. One was to sort out and structure the citizens' material according to physical entities such as houses, park, quays, etc. Another was to try to interpret the content of expressions such as 'to feel like home in the area and not just as a temporary visitor'.

Step 2: Invited teams for parallel urban studies

A way forward to handle and take care of all of these proposals was to invent a second step in the *Dialog*: *parallel urban analyses*. Citizens and professionals with varying professional and disciplinary backgrounds were invited to set up mixed teams to analyse the proposals that had been produced so far and to translate them into visions. Diverging opinions existed in the steering group: one regarded the citizens in the teams as a reference resource to react to the visions that were developed by the professionals, and another regarded the citizens as equally good team members who could take part on their own merits in developing visions – together with the professionals. A decision to pay the teams was taken. Every team leader had a budget of 350,000 Swedish kroner (approximately 3500 Euros) to pay professionals, and every citizen received 10,000 kroner for lost working hours. All money was taken from NUAB's budget.

A public invitation was sent out via newspapers and a local radio station. Team leaders were invited to propose a team with varying professional backgrounds and citizens were invited to become members of teams. The ambition was to create the citizens' teams so that they were not too biased in relation to the age, gender, ethnic and professional background of the local population. Every applicant had to give a short statement on why they wanted to participate. The interest from both professionals and citizens was overwhelming, and six teams with different profiles were chosen. The ambition was to get teams formed with a mix of professional backgrounds even though many architects and planners applied.

Six teams were formed. One group had the ambition to bring experiences from the north-east immigrant-dense suburbs of Gothenburg. Another team was made up of young people and children. The other teams had different profiles and all teams had at least one architect. The teams were asked to document the process and make logbooks for the sake of process evaluation. There were great differences between the teams' ways of working. One team used role play. Another used a more philosophical approach and discussed basic values for future urban life. The architectural firms worked with standard methods for project development, where the normal client was replaced by a team of citizens.

The outcome of the teams' efforts during autumn 2005 was presented to the general public in December 2005. The presentation was, to some extent, problematic due to the format and the time allocated to each team for presentation. The required format was very similar to that of an ordinary architectural competition and each team had 15 minutes for their presentation, without the possibility of discussions or questions. Several of the teams felt that this was too little and that they wanted to hear reactions.

The evaluation process

Many team members would have liked to continue with the work, but the municipal planning office and NUAB had to start an evaluation process and the production of a planning programme, and the dialogue was closed. The evaluators had no new instructions on how to continue with their work, and concentrated their efforts on questions that could formally be dealt with in the planning programme. The *Dialog* teams were eager to get reactions or comments from the city representatives, but there was silence. The evaluation work took much longer than expected. The silence became frustrating for some of the team members.

A cleavage emerged between different understandings of what kind of process the *parallel urban analyses* had been. One group felt that it was comparable with ordinary parallel architectural commissions, in which team members had been paid and their work was finished. Another group felt that the outcome of the evaluation was part of the public dialogue. When the evaluation document was presented, a debate started about what kind of questions could be dealt with by a municipal planning office. The evaluators pointed out that all *technical aspects* could be dealt with, but questions of a *political nature* needed to be sorted out and dealt with in other contexts. So what was considered to be political by the evaluators? This, for example, could involve questions concerning subsidized affordable rented housing versus more exclusive owner-occupied flats in a prime location. The politicians kept silent. The evaluators delivered a 'diluted' planning programme for which, after compulsory exhibition and opportunity for public debate, a political decision was taken without any public debate – the public interest had cooled down.

Is *Dialog Södra Älvstranden* an example of a new deliberative and collaborative way of planning or is it an extended planning process, including commissioned work to citizens to deliver their views? The name *Dialog* gave the impression that it was meant as a discussion about the future of the area

Figure 5.5 *The visions provided by the architectural firms in the parallel commissions have not much in common with the dreams of the citizens six years earlier*

and its use. But there was never any other response from authorities than the planning programme. An article in the local newspaper had the headline: 'The death of dialogue and democracy in 15 minutes'.

In May 2007, four architectural firms were invited to parallel commissions to develop sketches for detailed plans for part of the *Dialog Södra Älvstranden*. The firms presented their solutions in the autumn of 2007 (see Figure 5.5). The evaluation of these proposals was presented in spring 2009. In late 2011, the municipal planning office was still developing the ideas, and the first detailed plan was expected to be exhibited in public during autumn that year. Will the public interest be resurrected?

Långgatorna

In 2002, the Gothenburg Planning Office produced a new 'programme for detailed development plans' (a planning tool placed between the comprehensive and detailed levels in the Swedish planning legislation) for the 11 quarters of the Långgatorna district, located next to the Järntorget square and public transportation hub in the western inner city and near the Göta Älv River (see Figure 5.1). Historically, the vicinity near the water was important in the way that it created a vivid city life. This historical feature was called upon when it was contemporarily performed (in planning documents, newspapers and magazines, and at seminars and hearings) around the time of the planning efforts discussed here. The programme, a format in which to formulate overarching agendas for a city district, for instance, came about as a consequence of a real-estate owner applying for a building permit at the planning office. The available and legally valid document was a plan from 1948 against which the application was to be judged, which poorly represented the current context of the district, both in terms of physical appearance and content. In the latter sense, this meant that the separation of functions suggested in the plan was still to be pursued after more than 50 years. Långgatorna, however, is a district described by many as particular, compared to other districts in the city; through multiple actions of many different actors – again, media articles, public seminars, writings in official document, maps, etc. – it is portrayed as 'continental', 'exciting' and 'mixed' (Latour, 2005). Around the turn of the 20th century, function separation was anything but ideal; new planning ideas had made it obsolete. Långgatorna was repeatedly discussed as a great prototype for the city life so many city conversion professionals were hailing. It hosts a variety of small-scale businesses: designers, retailers selling alternative records, books and independent garment brands, alongside research collectives, club managements, music studios, artists and antique dealers. This, and a high density of restaurants and bars, gives the district a vibrant round-the-clock life. In some of the articles produced during the planning process, Långgatorna was put forward as a 'good example' of 'the mixed-use city' that planning authorities wanted to achieve.

The planners assigned to work with the programme were looking for ways to deepen their knowledge of the district, and Joakim Forsemalm, one of the chapter authors, had just begun a study with an interactive methodology in focus, seeking to use a cooperative or interactive knowledge structure (cf 'participatory research', Whyte, 1991).[1] The desire, shared by both the planners and the researcher, was to create a mutual exchange of knowledge. A focus

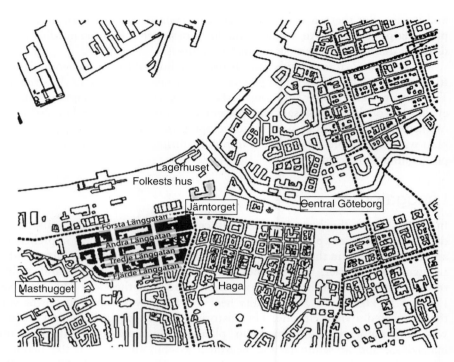

Figure 5.6 *Långgatorna, Gothenburg (highlighted in black)*

Source: Map by Oskar Götestam

group was conducted with real-estate owners, retailers, inhabitants and representatives from the city district office. The group met on four occasions. Set as a focus for discussion was the district's particular 'character'. What did that really mean? In the efforts to get to grips with lofty and vague descriptions, what was found were particular and site-specific networks, elements and actions (Czarniawska, 2004; Latour, 2005). For instance, retailers in close collaboration turned out to keep intact the district identity as 'cool' and 'happening': the independent trade and industry activity in Långgatorna was filling empty retail space with more and more city life-producing content (skate retailers, alternative music store with in-store gigs and parties, cafés owned and run by friends of the other retailers, etc.). Eventually, all networking, using both Facebook and flyers, ended up in an annual street party that celebrated the uniqueness of the district. Another important element, which became apparent through the focus group discussions, was that the fact that this was a 'porn-district' (half of the city's porn retailers and strip clubs are located here) kept rents low, keeping the retail spaces affordable to small-scale and independent businesses. The small-scale businesses' dependence on cheap rents and the cheap rents being a consequence of the porn shops in the district was a key learning process. This was connected to a design discussion in which the suggested pedestrianization of the main street became problematic. The porn consumer's need to park in front of the porn shops was threatened. A change from asphalt to paving stones might create a possible negative domino effect (see Forsemalm, 2007, for a more detailed discussion).

These were not the only important insights gained from this cooperation. The varied heights in the district were another feature of importance. The seemingly wasted economic potential in the unused building permits (one-storey buildings in central locations despite the fact that building permits allow up to four stories), as the focus group discussions made apparent, afforded another quality. Sunbeams shining down between buildings were mentioned as a particular quality corresponding with certain ideas about quality of life. For one of the sessions, the participants had been asked to bring their own photos of good and bad elements in the district. The discussion focused on a one-storey wooden building on one of the four parallel streets in the district containing a small shipyard, music studios and cheap plain apartments. This building's neighbour is a stone house from the beginning of the 20th century that had recently been renovated. Also discussed was a similar building one street up, a one-storey wooden house housing the district's round-the-clock strip club:

Inhabitant: I guess the picture didn't come out that well, but it's this particular light beaming down through the trees, when you stand on the street looking straight ahead. The light comes from all possible directions because of the houses being of such varied heights. Especially at night, too, a very particular light phenomenon appears.

Real-estate owner in the district: Yet, there is a need for more housing [in the city at large] and with such a place [the strip club...] I cannot see the end in itself with such a business or such a building.

Planner: Perhaps not, perhaps not that particular building; but maybe you don't erect a building as high as its neighbours (five to six storeys), you know? I guess that is to be studied in detail in the detailed development plan. I guess you suggest some storeys, but not five or six.

Inhabitant: It's interesting that this could be discussed at all, bearing in mind the probable amount of pressure on this site in a few years – I mean, on the unused building permits. But speaking of shape and form, this is a particularly exciting cityscape, the higher and lower buildings in a mix, letting light in in a peculiar way and whatnot. Yeah, but then, I don't find it self-evident that this is a form and structure for all eternity either.

The participatory model, in this case a focus group, contributed to a strengthened and more nuanced comprehension, both of the physical environment and of the life going on in different places in the district. With these discussions, the characteristics that had been abstract to the planners were made concrete and possible to express in a planning document – in this case, a document that prescribed cautiousness, sensitivity and a preservation of not only the physical, but also the cultural environment. One of the planners summarized her views at the end of one of the focus group sessions:

Planner: We have begun to weigh up and discuss after the consultation period [legally required procedure in the Swedish planning and building act] and are picking up as much as we can from these meetings, too, to be added to the final suggestions [i.e. the programme]. At the moment, it feels like we're to suggest as few alterations as possible, rather try to adapt new ideas to what is working fine as it is today. Perhaps we ought to make a plan that controls a usage of the ground floors for retail, to be able to maintain such a character. ... Since there are many calling attention to the fact that one of the characteristics of the district is the varied house heights, that there are both higher and lower buildings here.

Figures 5.7a and 5.7b *Retail (top and bottom) and low-density buildings (bottom) in Långgatorna, Gothenburg*

Source: Joakim Forsemalm

This preservation course laid out in the programme was less about preserving particularly important houses and more about making sure that the different important features of the district would withstand the growing city. It meant that the planners and politicians had to think twice before saying yes to suggestions (building permit applications) that would jeopardize a district that everyone thought about as comprising a particular quality in Gothenburg – a quality that, coincidently, would rhyme well with the planning discourse's ideal at the beginning of the 21st century (e.g. Jane Jacobs's ideas of the mix between old and new buildings, short blocks and the significance of a vivid sidewalk-life for street safety; and Richard Florida's ideas of the creative class as what ought to be in focus for a city with ambitions).

In this case of cooperative learning, planners were given – and were pleasantly welcoming of – an opportunity to penetrate particularities in this planning assignment in a new way. This knowledge process made them sensitive to the delicacies of the area's character: Långgatorna is not like any other district in Gothenburg, nor in Sweden at large. The assigned planners had learning in focus and found an opportunity to develop their knowledge. This was no isolated case: a couple of years later, once the programme was to be broken down into detailed development plans for each of the district's 11 quarters, the planners not only held on tightly to the direction set out in the programme, but also again sought knowledge through cooperation – this time with different academics and private parties (a property owner) able to supply more in-depth knowledge about the previously known and, for the district character, important relation between the activities at shop-floor level and the vibrant and widely loved city life.

One can here claim that the popular ideas of Långgatorna, an area historically characterized by a vibrant port and harbour life, were translated to also become part of the planners' agenda (Latour, 2005). The mental model of the district's features that was performed again and again in various contexts constituted the foundation for how the organization worked in terms of decisions for the future (cf Jenkins and Smith, 2001). The particular and repeated mental model of the public became, to use a term from Charles Goodwin, part of the vision, the image created by the professionals involved (Goodwin, 1984). The learning process, the idea to listen more in-depth than usual, was successful in the sense that the organization made operational a mental model that highly stemmed from the public perception of the district. To paraphrase Hall and Taylor (1996), in this case of conversion of a waterfront area, there were many cognitive scripts performing what turned out to be a normative frame of meaning for the organization to relate to, and depart from, in its work.

In the next case to be discussed in this chapter, an equally strong connection between mental model and the organization did not exist. Instead, there was seemingly only the professional vision put out to do work for the organization. The mental models produced had not been made operational and the planning office sought new solutions to an old planning problem. We move across the Göta River in Gothenburg to find a district not as favoured as Långgatorna.

Östra Kvillebäcken

Östra Kvillebäcken is a former industrial district located centrally on Hisingen Island in Gothenburg, closely connected to a large-scale shopping area (Backaplan) and only seven minutes from Gothenburg city centre, but mentally far away from it – on the 'wrong side' of the river (see Figure 5.1). For a long time, the municipality had tried to achieve a change in the district, which was becoming more and more plagued with crime as a result of poor maintenance (in turn as a consequence of the municipality refusing to give the real-estate owners anything other than short-term contracts on the land; cf Olshammar, 2002).

A Programme for Detailed Development Plan was established in 2003, but this was not followed by any legislative detailed plans. When the National Board of Housing, Building and Planning asked Gothenburg to join the Waterfront Communities Project (WCP) in 2003, it was eventually this site that was selected as a case study area. As waterfront conversion projects, both the northern and the southern riversides would have been a more distinct case, not least in a geographical sense. However, the northern riverside (Norra Älvstranden) was too near completion and its southern counterpart (Södra Älvstranden) had not yet, at the time of the municipality filing for its participation in the WCP, undergone some necessary overarching discussions to make it suitable as a case study area. Östra Kvillebäcken, thus something of an emergency expedient and not exactly the waterfront, came up as a possibility. The prerequisites for this district were quite different from those for Norra Älvstranden, as well as Södra Älvstranden:

> *Planner:* Here was a project where something needed to be done. There were intentions in the area and investment interests, but they were piecemeal. How could you get a unified grip on it? There had been a number of attempts throughout the years to do something, but somehow the visions had been constructed without anyone having the stamina to follow it through.

The 2003 Programme for Detailed Development Plan had formulated a direction for the district in terms of a 'mixed-use city' focus. This was, to use Jenkins and Smith's analytical tools again, the mental model for the operational organization of the local planning office (Jenkins and Smith, 2001). However, interest from the developer and landowners was absent, and as time passed, a bleak image was generated in the media, increasingly covering the criminalization of the district (Ristilammi, 1994). Regeneration through implementation of an overall municipality-created vision had been successfully conducted at Norra Älvstranden. Could the experiences gained from that conversion process finally be of use to (after years of work in the local planning office, leaving plans and cooperation behind) make something of Östra Kvillebäcken, by now a severe problem in the city due to rising criminal activities (Forsemalm, 2007)?

A WCP project team consisting of planners and 'academic partners' was put together.[2] Initially, quite a lot of time was spent discussing how the district should be approached. The task that the planning office had committed itself to – namely, the conducting of a visioning process – was not an easy one. The project team worked through several knotty problems in order to get to the

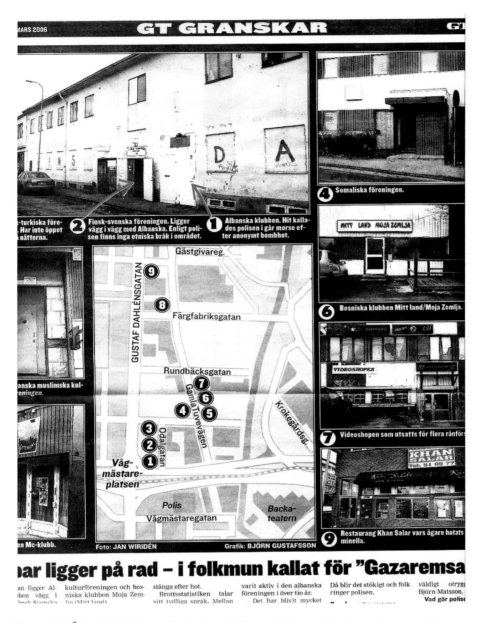

Figure 5.8 *Östra Kvillebäcken – Gothenburg's 'Gaza strip' according to popular perception as covered by local media*

point where such a process could be sanctioned. Numerous meetings took place within the project team, sometimes also in conjunction with so-called 'local partners' (i.e. other municipal administrations concerned with this regeneration, such as city district officials, traffic planners, property officials, etc.) and sometimes with external experts. From the outset, the idea was to incorporate the entire district (i.e. according to the demarcation indicated in the 2002 programme). At the end of 2004, an extended project team met to sort through the ideas and possible obstacles for the visioning process that the municipality had promised to carry out for the WCP. At the meeting, the project manager outlined a background and motives as to why this district was again in focus. The district was one of those highlighted in the existing Comprehensive Plan (ÖP99) as suitable for development.[3] All people attending had the opportunity to respond to and reflect upon this task-framing.

Consultant, expert on dialogue processes and city history: It is important to really get to know the character of the district, that's number one. Second, it has to be clear to each and everyone taking part in the dialogue what mandate they have in these discussions… 'Mixed-use city' is a rather woolly expression nowadays. What should be part of the mix? Is it a change in the already existing mix that is the objective here?

Researcher, with extensive knowledge of the district: What room to manoeuvre is there in the part or parts of the district we are to work with in the WCP? We need to map the businesses in the district in order to understand what the existing delicate prerequisites are. What kind of dwellings and how many do we need to build to supplement the existing businesses?

Project manager: We're not doing the same things today [as in the previous joint venture project] since there are other kinds of expectations for development of the area.

Academic partner: Haven't many demarcations and prerequisites already been decided upon? Aren't there already lots of different visions?

City district representative: This district is interested in generating positive spinoff effects for the problematic surrounding districts. One example is Kvillestaden [a district south of Östra Kvillebäcken] and its surroundings, where criminality is an enormous problem, as it is in Östra Kvillebäcken.

Project manager: There are expectations among both developers and property-owners; but at the moment, nothing has been specified.

Planner 3, member of project team: There is by no means a 'dead hand' laid on the district. The building permits that reach us at the office are validated against the existing programme, and in the southern part there are actors improving their facilities.

City district representative 2: You have to reach significant interested parties in the area, the ones that own land and the properties.

Planner 2, member of project team: It is very much about anchoring this project to the existing plans. To which financial accounts should the different commodities be accredited? 'Bohemian index' is rewarding – and economically capable in different ways. There is not one economic commodity, there are several.

Project manager: Sure, but where does the city benefit the most in the locating of districts such as this? There are different cycles at work in the city concerning where cheap premises should be located – the gentrification process.

Researcher: We need a proper analysis of the desires and wishes of the actors in the district.

Project manager: There might be inconveniences in introducing a frame that would be totally different from the existing expectations.

Planner 1, member of the project team: Does the city district have any particular wishes?

City district representative 1: Our hope is that Norra Älvstranden will spill over into Östra Kvillebäcken. We are working closely with the property-owner associations in the district on these issues.

Planner 1, frustrated by the volatility of the discussion: What other concrete interests are there?

City district representative 1: Well, the police go: 'Level the district to the ground!' Building dwellings is not an end in itself; the city district office objective is to create a safer environment in the Lundby district as a whole.

After a short break the discussions continued within the project team itself. The task facing the group – sorting through all the impressions, documents and prerequisites available – seemed overwhelming. Was this really the right forum for a visioning process and was the timing right? Was it at all possible to conduct such a process within the timeframes of the European Union project?

Planner 1: We do have the right to change our minds, don't we? What is it that we really want? Maybe we don't have time to conduct a visioning at all?

Academic partner: What is really governing this project? How strictly is it regulated? Are there any clear demands in the WCP plan?

Project manager: Might the visioning process contribute to the planning process by raising such questions?

Planner 3: Uh... replacement... the politicians, of course, have to be on board, especially those on the Planning and Building Committee; otherwise it won't be possible to incorporate the knowledge-building process of the focus group.

Project manager: There is no real working team in place yet, and no definite assignment from the Building Committee, at least not yet, although there are expressed interests from contractors.

Planner 1: The only existing initiative, then, is about the need for housing? The question, then, could be 'who should live here'?

Project manager: To get this conversion going, a catalyst of some kind is needed.

The planning office, as revealed on several occasions during the WCP, was not the only municipal office involved. It was the property office that the property and landowners were primarily dealing with.[4] Since the WCP working group did not include any representative from that office (they were invited to the meetings but did not turn up), there was a consequent and constant lack of mandate and information in the project team discussions. The project group tried to guess its way forward and started to perceive of itself as a spanner in the works, holding development back rather that moving it forward. A frustrated project work group tried and tried to get something done in the WCP, but seemed to face obstacles wherever it turned. The anchoring work continued, however (Czarniawska, 2000). The project manager and planner 1 met with the Planning Office Executive Group to try to sort things out and gain both guidance and clearance. A new obstacle loomed on the horizon. The Executive Group claimed that a 'visioning process' in this district at this point in time was obsolete since a politically sanctioned vision, thus a 'mental model', already existed in the outlined 'mixed-use city' objective in the 2002 programme.

Figure 5.9 *Östra Kvilleäcken, Gothenburg: City centre to the lower right end along the dotted line, representing the tram line*

Source: Map by Oskar Götestam © Digressiv Produktion

The Executive Group told the project team that the EU project should instead focus on a realization of this existing vision.

The project clock was ticking. The Gothenburg Planning Office had signed a contract to supply the 'best practice database' with knowledge concerning the chosen work package's complex of problems. But as yet no knowledge was being produced in the project that could serve as 'best practice' examples. The planning prerequisite had slowly transgressed from a broad point of departure, in terms of both geography and content, to a more narrowly demarcated task. In the quest to harness part of this district to the WCP, the planning office decided to focus on what it felt could act as a catalyst in this situation of stagnation. In the northern part of Östra Kvillebäcken, the municipality owned the land currently being used as a park and a cycle-lane. After having been earmarked as future road reserves as early as 1941, this stretch was again highlighted in the 2002 programme. The idea was to turn this stretch into a road that would support the nearby shopping district of Backaplan and link the northern parts of Hisingen Island to the city by creating an infrastructural crossbar to the adjacent city district of Tuve. By relieving pressure on the existing roads, noise and pollution levels could be sufficiently reduced to make it interesting for both contractors and landowners to construct buildings in which people would want to live.

The project work group thus initiated a focus group with the landowners and property owners around the road reserve to discuss prerequisites for it to come into existence. Several issues were discussed, the most important one concerned with financing. Who should pay for the road? And when could this conversion begin to take place? Again, there were uncertainties. No exact answers could be given and key persons (i.e. professionals, mainly other municipal administrators) who were able to answer some of the questions either failed to show up at the meetings or were overlooked in invitations to participate. The project manager claimed that there were many ways of perceiving how the cost should be divided (between the city, the land/property owner and others); but when asked to be more specific, answers were lofty. The land/property owners did their homework, producing sketches of possible stretches and locations of roundabouts and bus stops. This was a group of stakeholders who, although being mainly sceptical towards the idea of a road coming into existence and thus affecting their properties in different ways, wanted to cooperate and contribute. In the end, just as in the other cooperation projects for this area, the efforts made failed to result in any change, in any conversion of the district. Instead, the municipality returned to the model used to convert the northern riverside (Norra Älvstranden) – a model that gave power back to the municipality. In this way, the small-scale landownership – which was discussed as problematic due to stakeholders not wanting to follow the same path as the 'professional vision' – could be handled through the municipal development company, buying up these landowners to get a better negotiation position *vis-à-vis* the larger landowners – the ones who turned out to be those to whom the municipality *had* to listen. A consensus already existed around the previously decided 'mixed-use city' framework. This, thus, left little room to actually cooperate around a vision: it was, rather, a matter of transferring a vision *to* stakeholders and the interest in learning *from* these was marginal.

Conclusions

As everyone involved in city planning knows, there are always uncertainties, things happening along the way, which are not possible to foresee in the beginning of a planning process. This chapter has examined three different dialogues – cooperation projects within the same organization: the local planning office. As discussed and empirically found, uncertainties are not only a matter of things happening along the way being hard to predict. Uncertainties are, as discussed in the first and third cases, produced as a consequence of an undetermined knowledge-making structure. How should the city and its officials engage with the knowledge that is to be produced in a dialogue process? What measures must be taken in advance to ensure that the time spent by participating actors amounts to something real and valuable?

In none of the three cases presented here were such issues addressed beforehand. In the first case, the process was managed in a thorough way while it was in the experimental forums *Dialog Södra Älvstranden* and *Parallella Stadsanalyser*. The problems appeared when the new ways of working were to be linked to the standard and legislative operating procedures and routines in the municipal planning office and in NUAB. There was no preparedness for addressing the ideas and contents from the broad visioning processes that, in fact, had been asked for from the citizens and the teams. The content of the proposals was scrutinized by the evaluation team in order to 'cherry-pick', and was sorted into two groups. One comprised questions that fell into the area of responsibility of the planning permission committee – questions concerning what kind of buildings, floor area-to-ground ratio, etc. Other questions such as subsidies for affordable housing or citizens' representation on the board of NUAB were classified as political questions which could not be dealt with in the programming and planning process and were thus put aside; in reality, these questions have not been followed up on. An official evaluation report for the content of the visions (Stadsbyggnadskontoret, 2006) and another for the process (Bialecka et al, 2006) were produced as background material for the Programme for Detailed Development Plan, which was presented, exhibited and open for public consultation, and then politically decided upon. However, the interest for this part of the urban development process was minimal among citizens and mass media. The handling of the initial stages by the planning office had created a vast critique that, as of 2011, still existed.

Case 2, Långgatorna, might be said to be a more successful venture due to the fact that the planners involved actually used the dialogue in a constructive way: what was learned during the focus groups was of importance for what was decided later. Here, a real interest for the different actors' ideas was evident, and in several ways. The planners sought to understand the particular prerequisites for this district. This meant a way forward for the district in tune with the public idea and perception of the district's features and character. At the time of writing this chapter, this knowledge is the foundation for decision-making processes – for instance, negotiations with real-estate and/or landowners having interests in altering the structure that had been discussed by so many as worth preserving as much as possible.

In the case of Östra Kvillebäcken, on the other hand, there were several opportunities to learn from actors concerned and an ambition from the planning office to listen and have a dialogue. There *was* an interest, too; a particularly problematic district needed new input and the office sought knowledge through several cooperative processes throughout the years. What was learned and created in these processes in terms of knowledge did not, however, become part of any way forward. Instead, the professional vision constructed some years later put forward the 'mixed-use city' as an aim and objective, and although there were great possibilities of realizing that vision by keeping some of the existing buildings (and businesses), the programme from 2002 said nothing about such a way forward. Instead, everything was to be torn down to make way for a completely new district. This clear agenda became a problematic aspect in the WCP work in Gothenburg; there already existed a 'consensus' in the sense of the established direction. This left the project with no visioning space. If the planning office had had a better learning platform, such an error – there were many actors engaged before the problem with the already existing vision ('mixed use') was put on the table – might have been avoided. This might have saved time, money and, above all, confidence. The risk is that dialogue ventures become counterproductive as actors become reluctant to take part in them if things are decided beforehand or if the prerequisites are poorly researched, possibly creating obstacles along the way that, as in the case of Östra Kvillebäcken, might jeopardize what might otherwise be a fruitful, and mutual, learning process.

Recommendations for municipal dialogue processes based on experiences from Gothenburg include the following:

- Establish clear instructions for what issues can be dealt with in the public dialogue.
- Make clear from the beginning when the dialogue will start and finish.
- Make clear how the outcome of the dialogue will be linked to ordinary and legislative planning procedures.
- Establish some kind of open municipal institution to address ideas, visions and proposals from citizens.
- Establish a function within the municipality that can accumulate and distribute experiences from dialogues to politicians and planning officials.

Notes

1   This was an ethnographic study of identity-making processes in city conversion projects. Amongst other things, media debates, planning efforts and, above all, networking practices between property owners and retailers were studied between 2002 and 2007 using interviews, observations and text analyses, alongside focus group discussions.

2   The task of these partners was to 'monitor' the project and extract key learning points from it. The intention was also to supply methods for 'mutual learning' processes: a central objective in the project outline.

3   This is further emphasized, ten years later, in the proposal for a new municipal comprehensive plan, ÖPXX.

4   The property office manages council-owned assets, foremost properties of different kinds.

6
Experiences in Participation in the Port City of Hamburg

Harry Smith and Maria Soledad Garcia Ferrari

Introduction

Across many parts of the world, citizen participation in decision-making for urban development has become increasingly established in law and in practice, though often not going far enough, according to its critics. Waterfront regeneration projects pose particular challenges due, among other things, to the strategic importance that their development can often have for the city or the region as a whole; the large stakeholders that often own land and other assets in the affected areas (such as ports, railways, industry, etc.); and the variety of scenarios in terms of resident population, ranging from the total or partial absence of local residents, to resident port-related workforces who may feel threatened and displaced by regeneration proposals.

Recent and on-going major waterfront regeneration projects in the City of Hamburg provide a good illustration of such scenarios and challenges. Here the highly successful HafenCity project close to the city centre encountered the fairly common scenario of having practically no existing residents who may play a part in shaping the development. The city government, who was the major landowner, took the initial strategic decisions regarding the development of this area with minimal consultation, and invested stringent authority in the public development company that was tasked with regenerating the area. This is seen as a way of securing benefits for the 'public good', through strong controls on the design and management of developments that are approved.

A different scenario can be found on the south side of the Elbe, where regeneration that started after the launch of HafenCity, and on an even larger scale, is to encompass a variety of inhabited areas. As part of the city's wider 'Hamburg – The Growing City' long-term development strategy, the 'Leap across the Elbe' framework plan covers three very different harbour development areas spanning north–south across the Elbe island Wilhelmsburg. Large parts of the framework plan are derived from creative design proposals of expert and citizen groups who participated in an international design workshop focused on drafting urban design scenarios in 2003. The public dialogue established at the workshop and through other on-going fora fed into the Convention for the International Building Exhibition IBA 2013.

Hamburg also provides the setting for a new approach to dealing with the long-term management and maintenance of privately regenerated areas in

Germany, mainly through an adaptation of the Business Improvement District Model, which gives an active role to local property owners. Experimentation is also under way with transferring aspects of this model to the management of residential neighbourhoods. These experiences may hold lessons for the sustainable management of waterfront areas.

This chapter first provides a brief summary of some key theoretical considerations which are relevant to the analysis of citizen participation in planning and regeneration. It then describes and assesses these three experiences in waterfront regeneration and urban management in Hamburg from the perspective of civic engagement. The chapter highlights how different approaches to participation emerge from different context-specific scenarios, as well as the impact that the existing authoritative structures have upon the definition of such approaches – with the strong legislative and economic powers invested in the city-state of Hamburg, in this case, having been a key factor.

Public participation in the planning of waterfront regeneration

Public participation in planning emerged initially as a demand and later as a practice as part of the reaction to, and critique of, post-World War II top-down rational planning. During the 1970s, it became embedded in the planning legislation of countries around the North Sea (as well as elsewhere), where the existence of democratic political systems provided the basis for the right to participation to be acknowledged in relation to urban development processes. Forms of citizen involvement in urban development had existed in the US since decades earlier, and here the critique of these focused on the unequal access that different social groups had to the existing mechanisms of participation. Much of the academic critical writing of the time, underpinning approaches such as 'advocacy planning', originated from the US. Arnstein's (1969) classic text on participation analysed citizen involvement in social urban programmes in that country from the perspective of the redistribution of power. Application of her 'ladder of participation' showed that, in most cases, participation was used to manipulate or inform the public (bottom rungs of the ladder) rather than to give them the power to take decisions and have control (top of the ladder) (see Smith, 2005, and Figure 6.1).

The implementation of public participation in urban planning during the 1970s and 1980s was criticized for becoming procedural, instrumental and mostly not reaching the higher rungs of Arnstein's ladder. In addition, particularly in the Western and Westernized worlds, there was a shift from community-centred participation to approaches which responded to consumerism, which implicitly included a strong element of protection of property owners' rights (Smith, 2005). From the 1990s there was a conceptual shift (mainly in academic discourse initially, and later in policy) from participation to governance. The latter, which conceived of society as composed of different types of 'stakeholders' with varying capacities and degrees of involvement in urban development processes, provided a basis for the development of ideas around participation based on 'communicative rationality'[1] and the practice of collaborative planning, which required dialogue between the relevant stakeholders in appropriate arenas (Healey, 1996, 1997).

Ladder of citizen participation		
8. Citizen Control		
7. Delegated Power	>	Degrees of citizen power
6. Partnership		
5. Placation		
4. Consultation	>	Degrees of tokenism
3. Informing		
2. Therapy		
1. Manipulation	>	No power

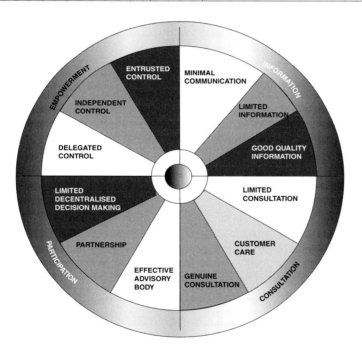

Figure 6.1 *Ladder of participation (top) and wheel of participation (bottom)*

Source: Respectively drawn by the authors based on Arnstein (1969) and by Mike Roper based on Davidson (1998)

In this context, alternatives to Arnstein's ladder were developed, such as the 'wheel of participation' used by South Lanarkshire Council in Scotland. Rather than setting out forms of participation on an ascending scale towards increasing empowerment, the wheel of participation presents a 'menu' of choices that encourage 'the right participation techniques to achieve the identified objective' (Davidson, 1998, p.14). This responded not only to an increased government demand for community involvement and to the development of new techniques for participation, but also to what was seen (at least in the UK) as a disappointment with delays through participation processes, tokenism and citizen apathy. The 'wheel of participation' was therefore specifically designed to identify the level of community involvement that was appropriate to a given scenario, without necessarily aiming to reach the top of Arnstein's ladder.

However, approaches such as the 'wheel of participation' deliberately sideline an issue that was central to Arnstein's analysis – that of power. As Flyvbjerg (1988) and Sandercock (1988) note, power is central to planning and urban development processes, and the exercise of power affects the choice and design of participatory approaches, as well as the way in which these play out. In fact, the very notion of participation as a process that is 'implemented' (usually by government or by developers) entails a preconception of the balance of power(s).

Waterfront regeneration can present a range of scenarios relevant to participation in the process, with power always being a central determinant. It is generally initiated by key organizations with a large 'stake' in the process, which tend to be government (central or local) and port authorities, as well as other major landowners when the land is in industrial use or similar. Often such organizations then form partnerships and special delivery vehicles to undertake the regeneration. These all are therefore the agencies that normally 'implement' (or commission the implementation of) participation processes. Such processes may be influenced by the balance of power and agendas among the key initiating stakeholders, as well as by other stakeholders affected. Such stakeholders may be present in the location to be regenerated or in its vicinity. This may or may not include a resident population, depending upon the use and historic pattern of occupation of the area, with possible affected parties being the population who worked in the port or industrial facilities, other residential provision and small businesses, among others. If the regeneration is seen as having strategic importance at a city or region level, then stakeholders may be defined on a wider scale, including residents and businesses across the city or region.

The City of Hamburg has carried out, and is continuing to plan, extensive regeneration along its waterfront and its hinterland. It provides a particularly interesting example of different regeneration processes, responding to different contextual scenarios and power dynamics between stakeholders, with correspondingly different approaches to public participation in the process.

The City of Hamburg and its waterfront

The 'Free and Hanseatic City of Hamburg' is a city-state resulting from the amalgamation of former port cities and a variety of urban areas with different characteristics across 50km of urbanization. It is the largest city in Germany after Berlin, with a population of approximately 1,730,000 in the city, which covers an area of 755 square kilometres, and approximately 4.3 million in its metropolitan region. The city is home to a large migrant population. Located around 80km from the North Sea, the city straddles the Rivers Elbe and Alster, and includes several islands in the former – the largest of which is Wilhelmsburg. The land north of the Elbe is higher, with that south of the Elbe being low lying and prone to flooding, making it suitable for the development of dock facilities, but also imposing constraints on other forms of development. The overall area of Hamburg's port contains high levels of immigrant population and a diversity of physical features, including scenic waterfront locations.

Hamburg city-state is one of the 16 German federal states, which have a degree of autonomy and legislative powers, the only other city-states being Berlin and Bremen. Hamburg therefore has its own parliament and government (the Senate), and therefore a high degree of independence in determining economic and urban development policies. Urban development is guided by the city's Ministry for Urban Development and the Environment.

Hamburg port is the second largest and third busiest port in Europe, offering modern equipment and efficient management. As a hanseatic city, port activities have historically been the driver for the city's development and have given Hamburg's politics a strongly maritime orientation (see Figure 6.2). The shift to containerization and larger ships posed challenges to Hamburg as a port, given its location far from the sea and the maintenance required in fluvial docks, such as continual dredging, etc. The city's strong reliance and focus on its port have meant continuing investment in maintaining and improving its position in maritime trade. Although, as in other port cities, other economic sectors – services and media, in the case of Hamburg – grew in importance in both absolute and relative terms, dock-related activity has remained central to the city's economy. Following the reunification of Germany at the beginning of the 1990s, Hamburg's strategic position as a gateway to former East Germany and other parts of Eastern Europe brought about a boom in port activity, which has since been sustained. Though the new requirements of containerized shipping have led, as elsewhere, to former centrally located docklands becoming redundant, the continuing strength of port activity and the support for this from local dominant social groups influenced how the city went about initiating the regeneration of such brownfield sites. On the other hand, the City of Hamburg has had a strong position as landowner of the port area, which has been to its advantage in steering the regeneration of parts of the port (Harms, 2003).

Waterfront regeneration started in Hamburg during the 1980s, with promotion by the city of the so-called 'String of Pearls'. This comprised a series

Figure 6.2 *View of 19th-century buildings in Speicherstadt, the historic warehouse district*

Source: Harry Smith

of sites along the north bank of the Elbe, west of the city centre, which were developed in a market-led approach over a lengthy period of time and significantly gentrified the area (Schubert, 2011). A more strategic approach was taken from the mid 1990s onwards in the development of HafenCity ('harbour city'), a new urban quarter on the north bank of the Elbe that was masterplanned as a major extension to the city centre. Here the city took a more proactive and planned approach to converting former port areas into 'city'. The successful implementation of HafenCity was followed in the mid 2000s by the proposal of the Leap across the Elbe initiative, within a regional development perspective. The Leap across the Elbe development framework covers, from north to south, HafenCity and Harburg Inner Port, with Wilhelmsburg Island at its core. This framework is one of the five key projects of the Metropolis Hamburg – Growing City strategy, initiated by the Senate of Hamburg and pursuing the concept of 'smart growth'. Leap across the Elbe has important implications for the city as a whole. It departs from strategy that was predominant during the 20th century where residential development was kept to the high ground north of the Elbe, and port-related and industrial uses were located in the lower marshland around, and south of, the Elbe; and it proposes a new north–south urban development axis (Schubert, 2011).

The City of Hamburg has promoted and implemented different strategies for citizen participation in both of these major waterfront regeneration initiatives, but confronting different realities, from securing benefits for the 'public good' in HafenCity to creating experts and citizens groups to participate in international design workshops in the Leap across the Elbe initiative. These are explored, in turn, next.

HafenCity[2]

The 157ha of land developed as HafenCity are located close to the city centre of Hamburg, separating it from the northern branch of the River Elbe. The area was previously used by the port and contained port-related infrastructure but had almost no permanent inhabitants. As elsewhere, the obsolescence of small-scale harbour structures and the need for larger sites required due to the development of container technology had led to the decline in port activity in the area. Although surrounded by neglected housing estates, the wholesale market, industry, port facilities and railway lines, the location had great potential because of its proximity to the commercial centre of Hamburg. The main objectives of the City of Hamburg for the development of HafenCity were focused on the expansion of the city centre by around 40 per cent, aiming to strengthen Hamburg's competition with other major European cities (HafenCity Hamburg, 2010). The overall aim of the city was to generate a dense, mixed-use, economically and physically attractive extension of the inner city and contribute to the positioning of Hamburg on the map internationally.

Interestingly, the redevelopment of the waterfront in HafenCity is connected to increasing harbour activity in Hamburg and new opportunities that emerged with investment in the function of the port. A newly developed container terminal in Alternwerder, financed through income generated by the HafenCity development, was located downriver, releasing land in the area for other uses. In addition, as indicated above, the development of HafenCity is linked to national strategic decisions related to the economic significance of Hamburg in Germany and in Europe and the outcome of a German port growth policy. The growing strength of port activity underpinned the continuing influence of port-related social groups in the city's decision-making, a factor that was affected by the city authority's approach to the regeneration of the area, as is seen below.

The original masterplan for HafenCity area was approved by Hamburg's Senate in 2000, but this proposal had taken almost ten years to develop. Initial ideas for regeneration of the areas surrounding the port in the central part of the city emerged during the 1990s, responding to the changing role of Hamburg in the European context with the fall of the Berlin Wall and the Iron Curtain. In 1991, the city's mayor unofficially commissioned a study into the inner-city port fringes and its potential for transformation. Concentration of port activities had built up south of the River Elbe, leaving centrally located sites on the north banks of the river underused, as they were unsuitable for new operations based on the use of containers (HafenCity Hamburg, 2010). This initial stage in the regeneration process was treated with discretion due to possible resistance from the port industry and possible speculation and rise of land value, which would have made the project unviable.

Although the majority of the land belonged to the City of Hamburg, most buildings in the area belonged to private business. During this initial stage the buildings were acquired through a company wholly owned by the city and formed in 1995: Gesellschaft für Hafen-und Standortentwicklung (GHS), since 2004 HafenCity Hamburg GmbH. The initial study on the regeneration of the peripheries of the port was presented in 1996 by a Hamburg architect, Professor Volkwin Marg, while the project was still confidential. The principles for development presented in this study were adopted in the final masterplan, such as the urban structure proposed and the principle of mixed uses (HafenCity Hamburg, 2010). The project was introduced to the public in 1997 under the title 'Vision HafenCity', proposing a plan for the city to regain its connection with the waterfront. The areas affected initially were only narrow sections of the 157ha that are now being developed.

With the objective of financing the HafenCity project and its infrastructure, as well as a modern port facility at Altenwerder with a new container terminal, a special fund was established by public law to hold 'city and port assets' public land in the ownership of the City of Hamburg. The establishment of this fund also contributed to providing political legitimation for the project through removing the HafenCity area from the umbrella of the port without conflicting with the port industry.

In April 1999, an urban planning ideas competition for HafenCity masterplan was launched, and after a series of studies carried out by the municipality and GHS, the winner was announced in October1999: a Dutch–German team. The proposed masterplan was then approved by Hamburg Senate in February 2000. Among the principles of this masterplan were a strong interaction between buildings and the water, the elevation of buildings for flood protection, the public character of a majority of ground-floor uses and the mix of uses (see Figure 6.3). The masterplan also defined the development of new neighbourhoods within HafenCity and the long-term realization of these developments into the 2020s. HafenCity also aimed to be the leading example for a new business, social, cultural, urban and economic image for the city in a

Figure 6.3 *Model of the HafenCity project in the HafenCity InfoCentre*

Source: Harry Smith

21st-century European context. Some degree of flexibility was also embedded within the masterplan, which aimed to be highly adaptable to unforeseeable future changes. Implementation was to require an element of public subsidy.[3]

A development corporation was formed in 1998 to undertake the development process.[4] It is a quasi-autonomous non-governmental organization (NGO) which is fully owned by the Free and Hanseatic City of Hamburg. The land was originally owned by the City of Hamburg and transferred to HafenCity corporation. During the development, all land is sold and the revenues are used for public investment such as sewerage, renovation of the historic quays and design of public spaces (Zandbelt&vandenBerg, 2005).

While providing an opportunity for the expansion of the city centre, the vision and the masterplan did not propose simply to add to its mainly office and commercial facilities, but also to strengthen its residential function of the centre. The plans for the area mostly offer both office and apartment buildings, including combinations of office and houses in one block as well as work–live housing units, resulting in homes for 12,000 inhabitants and scope for 45,000 jobs. Since its initial masterplan, the aim was to provide a broad range of housing types and to include a flagship cultural centre. These developments are being delivered in a phased sequence of neighbourhoods with their own identity, spreading eastwards and southwards from the city centre. Individual city blocks are developed through competitions for land where the key factor is the quality of the proposal rather than price, as this is usually fixed at the outset. Actual sale of the land to the winning bidder is controlled through a process that ensures that conditions are met, including the holding of architectural competitions for the buildings and securing of building permits (see also Chapter 3).

HafenCity had almost no inhabitants, but development required citizens from elsewhere in the city being informed on the area and the strategy was to use different means of publicity, while creating opportunities for public involvement. When the Senate approved the masterplan in 2000, this was then presented to the public through a series of exhibitions and talks. That same year an information centre was established in the former power station of the historic warehouse district – the Kesselhaus – where a regular local public discussion forum, the *Dialog im Kesselhaus*, is held on different aspects of HafenCity development, such as arts and public spaces. The move of Katharinen School from the old part of the city centre to HafenCity, planned to become a centre for the new community with a comprehensive programme of uses, was also among the strategies to encourage public participation. As part of a research programme sponsored by the German Ministry of Education and Research, a project was put in place aiming to study different patterns of work and life. The project maps these patterns using a computer program that is able to identify possible conflicts and interrelations with urban spaces.

A substantial part of the participatory initiatives are focused on informing and raising awareness. The Viewpoint is an observation platform containing information boards and introducing the entire HafenCity project. This temporary structure is located at the end of the Kibbelsteg in western HafenCity, with the aim of informing the public on the progression of the project and the dynamic growth of a new district in the city. Regular cultural events and temporary art installations are another instrument used to raise the profile of the area. Examples include a charity run through the site, the visit of large cruise ships, such as *Queen Mary 2*, and the opening of specific new developments, such as the Magellan Terraces public space in 2005, for which a two-day celebration was held (Waterfront Communities Project, 2007).

Design of public space has also been used as a tool contributing to the participation and integration of the wider citizenry of Hamburg in the area. The main open spaces in western HafenCity – Magellan Terraces, Sandtorpark open space and Marco Polo Terraces – were designed by the Spanish architecture firm EMBT and are an integral part of the overall open space planning in HafenCity. These open spaces and parks redefine the borderline between the water and the riverbank by using different levels; generate a sequence of overlapping land and river spaces connecting the various green areas, with the water integrating harbour elements; and integrate the work of local artists. Sandtorpark open space was developed in 2010 and opened in 2011, by which time residents had moved into the area, influencing aspects of its detailed design.

As buildings have been completed and occupied and a population has begun to establish itself in the area, new forms of public involvement have developed, focused on the smaller-scale issues directly affecting these new residents. For example, the specific location of the old harbour cranes that were kept onsite and restored through a heritage project was negotiated with the new residents in the buildings that lined the affected docks (see Figure 6.4). A new play-building provided as part of the first neighbourhood to be developed is now managed by parents. An informal advisory board for the neighbourhood (*Quartiersbeirat*) was established as a forum for debate, and owners and tenants formed a joint association prompted by the development company. A dedicated neighbourhood manager is employed by HafenCity Hamburg GmbH, who is responsible for cooperation with, and the participation of, residents and other stakeholders in the area. In addition, a person has been designated to supervise open space on a daily basis (*Wegewart*), coming into contact with residents and acting as a channel for their views (Kreutz, undated).[5]

Figure 6.4 *Dalmannkai, the second quarter to be completed in HafenCity, with floating pontoons in the foreground and a historic crane*

Source: Harry Smith

HafenCity Hamburg GmbH takes on a strong role as 'guardian' of the public interest in the conditions that it places on new developments, ensuring that certain standards of provision of public space are met. This has even involved making privately owned space publicly accessible, such as the atrium in the new Unilever HQ building for German-speaking countries, completed in 2009. These strict conditions are possible because of the development company also being the landowner.

During 2010, the masterplan was revised, with a focus on redefining development of the eastern neighbourhoods. Public presentations and discussions of the proposals were used to gather feedback. Following the consideration of these inputs and further refining of the proposals, the masterplan was presented for approval by the city Senate in 2011.

The experience in HafenCity shows an ascending scale in relation to Arnstein's ladder. This started with no direct power being given to the citizens in the early stages, when the key strategic decisions regarding the development of the area were being taken by the city authorities. Participation then rose to mostly information, once the masterplan was approved and the development was given the go-ahead by the Senate. Levels of consultation and, in some very particular small-scale initiatives, forms of delegated power have emerged around more detailed issues during implementation. Information and consultation have also been used in the revision of the masterplan ten years after its first approval. Against the 'wheel of participation', it is clear that the

City of Hamburg, which is in control of the regeneration, has chosen different approaches according to the nature and scale of the decisions, ranging from minimal communication in the early strategic stages, to various forms of consultation later (and, again, some form of delegated control in relation to more detailed management issues, such as, for example, the running of the play park by parents).

This approach was very much a response to the political sensitivities at the outset around the possibility of transferring traditionally port-related expanses of land and water to the city, as well as to the minimal inhabitation of the area at the time. A very different scenario was faced when developing the Leap across the Elbe initiative.

Leap across the Elbe

At the centre of the Leap across the Elbe project, which aims to extend urban development between the city centre of Hamburg and the old port of Harburg, is the island of Wilhelmsburg. This low-lying area, which suffered devastating flooding in 1962, consists of a patchwork of port-related, industrial, commercial, infrastructural and residential uses, including large-scale post-war social housing. Its approximately 50,000 residents include port and industry workers, and a large proportion of migrants. It is seen as a 'problem area', with economic and social decline brought about by the westwards move of port activity and the failures of some of the 1960s social housing. In the official discourse it is also seen as an area of opportunity for the development of 'a versatile and living city' due to the physical, cultural and social contrasts to be found in the area, where harbour, city, village and particular landscapes are juxtaposed (see Figure 6.5).

The challenges faced in the development of Wilhelmsburg are very different than those surmounted by HafenCity. The latter's location and infrastructural connections made it a magnet for private investors in a way that Wilhelmsburg would find hard to rival. In addition, the very success of HafenCity has drawn potential private investment away from Wilhelmsburg. A study for the European Investment Bank (EIB, 2009) concluded that the majority of measures proposed in the Leap across the Elbe initiative (such as traffic infrastructure, green space, public realm, social facilities, etc.) would have to rely on public subsidy.

Leap across the Elbe proposed a range of interventions, including the development of inner-city wasteland and the upgrading of public spaces, social infrastructure and educational institutions, especially in deprived areas (EIB, 2009). The project objectives are to adopt investment-related measures with reference to labour market and employment; create the infrastructure needed to develop local economies; and increase the attractiveness of local district centres. It is seen as an opportunity to develop a 'model for sustained, forward-looking, internal development' (EIB, 2009) which would benefit the rest of Hamburg's inner city. The long-term perspective for the Leap across the Elbe initiative spans a century of urban development and redevelopment, to be kick-started by two key events in 2013: the International Building Exhibition (IBA) and the International Garden Show (IGS).

Figure 6.5 *From the Marco Polo terraces in Western HafenCity, the port and industry of Wilhelmsburg were visible in the distance before western HafenCity's southernmost plots were developed*

Source: Harry Smith

International Building Exhibitions have been used in Germany as vehicles to explore new forms of architecture and urban development since 1901. Successive IBAs around the country have tended to be critical of previous experience in building and urban development, and developed or showcased new models. Thus, the first IBA in Darmstadt (1901) created an artists' colony as a response to mass housing and overcrowding; the Weißenhofsiedlung in Stuttgart (1927) showcased Modern Movement architecture and housing; two consecutive IBAs in Berlin (1957 and 1987) built models of city development, the first applying the principles of the Modern Movement to buildings in an open urban structure, the second criticizing this and proposing a new urbanism based on the city block and contextualism, mostly based on Post-Modern design. The more recent IBAs in the Ruhr (IBA Emscher Park, 1989), Niederlausitz (IBA Fürst-Pückler-Land, 1999) and the state of Saxony-Anhalt (IBA Stadtumbau, 2010) have tackled regeneration of industrial and other landscapes, with a strong focus on innovative economic renewal and environmental rehabilitation. IBAs have tended to increase in scale, from the early colony and small district developments to the latest federal state-wide approach in Saxony-Anhalt.

Germany has also developed a strong tradition in garden shows at various levels (regional, national and international). The history of Hamburg's International Garden Shows goes back to 1869, and there have been six more since. These have had an important impact upon the quality of open spaces in the city and have contributed to Hamburg being known as the 'Green City on the Waterfront'.[6]

The IBA and IGS are not the only activities taken forward to implement the Leap across the Elbe initiative. Complementing these, Wilhelmsburg is also the location for the initial activities of other programmes with wider application throughout other parts of the city, some of which have been running since the 1980s: City Renewal, *Soziale Stadt* and City Renovation West. Taken as a whole, the composite vision across all of these initiatives is to integrate the Elbe islands within the city structure, developing and restructuring these internally, as well as better linking them to the city through new transport infrastructure (e.g. a possible new bridge linking directly to HafenCity, and a planned extension of the new Metro line from HafenCity to Wilhelmsburg/Harburg). This vision includes the following aspects: quality development of inner-city districts; integration of work places within urban development; forms of housing suitable for families and mixed ages; water and green spaces, architecture and aesthetics; and intelligent infrastructure (EIB, 2009).

Realization of the vision comprises a wide and ambitious range of projects, including, for example, a new central public park creating a link between the various districts of Wilhelmsburg and new international gardens; experimental housing, including on the water and landscape-based forms; educational facilities, including a new international school; new sports facilities as a basis for a potential Olympic bid; waterway links, continuous waterfront promenades and green bridges; land decontamination; and renewable energy production (EIB, 2009).

The Leap across the Elbe initiative emphasizes the opening up and developing of the old harbour, including areas dedicated to port activities and Elbe Island. Therefore, the development strategy required addressing both port development and urban planning, with individual implementation strategies for a variety of sites. The approach has been to link 'soft port activities' with urban environments (Zandbelt & vandenBerg, 2005). The framework also needed to incorporate existing transport infrastructure and future transport projects.

Particular focus has been given to the implementation of participation strategies, responding to the different characteristics of the sections within the area, with, for example, Wilhelmsburg Island experiencing, in parts, social difficulties with high levels of unemployment, poverty and crime. One of the key areas for action in Leap across the Elbe is 'Citizens for Hamburg', which aims to develop citizen participation processes.

These approaches to citizen participation include (Waterfront Communities Project, 2007):

- Active involvement of citizens, authorities and different committees during the development process. The purpose of this was to generate confidence, political involvement and to implement the notion of self-help and self-responsibility.
- Use of the already established Advisory Board for Urban Development (*Beirat für Stadtentwicklung*), which includes representatives of both formally constituted groups and institutions and informal, as well as *ad hoc* groups from different neighbourhoods, and has been working since 1994.

- Setting up of an onsite office.
- Mechanisms for close cooperation among all levels of government involved in the strategic development programme, including the Senate of Hamburg.
- Organization of national and international conferences and workshops with a variety of focus themes.

As part of participatory mechanisms, a series of regular meetings between the local administration and stakeholders was held in order to identify relevant problems and to address questions. These meetings included researchers, practitioners and end users, allowing for continuous professional communication and cooperation, and helping to build up trust-based relationships in order to underpin the mutual translation of different logics and languages across actors involved in the projects (Waterfront Communities Project, 2007).

In 2007, Hamburg's Ministry of Urban Development and Environment established a company to develop the IBA: IBA Hamburg GmbH. This company, together with a sister company in charge of the International Garden Show (IGS Hamburg 2013 GmbH) took on the management of the process. These identify and develop projects, but have no planning authority, which still resides with the City of Hamburg (Stock and Tummers, 2010). IBA Hamburg established a permanent 'participation council' (*Beteiligungsgremium*), composed of 24 citizens[7] and 7 political representatives from the area, which once a month holds meetings that are generally open to the public and is the main channel for residents' views. In addition, the two companies jointly organized a series of large-scale forums for citizens (Dialogue with the Citizens), which take place once or twice a year and involve interested citizens through open invitation. IBA Hamburg's public involvement programme also includes bringing together residents with national and international experts through special workshops focused on specific themes, which are referred to as 'laboratories'. The IBA website reflects the importance attached to citizen participation in this project: 'No major decisions are to be made without the support of the people living on the islands, nor against the will of those who are personally affected by the plans, building work and events.'[8]

The establishment of the IBA was accompanied by the signing of a convention, also in 2007, involving over 50 organizations (from both government and market sectors) who became partners in supporting the project. This 'partnership' then grew with the addition of further organizations over time.

A mid-term assessment of the IBA suggested that it tried to enhance the lives of local residents, including the large proportion of immigrants with their large families, through both housing and education projects. However, it also noted the problems raised by residents' temporary disengagement from their local community due to displacement during the construction of new housing, as well as the lack of success in making local facilities available. In addition, some of the changes in transport links require the relocation of federal motorways, which have generated citizen opposition (Stock and Tummers, 2010).

Stock and Tummers's (2010) assessment of participation in the IBA Hamburg was that, though the complex context of Wilhelmsburg suggested that strong participation and partnership with local stakeholders was needed for a successful process, in practice citizen participation was institutionalized and did not go beyond information and consultation (i.e. the middle rungs of Arnstein's ladder of participation). The approaches seen here appear to map onto 'good-quality information' and two forms of consultation ('limited' and 'genuine') in the 'wheel of participation'.

Business improvement districts and neighbourhood improvement districts[9]

The Leap across the Elbe initiative forms part of a wider drive for regeneration across the city, which is taking place within the context of Hamburg's 'Growing City' vision, approved by the city-state's Senate in 2001. Some approaches to such regeneration are increasingly responding to a wider conception of governance that has developed during the first decade of the 21st century in Germany. This is happening in the context of a policy of transformation of the German welfare state, with increasing calls on private responsibility (e.g. with regard to health insurance and pensions), public–private partnerships for the delivery of infrastructure and urban development, and the sale and privatization of public assets, such as social housing. This has been the background against which public–private partnership models for urban management have been adapted from elsewhere (primarily the US) and provided for in federal legislation. Hamburg is among the pioneering states in developing state-level legislation for, and implementing, German versions of business improvement districts (BIDs) and neighbourhood improvement districts (NIDs) (Kreutz, 2009).

Hamburg's BID law was the first to be passed by a state government in Germany, in 2005. This established BIDs as time-limited partnerships between real-estate owners in a designated area in order to procure services (such as cleaning and maintenance, security and promotion) and to undertake capital improvements in the public realm. Such partnerships are limited to five years, are funded by a levy that is paid by all real-estate owners in the designated area, and can only provide services and improvements which are over and above the public 'standard'. Declaration of a BID requires a proposal to be backed by at least 15 per cent of proprietors (in number and in area), and approval of its business plan through a ballot of all affected proprietors, with the BID being designated by public statute if less than one third of proprietors reject it. For the BID to continue beyond its five-year period, it must be renewed by another ballot. The public sector is involved in the initial stages of setting up a BID; but once it is approved (by the district council), its role is limited (e.g. to facilitating the BID tax collection, by the Ministry of Finance, and subsequent BID continuation ballots, again by the district council), while the BID is run by an appointed management body or individual (Kreutz, 2009, 2011).

By the middle of 2011, six years after state legislation had allowed their designation, 12 BIDs had been established in Hamburg, two of these having entered their second term. These have all been in 'attractive and more or less prominent locations... with high property values and economically viable properties' (Kreutz, 2011, p13). The initial BIDs were widely dispersed across the city; but those in preparation in 2011 were more concentrated in the city centre and not far from HafenCity. One had been established in the old city centre of Harburg, which is close to the south Elbe waterfront that will be linked to Hamburg city centre via the Leap across the Elbe initiative.

Hamburg is also experimenting with adapting the principles of BIDs to housing areas through the implementation of NIDs. This initiative has responded to demands from the real estate and public and co-operative sectors for development of models based on the BID experience, within a context of housing stock transfer (from public to private ownership), which is leading to loss of public influence on area-based development of residential areas (Kreutz, 2007). Hamburg Senate passed a law in late 2007 which allows what it calls 'innovation neighbourhoods' to be established, and the implementation of NID schemes that are very similar to BIDs. The key difference is in the quorum required to take a NID proposal forward, which is raised from the 15 per cent applicable in BIDs to 30 per cent of property owners. Only property owners have a right to vote – not tenants or other stakeholders.

When the legislation came into being, a pilot project had already been initiated in the housing estate of Steilshoop. Built in 1969, this large estate, with 6380 housing units arranged in a scheme of medium- to high-rise large-scale perimeter blocks with a shopping centre on its central axis, had already been the focus of much public investment in regeneration during the late 1980s and 1990s; but problems persisted. Property ownership spans almost the entire range of what is possible in Germany, with the largest owner being an international stock-listed corporation, followed in size by council housing owned by a community housing association, and then a range of housing co-operatives, private housing companies and owner-occupiers (Kreutz, 2009). HafenCity University's observation of the pilot project showed differences in the levels of participation of the various property owners in the process of setting up the NID, with larger housing associations and co-operatives being more involved, and the smaller landlords (owner-occupiers, private landlords and smaller private housing companies) not initially engaging. It also noted differences in the decision-making powers of public and private stakeholders, which did not facilitate the process (Kreutz, 2009). One particular aspect that shows commonality with experience in HafenCity is the approach to open space management, with a person being designated in Steilshoop to take daily responsibility for this on the ground (in this case called the *Kümmerer*) who is the point of contact between owners and residents, on the one hand, and the city's sanitation department, on the other (Kreutz, 2010).

BIDs have generated mixed reactions among those who have analysed them. In their favour it is argued that they provide improvements on the ground and, in some cases, show economic performance having been increased, though this is not always easy or possible to measure; and that they provide one possible way of achieving new management and partnership structures, which are seen as necessary to achieve urban regeneration (Findlay and Sparks, 2008). The main concern is the extent to which BIDs constitute a privatization of public space, and therefore a loss of democratic control over this and subsequent impacts upon social cohesion and inclusion (Findlay and Sparks, 2008; Minton, 2009). In the case of the Hamburg experience, it is argued that some positive indicators for BIDs, to date, are instances of improved performance and the fact that BIDs are being rolled forward in second ballots. Regarding the loss of accountability, it is argued that the public administration retains control over urban development, therefore safeguarding democratic accountability (Kreutz, 2009).

As for NIDs, the Hamburg experience suggests that deprived neighbourhoods are perhaps not the best suited to this kind of mechanism, as the limited financial capacity of private owners requires considerable public support. But the Steilshoop experience also shows that initiating a NID process has contributed to better communication and coordination among stakeholders, which has resulted in improvements in maintenance on the ground, without additional funding required (Kreutz, 2009).

Although these experiences have not taken place directly at waterfront locations or within waterfront regeneration areas, they hold potential for implementing partnerships for regeneration and long-term management in the different scenarios that can be found in places such as HafenCity or Wilhelmsburg.

BIDs and NIDs would rank very low on Arnstein's ladder if they were to be analysed from the perspective of wider citizen participation, as residents and even businesses are not directly involved at all. Their power as citizens appears to be exercisable only in a very indirect way via the local authority. On the 'wheel of participation', they would appear to fall in the 'information' quadrant, as information is readily available on all the BIDs in Hamburg. On the other hand, if Arnstein's ladder is applied only to the stakeholders who are directly involved in BIDs (i.e. property owners), these are given a role that could be seen as somewhere between having 'delegated power' or even 'control' (though not 'citizen control') – that is, at the top of the ladder. In the 'wheel of participation' they would be classified within the 'empowerment' quadrant. This again raises questions over where power lies and how this is allocated through urban development and regeneration mechanisms, and who should be included when 'citizen participation' is considered, given the multiple 'roles' that stakeholders can have (e.g. as both property owners and residents).

Conclusions

These three experiences in city-building and city management in Hamburg are examples of a range of approaches to participation, linked to different scenarios with varying balances and types of power.

The development of HafenCity shows the key strategic decision-making processes being initiated almost in secret by the city government in a (successful) attempt to avoid the initiative running aground due to potential opposition from port and port-related bodies, as well as possibly the wider population, and the risk of increases in land value. The process has become increasingly participatory at levels where the scale and strategic significance of decisions became more limited. This approach was possible in great part because of the land being mostly under City of Hamburg ownership and the virtual lack of resident population in the area affected. Power, in this case, was concentrated in the city and the port authorities, and the former manipulated the scope for manoeuvre of the latter.

The existence of a resident population, with some history of protest, to boot, painted a different scenario in Wilhelmsburg. The Leap across the Elbe initiative could not be launched without wide engagement of the variety of stakeholders affected. The range of decision-making bodies and the integration of residents' representatives within these are greater. However, the complex institutional framework has been designed in a way that still retains key decision-making power with the city authorities.

Finally, the BID schemes strengthen the power of property owners to manage limited and clearly defined local areas, potentially side-lining the views of other stakeholders who use such areas. The level to which power is delegated here is arguable.

In all three experiences, the strong position of Hamburg's government is notable, making use of its legislative and financial powers, as well as of its strategic leverage as landowner (particularly in HafenCity). Its room for manoeuvre is strengthened by the booming economy of the city and the continuing contribution to this from its port activities. It is therefore in a good position both as an authoritative structure and as an allocative structure. Its high level of power as an organization is accompanied by the continuing strength of the mental model of the state as guarantee of the public good – which underpins HafenCity Hamburg GmbH's negotiations with developers on behalf of the wider population, as well as the view that the local authority still ensures democratic control over the public spaces that are included in BIDs.

It is an entrepreneurial state, however, reflecting the increasing power and influence on market-based models. This is evidenced in the use of arms' length companies to implement the city's plans for the regeneration of the waterfront areas, as well as of private-sector (and public-sector) property owners to manage and bankroll district improvements. What is perhaps less developed overall, despite the 'Citizens for Hamburg' theme of participation in the Leap across the Elbe initiative, is an approach to participation that extends citizen control and management to higher levels of decision-making, beyond representative democracy mechanisms.

A sign of this and the discontent that it can generate is the 'Not in Our Name' manifesto produced by a group of artists, intellectuals and concerned citizens against the city model being developed in Hamburg, particularly in the waterfront areas, which through gentrification is said to be driving out the 'creative class'. They call for the city as a community as opposed to seeing it as a corporation and a brand (Desfor and Laidley, 2011; Novy and Colomb, 2011).[10] The experiences of Hamburg raise hard questions regarding whose priorities should (and actually do) guide and influence such ambitious projects as HafenCity and Leap across the Elbe, within the context of current shifts in governance environments, balances of power and mental models of the city.

Notes

1   See Flyvbjerg (1988) for a good discussion of Habermas's concept of communicative rationality.
2   This section draws on Carley and Garcia Ferrari (2007) and www.hafencity.com/en/overview/hafencity-the-genesis-of-an-idea.html, as well as on information collected during visits to HafenCity by the authors in 2008 and 2010.

3 At least 774 million Euros in public subsidies are calculated for the HafenCity development (August 2009) (see Krüger, 2009).

4 Initially called GHS (Gesellschaft für Hafen-und Standortentwicklung mbH), this later became HafenCity Hamburg GmbH.

5 See also www.hafencity.com/en/management/communication-and-dialog-in-hafencity. html (accessed 18 July 2011).

6 Interview with the managing director of IGS Hamburg 2013 GmbH, available at www.igs-hamburg.de/134.0.html?&L=1 (accessed 14 July 2011).

7 These have to be resident or working in the district.

8 See www.iba-hamburg.de/en/02_gemeinsam/3_beteiligung/beteiligung_gremium.php (accessed 12 July 2011).

9 This section draws on the research on urban improvement districts undertaken by HafenCity University Hamburg. More information on this research is available at www.urban-improvement-districts.de/?q=English.

10 See http://arafiqui.wordpress.com/2009/11/26/not-in-our-name-hamburg-artists-speak-out-against-a-segregated-city/ and www.signandsight.com/features/1961.html (both accessed 18 July 2011).

7

Harbourscape Aalborg
Design-Based Methods in Waterfront Development

Hans Kiib

Introduction

How can city planners and developers gain knowledge and develop new sustainable concepts for waterfront developments? The waterfront is far too often threatened by new privatization, lack of public access and bad architecture. And at a time when low growth rates and crises in the building industry are leaving great parts of the harbour as urban voids, planners are in search of new tools for bridging the time gap until new projects can become a reality.

This chapter presents the development of waterfront regeneration concepts that resulted from design-based workshops – *Harbourscape Aalborg* in 2005 and *Performative Architecture Workshop* in 2008 – and evaluates the method and the thinking behind this. The design workshops provide different design-based development methods that can be tested, with the purpose of developing new concepts for the relationship between the city and its harbour, as well as generating easily grasped images of a coherent harbour transformation (Kiib, 2007).

The lessons learned in the course of these workshops in Aalborg indicate that comparable methodological achievements require a consistent line in the professional approach of team leaders. Design-based development can make an independent contribution to the visioning process on urban development, city life planning and landscaping; but this has to be based on a 'non-dogmatic' approach in architectural and urban space design. This involves, amongst other aspects, the combination of independent evaluation and discourse analyses in the regeneration of the harbour area, and a combination of methods and approaches used in order to achieve quality design and ownership from citizens, as well as commitment from professionals.

Waterfront challenges

The intensive battle for the control of waterfront redevelopment is taking place in many major cities and towns (Marshall, 2001; Dovey, 2005). In a manner similar to the industrial conquest of the harbour 100 years ago and its subsequent transformation into a closed industrial zone separated from the rest of the city, exclusive offices and residential buildings of cities are now well on their way to causing a new privatization of large parts of the harbour's surplus landscapes.

In all big coastal cities, as well as in smaller towns, the harbour is a grandiose meeting of the town and the sea, representing an interesting interface between local life and the big world. The waterfront could be a common gift for all citizens, a gateway for hopes for a better life and a meeting place between 'tradition' and 'the new'. The waterfront could be a fantastic interface between nature and the manmade world. Some political forces call for strategies that can prevent this privatization, and produce a series of public domains along the waterfront, including a great variety in its future use, meeting places for all and, finally, room for architectural experiments and arts.

But this is far from the strategies which predominate in current waterfront development (Bruttomesso, 1993; Marshall, 2001; Carlberg and Christensen, 2005). An intensive battle for the private control of waterfront redevelopment is taking place between stakeholders. Exclusive offices and residential buildings of the city are now well on their way to causing a new privatization of large parts of the harbour's surplus landscapes. A counterpart to the residential and office projects of developers' strategies is to be found in a balanced combination of different strategies for land use that ensure the particular status of the harbour as a port and as a public domain (Marling and Kiib, 2007).

Waterfront redevelopment strategies in Aalborg

This development also takes place in smaller towns such as Aalborg, where the area of waterfront regeneration covers more than 200ha of former industrial sites on both sides of the fjord (see Figure 7.1). Three big agendas and conflicts have been in focus here:

Figure 7.1 *The twin city Aalborg*

Source: photo-collage by Jens Rex, in *Harbourscape 2007*

1   Public domains: the privatizing of the quays or development of the
    waterfront as a new public domain along the fjord.
2   New crossings: should new crossings of the fjord be based on a new
    motorway or on smaller city-integrated bridges?
3   Breeding grounds for creative forces: the conflict between short-term
    development based on top-down strategies and a long-term regeneration
    approach based on bottom-up strategies and temporary use.

In 1999, the *Fjord Catalogue*, which provided the overall guidelines for the
relationship between city and harbour along both sides of the fjord, was
approved (Aalborg Kommune, 1999). The regeneration of the old industrial
areas on the waterfronts on both banks of the fjord focused on modern urban
housing and business areas.

The experience gained from the initial transformation of a central part of
the waterfront from industry to a 'private zone' of mixed residential and
office area gave cause for concern. The area bears the paradoxical street
name, since the beginning of the 20th century, *Ved Stranden* ('By the Beach');
but the buildings are tall and dense, and, in spite of vocal and forceful
criticism from local citizens, the block structure excludes public functions.
The building projects here can be described as project-initiated development
with fragmented programming and a frail architectural vision. Finally, the
projects were not linked within a distinct urban space policy or an inclusive
preservation policy. One might speak of a boomerang effect as these buildings
brush aside the bustle and atmosphere that make up the attraction of the
harbour. This public criticism and evaluation were the basis for the demand
for a more comprehensive planning strategy, which could focus on developing
public domains along the quays (Aalborg Kommune, 2004; Marling and
Kiib, 2007).

Another big conflict has been related to the crossing of the fjord.
Aalborg is a twin city along the Limfjord, with the main part of the city on
the south bank and the district of Nørresundby on the north bank, where
for more than 30 years there has been debate on the connection between the
two sides of the fjord (Jensen and Hovgensen, 2004; Kiib, 2004), including
on the nature of the next crossing. Should it be based on high-speed car
transport or should it be related to sustainable transport by bus, trains and
bicycles? This has been a major conflict between two agendas with
respective proposed solutions: on the one hand, a crossing as a new
motorway solution promoted by modernist planners and car lovers, and, on
the other, several city-integrated bridge connections promoted by
environmentalists.

Finally, there has been strong public resistance towards 'developer-driven'
demolition of the old industrial buildings – a 'tabula rasa strategy' – preparing
the harbour area for new expensive developments for residential and office use.
Most of the waterfront was owned by the municipality or by the public harbour
company; but the land has gradually been sold out to private developers and a
lot of the industrial buildings have been demolished, leaving the waterfront as
vacant land for years. The impact of this strategy has been that a rich heritage
of industrial buildings and warehouses has disappeared. Furthermore, a lot of

cheap built space, which could serve as a haven for creative forces, small upcoming companies and education, was removed.

In the wake of these highly criticized projects and policies, the City of Aalborg brought the harbour into focus again by asking for a more comprehensive strategy for regeneration. During the years following 2000, a reinterpretation of themes and strategies was put forward in the public debate (Aalborg Kommune, 2005). These included, amongst others:

- How can the harbour be developed from a privatized industrial zone into a public domain for the citizens?
- How can the harbour develop its own unique position in the city – not as a divide, but as 'a connecting element' between the twin cities of Aalborg and Nørresundby?
- How can the harbour contribute to the everyday life of different sections of the population, including artists and new business?
- How can harbour activities be continued?
- How can the industrial heritage contribute to design quality in private projects as well as in the public realm?
- How can the public realm be extended along the banks and quays, and how can it be a bridging element between different programmes along the fjord?

Harbourscape workshops: Design-based methodologies

From 2004, the City of Aalborg and Aalborg University joined the European Union-funded InterReg IIIB Waterfront Communities Project (WCP), including

Figure 7.2 *Photo-collage from the Harbourscape Workshop 2005*

Source: photo-collage by Jens Rex, in *Harbourscape 2007*

eight other cities around the North Sea (Carley and Garcia Ferrari, 2007). Each city experimented with new ways of tackling a particular challenge of waterfront development, and at joint meetings and through thematic research new learning was gained and communicated. Based on experiences from these cities, it was agreed that a series of design-based workshops should be organized by the university, focusing on the topics raised above.

In 2005, the *Harbourscape Workshop, Aalborg* event took place as three workshops and a conference at Aalborg University, with the participation of 45 architects, engineers and planners from Denmark, Norway, The Netherlands and the UK (Kiib, 2007). The aims were to develop visionary concepts and design proposals emphasizing the development and regeneration of the waterfront in Aalborg; to investigate a full-scale dialogue on concepts and architectural quality in the waterfront development among stakeholders in this process; and to illustrate how different design-based methods can serve as tools in the process.

The event was repeated in 2008 with the *Performative Architecture Workshop*. Some of the same questions were put on the agenda and three different workshops worked hard on new concepts for waterfront development and improvement of city life using design-based methodologies.

The design-based workshops were inspired by the Hamburg '*Bauforum*', which in many ways has served as the learning ground for design-based development strategies in urban transformations (Freien und Hansestadt Hamburg, 2003). Other inspirational examples hailed from Oslo and Copenhagen. The so-called Oslo-Charrette took place in 2004 – developing various design strategies for transforming the border zone between city and fjord (Fjordbykontoret, 2004). Oslo City Council assembled three design and planning teams to work with three different scenarios: Oslo Large, Oslo Park and Oslo Network. Each scenario gave an overall assessment of the possibilities for expanding the city's harbour area. Three sub-areas had been chosen in advance. Experience from Hamburg and Oslo demonstrated that architectural workshops have great potential in *developing new concepts in urban design*.

The workshops in Aalborg were organized using the following components:

1   a one-day mini seminar with open lectures by internationally acknowledged researchers and architects who theoretically and empirically illuminated the subject by way of international examples and the results of their own research;
2   a five-day workshop led by three teams of excellent architects;
3   an exhibition of the results, including interviews and public TV;
4   a one-day public hearing with participants from the local community (presentations were held highlighting the results of the workshop – intermediate results and finished products – and a panel of politicians and local representatives within building and planning answered questions regarding the future expansion of the harbour and the quality of construction); and
5   an academic conference evaluating the methodology used and presentations from research on waterfront developments.

Themes as a starting point for concept development

On the basis of international research and learning from successful waterfront developments in the North Sea region, the organizers of *Harbourscape Aalborg 2005* presented central themes summarizing the challenges that face the twin-city waterfront development. They were to serve as the starting point for the one-day mini seminar with lectures and discussions.

Multifunctional programming. Complex programming has the advantage of allowing space for programmes that assign priority to activities, such as existing industrial and artisan areas, and harbour-related cultural landscapes and event spaces, but also spaces for working and living. There must be room for functions that make a positive contribution to the new economy of the experience industry. Finally, by reserving some areas for temporary activities, this type of programming can benefit life at and around the harbour, thus keeping the harbour area open for future initiatives and ensuring that different lifestyle groups have reasons to use the area.

Movements and connections. This theme involved the overall physical design of the urban harbour, including connections and movement along the waterfronts and across the fjord, and how to build in a manner that avoids turning the fjord into an obstacle, but instead establishes it as a large connecting urban space in the core of the twin city.

Ten public domains. This comprised the physical design of locations and harbour spaces, passages along the quay progressing coherently with the harbour promenade, the bridges and surplus landscapes. The theme marked an attempt to find means of ascertaining the diversity of open as well as closed urban spaces and landscape spaces that could be established along the fjord.

In the *Performative Architecture Workshop* in 2008, the organizers focused on two further themes.

The city as a learning lab. This theme would combine a rich and experimental urban context with an informal learning environment and education. Creative and artistic education could be provided, together with music halls, theatres, art galleries, cafés and art workshops in order to minimize the distance between learning and artistic performance, and to ensure the production and consumption of different kinds of experiences. You could talk about the *city as a campus – a hybrid structure of layered programmes, interactive spaces and transparent architecture.*

Urban catalysts and temporary use. This theme was looking for small and large urban interventions, surprising use of existing buildings and the addition of *temporary architecture* in the transformation of urban design. Urban catalysts could be 'event-scapes', exhibitions or artistic performance, which could show new ways of going forward. The focus was on *temporary and permanent architecture and art that perform as urban catalysts in abandoned urban fields.* How could temporary use of abandoned urban fields involve, in particular, students, artists and cultural workers? And how could you transform former waterfront areas and industrial buildings into vibrant urban environments for cultural development?

Concepts and designs

In the five-day long professional workshop on concept development, each of the teams, comprising team leaders and 15 architects and planners, could choose what to focus on. The chapter now focuses on three of the teams, selected from both events, which presented unique conceptual developments:[1]

- The *Gehl Team* (Gehl Architects, 2005 workshop) focused on public space development, employing a unique methodology labelled 'city life development'.
- The *BIG Team* (Bjarke Ingels Group, 2005 workshop) focused on how to work with hybrid concepts in the development of new crossings. This team employed a pragmatic methodology with a firm grip of the development of hybrid architectural concepts.
- The *Urban Catalyst Team* (Studio UC and Raumlabor Berlin, 2008 workshop) employed a participatory methodology looking at the liminal zone at the harbour and focusing on a procedural planning strategy for temporal use and concrete interventions in the area.

Each of the three team leaders was responsible for a unique methodological approach to the work, the outcome was to be oriented towards strategies and concepts, and new urban proposals had to be quickly designed and implemented in sketches, physical models and direct interventions on the ground.

The Spine: The Gehl Team, 2005

The Spine concept developed by the Gehl Team presented activities which were intended to transform the harbour into a pleasant place teeming with activity. In all its simplicity, the method reversed the traditional focus on architecture, approaching first, *urban life*, second, *urban space* and, finally, *the edge* and *buildings* (Gehl and Gemzøe, 2000). In general, the buildings along the harbour were not treated as building volumes, but as edges and frames for public space. Thus, the focus was first and foremost on the spaces between the buildings, the transparency between the interior and the exterior at the ground level, and the function and activity of a given building rather than its form. This method had three steps (see Figure 7.3):

1   The *activities* at the harbour were programmed and spread out in a manner that highlighted the distinctive character of a given area. The circadian rhythm of the harbour and the change of the seasons were rendered visible and highlighted.
2   The dimensions and character of the various spaces were modelled in accordance with urban life conditions. The harbour space was defined across the water in order to combine land and water in a synchronized spatial experience and orientation.
3   Finally, *the edge* was represented on two scales. The harbour was not defined in terms of the quay, but rather by the façades that mark the edge

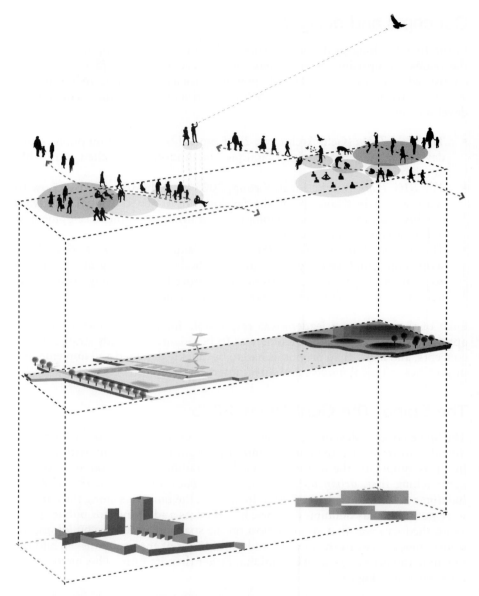

Figure 7.3 *The 'reverse-thinking' model: Life–space–edge–buildings*

Source: The Gehl Team, in *Harbourscape 2007*

of the city. At the local scale, in a context of urban spatiality, the edge was defined as three-dimensional surfaces that animate the urban space and imbue it with life. Thus, the circle was closed. The edge provided space for life and called for contact between inside and outside, between the public and the private spheres.

The 'Spine' metaphor (see Figure 7.4) provided a new overall design concept allowing an experience of the twin cities (Aalborg and Nørresundby) not as two

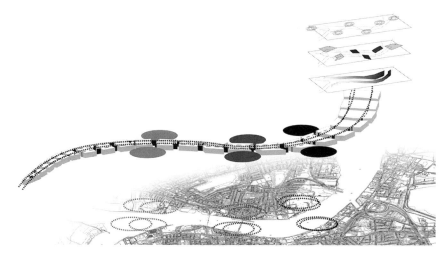

Figure 7.4 *The 'Spine' concept for the 'Fjord City'*

Source: The Gehl Team, in *Harbourscape 2007*

separate cities with a body of water in between, but as a unified urban landscape, where the water is the core connecting part of the city, and the two waterfronts are the 'edges of the big blue plaza' in 'the Fjord City', providing this city with its historical identity and pride. At a smaller scale, this workshop developed a range of new and interesting waterfront space concepts, taking the historical context into account and preserving some of its present spatial qualities (see Figure 7.5).

'Reverse-thinking'

The Spine concept was based on 'reverse-thinking' as a way of generating concepts on space development. The Gehl Team argued that every city and every developer wants life and a high density of people, which often results in even greater density. But the contemporary architectural answer to greater density is frequently bigger volumes and much larger spaces, resulting in a lack of human-scale environment and, thus, inevitably in a lack of people and life. This is a bad downwards spiral. 'Nothing happens because nothing happens as nothing happens…' (Kiib, 2007). It was almost possible to talk about 'a modern paradox' in urban development, and the circle had to be broken through a renewed focus on the architectural planning and design process.

Being very critical towards traditional city planning and towards the strong focus on form and volumes in architectural practice, the team suggested an 'upside-down' approach to planning. When developing a successful city area, whether a new or existing city area, life needed to be in focus from the beginning of the design process. By turning the traditional methodology upside down, people and city users could become more visible in the planning process.

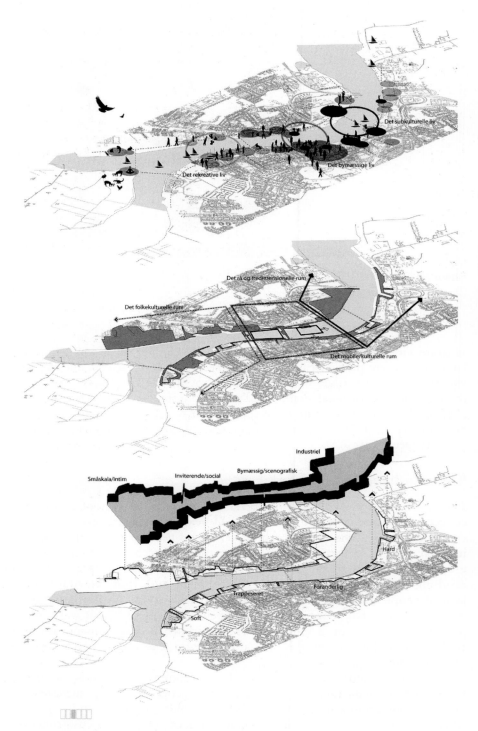

Figure 7.5 ' *'The blue square' in the middle of the twin city*

Source: The Gehl Team, in *Harbourscape 2007*

People, life and vitality were to be the biggest attractions in the city. It was argued that planning and design would start with people, and the quality of the urban environment had to respond to the biological preconditions of humans. There are certain conditions that can be found to be true for everyone regardless of cultural background.

Humans are 'a walking animal', and we move around at a speed of 5km per hour, they argued. This made the detailing of the urban environment at eye level very important. The public realm needed to respond to walking speed, the experiences and the need for stimuli of people and not, for example, cars moving at speeds of at least 60km per hour. People would seek shelter when needed, sun when it is cold and vice versa. People would prefer to sit on the edge of a space or a bench rather than in the middle. People would talk to each other at a social distance of 1.5m to 3m, etc. With reference to the methodology developed by Professor Jan Gehl, the concept was developed applying a lot of universal factors to be incorporated within the design, to ensure and invite social interaction between people (Gehl and Gemzøe, 2000):

> However, we cannot DESIGN or CREATE life, but it is possible to create the environment which invites human activities! The learning is that we have to take *urban life* as a starting point – not the buildings. Secondly we have to consider how we can improve city life and to densify it in *a series of spaces*. The third step is framing the spaces by designing *the edges*, the floor of the spaces and public space interior. The buildings give life, character and identity to a place. When looking at a space one should never separate the analysis of the floor from its edges. The activities, entrances and functions of the lower floors of a building are particularly important at the scale of pedestrians and people. At the end of the line in this methodology we find *architecture*.
>
> Gehl Team in Kiib, 2007

Bridging Aalborg: The BIG Team, 2005

The concept from the BIG team took as its starting point the physical and mental connection of the twin cities with bridges as architectural projects. Four new prototypes of hybrid bridges were proposed to jointly connect the two sides of the harbour, thereby laying the foundation for a new perception of the harbour as the common space of the city (see Figure 7.6). Specifically, an elevated bridge to the east, the Residential Viaduct, was remarkable as a new and innovative design. It consisted of a number of residential towers with an urban park and low-speed traffic and pedestrians on top, and a parking deck below the urban park and above the housing towers. It contained a total of 1000 residences and 1000 parking spaces.

The effect of all these new bridges was to brand Aalborg as a 'City of Bridges' and all the bridges were to be financed through double-programming. The Residential Viaduct, for example, was to be financed through the residential project.

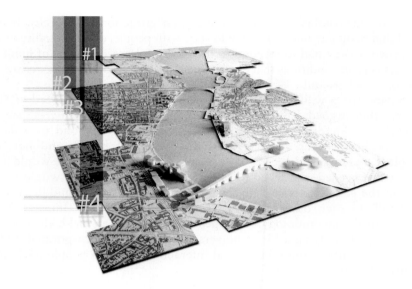

The proposed 1.5km long residential bridge would connect Aalborg and Nørresundby by way of a vacant industrial area to the north (see Figure 7.7). Of the four projects, this was possibly the one best suited to create quality for public and city alike, at no cost for the city. The idea was to utilize private willingness to invest and exploit the historically high value of building residential developments in order to create something extraordinary for the public. Primarily, it was a permanent traffic connection, which Aalborg sorely needs. Second, it linked two historical areas that contain a vast potential. If they were gradually developed into two different cultural parks, each with its own specificities and identity, they would comprise two fantastic poles for the bridge to connect.

The residential units would be located in the piers, and on top of them would be a parking deck. The bridge could then be crossed by cars and pedestrians and there would be access to the parking zone below the decks, from where the flats could be accessed by elevator. Here, people would be able to sit on their terraces and enjoy the view of the industrial areas, the fjord landscape or the city. People could watch the ships glide in between the piers. This bridge could become a landmark for cruise liners on their way to Norway, and thus attract thousands of tourists to Aalborg. Depending upon the size of the bridge, such a construction could contain up to 1000 residential units. This is a feasible amount since a lot of housing is currently being planned in Aalborg. By moving approximately 700 units from the waterfront on the Aalborg side and 300 from the Stigsborg area to the bridge, the project would become realistic within just a few years. The project would primarily be funded through private investments, but in a constructive symbiosis with the public authorities.

Focus on paradoxes

The BIG Team argued that there is a paradox built into waterfront development in a Danish context – between too much open space and too little need for new development:

(a)

(b)

Figure 7.7 *The Residential Bridge*

Source: The BIG Team, in *Harbourscape 2007*

The problem is, perhaps, the lack of pressure on urban development in towns like Aalborg – leaving the central industrial areas under developed. One could term it a 'surplus landscape'. Aalborg has a larger harbour area than Copenhagen – very much so if we compare the size of the cities. This could easily lead to a very low density due to the lack of pressure on the building market.

BIG Team in Kiib, 2007

Instead of low-density development, this team's proposals would lead to a concentration of the construction work on a few new spots and connections across the fjord, leaving the larger areas for recreational purposes, parks and spaces for alternative applications. Old industrial buildings have proved to be extremely well suited to cultural applications, galleries and temporary functions such as summer restaurants, concert halls and other types of events, etc. In this type of culture, budgets are typically low, and by leaving a large part of the existing wealth of buildings un-restored and, consequently, cheap and accessible, a sort of cultural magnet could be created, which could help to rebrand the City of Aalborg.

If there was a vast amount of these types of abandoned areas available, this could contribute to giving the city a new image as an alternative cultural city, rather like Berlin, where there is also a large surplus of buildings and environments that can be exploited in European cultural life – precisely because of its accessibility. At the waterfront in Aalborg a similar vast potential is also to be found because the city still has so much of the old mass of industrial buildings, and the option of ensuring that some of it remains unplanned exists (Andersson and Kiib, 2007).

In this way, the surplus landscapes could contribute to the definition of a cultural scene (Pine and Gilmore, 1999; Landry, 2000):

> Coming to Aalborg and discovering the large industrial 'dinosaurs' at the harbour is quite an extraordinary *Blade Runner* kind of experience in its own right. Consequently, developers' plans to demolish the large industrial buildings in the central part of the harbour are a bad idea since many other building sites exist, and it would mean a removal without replacement of one of the few real attractions of the harbour.

> BIG Team in Kiib, 2007 (see Figure 7.8)

In the course of the workshop, the BIG team developed an urban type that can add a lot of square metres without destroying the existing magic of the harbour, especially in the areas of industrial culture that remain. They perceived this as a successful part of the workshop.

Astonishing wealth of urban volumes and typologies

The team focused on the astonishing wealth of urban volumes and typologies, a vast variation in scales in the form of, for example, giant silos next to weird cranes:

> It is *a fantastic catalogue of typologies*, which might actually be suited to the contemporary city-dweller precisely because of this typological wealth. The block city does have a lot of different qualities, but it has also become somewhat restrictive for our way of conceptualizing the city.

> BIG Team in Kiib, 2007

The BIG workshop pursued a paradox in the way in which our harbours have been constructed until now. One part of this paradox was that the inner cities consist almost exclusively of one typology of urban structures and buildings: the five-storey block. This block, however, was housing a multiplicity of programmes – residences, nursery schools, businesses, etc. 'We are dealing with a physically and spatially very homogenous city with a multitude of programmes.' The other part of the paradox was that the harbour, on the other hand, contained many complex typologies, which nevertheless encompassed only one type of programme: industry. Thus, there was a paradox in the sense that the number of typologies was not related to the number of programmes.

(a)

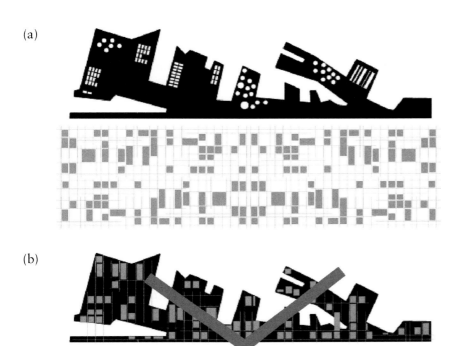

(b)

(c)

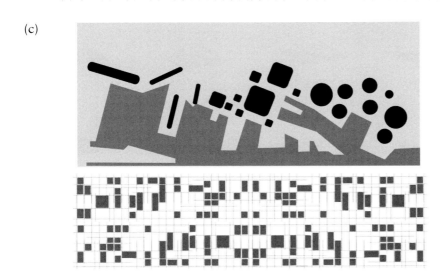

Figure 7.8 *Current plans to demolish the large industrial buildings in the central part of the harbour are a bad idea*

Source: The BIG Team, in *Harbourscape 2007*

The inner city was multi-programmatic but mono-typological, whereas the harbour was mono-functional but multi-typological. So, instead of simply adding to the familiar urban block structure, the team viewed the harbour as an exploratorium for new urban typologies (see Figure 7.9):

> In fact, the harbour's catalogue of interesting and unpredictable buildings simply consists of industrial warehouses that fulfil some very specific demands under certain very specific circumstances. If, through analysis, we are able to uncover some equally specific needs under specific circumstances, the potential for creating new and unpredictable urban typologies might exist.

BIG Team in Kiib, 2007

Hybrid concepts link the architectural heritage with new typologies

The proposed Residential Bridge was quite an innovation, and it attracted a great deal of attention at the presentation, partly due to the scale and design, and partly due to its residential content and its importance in terms of traffic. The hybrid bridge was a metaphor for the pragmatic way of thinking in urban

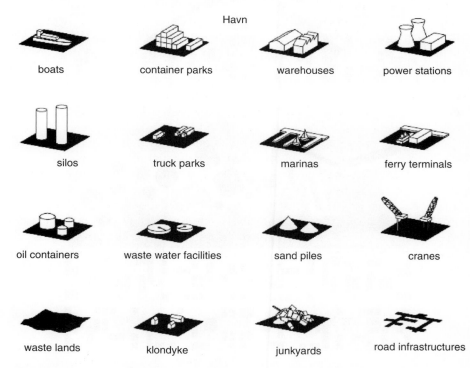

Figure 7.9 *The industrial waterfront – a mono-functional structure but with an astonishing wealth of typologies*

Source: The BIG Team, in *Harbourscape 2007*

design (Chung et al, 2001; Andersson and Kiib, 2007). 'Hybrid economy' and 'hybrid space' can be understood as linking 'a traditional economy' to a new 'experience economy', and merging 'traditional private urban spaces' with 'new types of public domains'. This coupling is the point of departure for the mental shift from an industrial mind set towards a new pragmatic philosophy in the development of our cities based on knowledge and culture. The term 'hybrid urban domain' breaks down the traditional division between public and private and seeks to choreograph the city as the space of experience, which serves both as a framework for traditional functions, while simultaneously taking on new roles, new meanings and new narratives:

> The bridge could constitute a futuristic landmark for the city and, to a certain extent, enter into a good dialogue with the industrial landscape to the south in terms of scale. Also, its romantic form creates a good contrast to the raw aesthetics of the practical on-shore works and surplus areas. Thus the project would also have a strong branding effect.

BIG Team in Kiib, 2007

Aalborg Catalyst: The UC/Raumlabor Team, 2008

The Aalborg Catalyst Team employed a participatory methodology in the liminal zone at the harbour, focusing on a procedural planning strategy for temporal use and concrete interventions in the area (Bader et al, 2009). This team focused on the size of the current urban voids (see Figure 7.10). So far, the municipality has focused on building up two big cultural institutions at the central waterfront – the Music House and Nordkraft – which combine multiple cultural, sports and entertainment players in one complex. This strategy is meant to create a dynamic impact for further development in the leftover eastern harbour. But the economic crisis has stopped the development of further office and housing projects.

As an effect of an on-going transformation process and the economic crisis, the city contains numerous areas of former industrial use. As more and more of these areas become derelict, urban voids evolve. A deep divide can be identified between the central part of the waterfront – programmatically diverse and well developed – as a fairly stable condition and the east undergoing severe structural transformation. The size of the current urban voids in the eastern part of the waterfront on both sides of the fjord now exceeds that of the whole city centre of Aalborg. With further economic recession and economic crises coming, more voids are to be expected. The way of dealing with these urban areas is crucial for the development of Aalborg in the coming 30 years.

A masterplan for temporary use

The starting point for development of a 'masterplan for temporary use' involved a paradox: there exist numerous plans for new developments in derelict industrial areas, but no demand for all the surfaces. The approach was based on a double strategy: on the one hand, a plea for a dynamic planning

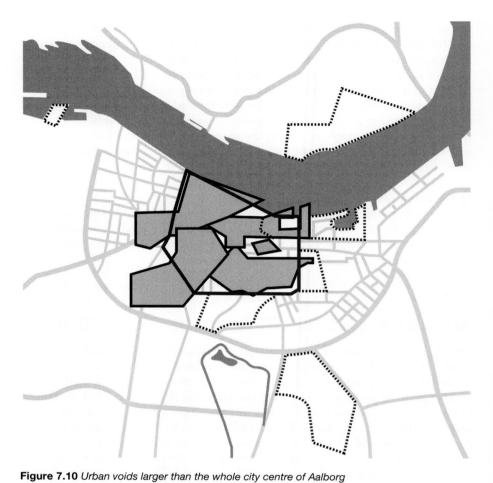

Figure 7.10 *Urban voids larger than the whole city centre of Aalborg*

Source: Urban Catalyst/Raumlabor Berlin, in *Architecture and Stages in the Experience City*, 2009

and, on the other, to adjust the development to current needs and to discover such needs and make them visible, finding new actors and turning them into developers:

> The central question was: when exactly was the masterplan set and who was in charge of which spaces. Until now, the existing instruments of planning were not just thought for an immediate appropriation of the space, but also for securing permanent structures. They had to be supplemented by new control tools, which on one hand could make handling unfinished or transitory situations easier and on the other hand diminish the users' chances to actively participate.
>
> Bader et al, 2009

The 'masterplan for temporal use' (see Figure 7.11) exploited the potential of the time gap between the present situation as a functional void towards a more permanent use. Instead of demolishing former industrial warehouses and grain

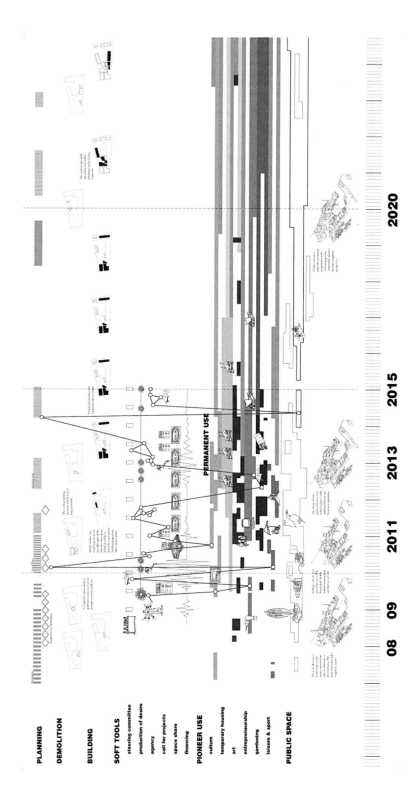

Figure 7.11 Masterplan for temporary use: the diagram exploits the potential of the time gap between the present situation as a functional void towards a more permanent use

Source: Urban Catalyst/Raumlabor Berlin, in *Architecture and Stages in the Experience City*, 2009

silos, it suggested their reuse by new agents (e.g. artists, galleries, performers and small upcoming firms, but also young people with new ideas in relation to sport, leisure and play). It was called 'pioneer use' (e.g. for culture, temporary housing, art, entrepreneurship and gardening).

A range of 'soft tools' was to be employed in the process, including the creation of a steering committee, setting up small agencies for distribution of space, space sharing, and establishment of a micro-loan system for the pioneers. Gradually, over a time span of 20 years or so, it would be possible to develop commercial projects in the area, and new building projects could emerge. Some of the worst buildings could be demolished and new buildings then erected.

Process planning

As suggested in the presentation of the workshop results, the following aspects seem to be essential steps in a dynamic planning process, as suggested by the Aalborg Catalyst Team (Bader et al, 2009):

1   Identify waiting spaces, time gaps and potential activist networks.
2   Make a strategic plan prioritizing focal areas for different temporary-use typologies.
3   Open up time gap spaces for spontaneous use.
4   Initiate public life at non-public place.
5   Reuse existing spatial structures.
6   Allow direct implementation.
7   Get key agents involved in supporting informal networks and strategic coalitions.
8   Make as many actors as possible become part of the process.
9   Create a negotiation platform to combine formal and informal development strategies.
10 Follow flexible strategies: allow temporary activities to become permanent, as well as closing them down if necessary.

Stimulation of planning. Dynamic planning, unlike traditional planning, aims at a gradual densification of activities, programmes and networks, which also become 'constructural'. Factors contributing to this could be consolidation of use, achieving a critical mass of actors, a change of location or altered basic economic parameters. It is important to identify milestones of development and to react in an appropriate way – for example, to change the form of organization and to invest in structural projects or new partners. The moment and the type of development cannot be previously determined. However, planning can help to design spatial, programmatic and economic scenarios. It therefore formulates a basis for making decisions.

Share control. To gradually densify concepts of utilization without limiting them by planning is, without doubt, for many actors linked with the distribution of control for available space, design and programmes. The loss of 'solitary development' that is assumed in this approach can also become a reduction of risk and a win–win situation for every person involved. Which role the principle of the divided control plays in a project depends upon the proportions of properties and the constellations of actors. The possibility of participation is beneficial (e.g. when the public sector provides an area to a group at low tenancy, or when the marketing conditions of an area are so bad that the owner is glad about any person who uses the area). The optimum situation would be when the user becomes an owner and an administrator – for example, by temporary finance via private investors. Development of projects with private owners is rarely given into the hands of users.

Sampling. It is necessary to enlarge the areas of action in city planning, to connect short-term as well as long-term planning, and to combine hard and soft tools in planning strategies. Calls for projects on pioneer uses, cultural activity in public spaces, the manipulation of accessibility, reprogramming of existing structures or the networking of actors are a complement to a number of facilities: local public infrastructures, open spaces and structural activities. There are several possible role models, which act as spiders in a web: they initiate projects, develop available spaces, build networks of actors and coordinate the development of areas. Or they act as service provider with specific planning tasks for the users, local authorities or owners. In other cases, they act as mediators between the involved parties through new proposals.

Acting. The duration, often very long, which is negotiated in the planning process renders the proposed object abstract and, for many, inaccessible. Despite his or her training, even the planner is in danger of losing the reference of the object in the working process. Through the construction of scale 1:1 objects, we could escape this danger. At the same time, it is important not only to negotiate the right subject but to independently act on the spot.

Conclusions

The graphics and models from the teams showed an impressive range of new designs that could represent a 'goldmine of advanced concepts and ideas' for future developments. The results of the five days of work were impressive, and the three methods proposed strategies and designs that could serve as a good foundation for further planning and debate in relation to the harbour as a public domain.

All teams worked with strong methodologies based on 'reverse-thinking' and a 'paradox approach' in the development of strategic concepts, where new hybrid urban spaces and new architectural prototypes are revealed. Many of the ideas and concepts have subsequently been discussed and implemented in the planning process at the municipality.

One key element to emerge was that planning policies and administrative procedures should have much more focus on the following points:

- There should be much more awareness of problems that have to do with privatization of harbour areas where a large number of housing stock and office space are located.
- Mixed use along the waterfront is essential in order to avoid privatization from housing and office programmes.

- Design quality in the public domain should have a special focus, using the methodology from the Gehl Team.
- Industrial heritage should not only be viewed as a question of preservation or not; rather, the scale and the typologies from waterfront industries form a fantastic catalogue of interesting typologies that are useful for new developments as well (the BIG Team).
- Temporal use and weak planning in areas suitable for artists, craftsmen, smaller industry and leisure activities, for example, are very much to be taken in by municipalities and developers because the pressure for new developments is limited and these areas can work as breathing zones for talented people and smaller businesses.

Furthermore, the three workshops provided detailed methodological knowledge of design-based development and how this could supplement traditional planning approaches. By promoting different set-ups, a variety of context-related designs emerged; in terms of approaches, the strengths as well as the weaknesses could be compared. However, comparable methodological achievements require a consistent line in the professional approach of the team leaders. The teams must be composed of people with different competences who are willing to work together and where strong leadership guides the professional focus. Design-based development can make an independent contribution to the visioning process and new sustainable discourses can be developed; but this has to be based on 'reverse-thinking' and a 'non-dogmatic' approach in the architectural development of prototypes and urban space design. This involves, among other aspects, the combination of:

- independent evaluation and discourse analyses in the regeneration of the harbour;
- strategic planning related to the waterfront development, combining this with an architectural policy, urban space policy, lighting policy and parking policy;
- independent forums of professionals, architectural workshops and competitions; and
- not one single method, but a combination of methods and approaches to be used in order to achieve quality design and ownership from citizens, as well as commitment from professionals.

Note

1   The Gehl Team was led by Gehl Architects, Copenhagen, www.gehlarchitects.dk; the BIG Team was led by Bjarke Ingels Group, Copenhagen, www.big.dk; and the Urban Catalyst team was led by Studio UC and Raumlabor Berlin, www.raumlabor-berlin.de.

8

How Visions of a Living City Come Alive

The Case of Odense, Denmark

Solvejg Beyer Reigstad

You are sitting on a comfortable bench in the sun, enjoying the weather and looking over the sea and at the children playing in the square. It is windy today, but here you have found a peaceful oasis in which to sit and have a break. You wave at your friends and decide that you can stay another ten minutes longer before you have to go – this is the good life.

Doesn't it sound nice? This is a description of what most people appreciate in public space: to have nice places in the city, where we can enjoy having a break, to look at or meet other people and where we can enjoy the weather and a nice view. Because this defines quality of life and well-being to most people, it seems strange that city planning often does not include planning of comfortable and attractive public spaces. But in Odense, Denmark, public space has from the start been a part of the planning of the new city area along the harbour front, and more and more cities are bringing the design and layout of the public space to the forefront in the planning process.

This chapter presents cases from Scandinavian cities where this has been achieved, with a focus on Odense harbour front, as well as tools that can support planners in creating living cities.

Visions of a living city by the waterfront

The challenge in waterfront development is particularly to manage visions of a living new city area and large-scale buildings, existing physical structures and infrastructural barriers, and often a bad image due to heavy industrial activities. All of these factors need to be addressed to ensure that people will be attracted to new urban areas at former industrial sites by the harbour front. Odense Waterfront is a best practice example of how this can be done.

Odense is Denmark's third largest city and is situated in the middle of Denmark, at the centre of the main island, Funen (Fyn). All transport on land between eastern and western Denmark passes through Odense. Odense has no coastline directly on the seafront but is situated at the end of a canal.

The history of Odense harbour as an infrastructural node for trade in the area is short compared to other harbour cities (Harnow, 2004). Until 1700, the harbour was only accessible by small ships – bigger ships had to anchor at the mouth of the stream, sending in goods to the city on small carts and horse wagons. In 1803, the stream was converted into a canal and from then on trade in Odense increased and the harbour grew in size and activity level. Industrialization was a turning point for the use of the harbour. Big industry was located at the harbour front, with easy access to shipping and close connections to the railway which had been laid out between the harbour and the city – now a barrier for traffic between the harbour and the city centre. In 1918, the big Lindø shipyard (Odense Steel Shipyard Group) acquired land and subsequently provided work to many people in the district for years to come. During the 1960s, the shipyard moved north along the canal – closer to the open sea – and other industries took over the location at the inner harbour.

During the 1980s, the industry started to move out of the area because the big modern ships could not sail into the harbour; instead, they located north of Odense by the shipyard. Meanwhile, the municipality, as in many other cities, discovered the high potential and qualities of being a city by the water.

Because the harbour had been closed to public access for many years due to heavy industry, the success of opening the harbour to its citizens depended upon good communication. Citizens had to be made aware that Odense is a city with an attractive and accessible harbour front, with many recreational and cultural qualities. Odense Municipality therefore started the harbour transformation project in close dialogue with the major landowners, citizens and other stakeholders in order to ensure that the functions and activities of the harbour were attractive to future users and residents in the area.

In 2002, Odense Municipality held a harbour-forum for landowners, planners, citizens, users and other stakeholders. The workshop resulted in the formulation of 13 consensus points for the development of the harbour. These points were then processed and integrated within the 'transformation plan' and municipal plan. During this process, a vision for the new harbour area was also defined in order to guide planning and any associated transformation: Odense wanted to have *a sustainable and living harbour area with mixed use as a vibrant part of the city* (Odense Municipality, 2006).

The vision for the new harbour area set out guidelines on what functions are needed – both overall and within each block and building – in order to ensure that the harbour becomes a varied, living and attractive city area of high quality. Aspects such as seasonal activities, open ground-floor façades and functions, integration of history, good design, definition of user groups and the use of the water surface are just some examples of the variety of topics which the guidelines addressed. The discussion of what user groups were wanted and what role the new area should have in relation to the older parts of the city resulted in a guideline stating that the original industrial structure and identity create possibilities for many user groups, but especially creative people, companies and start-ups, who will be attracted to the original industrial fabric, both temporarily and permanently.

The vision was ratified by the politicians and was published and distributed to citizens, users and other stakeholders. Thus, the vision is expected to serve as a documentation and background for future negotiations and decisions – the politicians can be held to their promises by the citizens and other stakeholders.

The planning process of transforming Odense harbour into a new city area involved many themes, projects, municipal departments and stakeholders. Due to its participation in the Waterfront Communities Project (WCP), Odense was able to develop and test new working and planning methods during the implementation of the harbour transformation project. Because of Odense's focus on creating a living city by the harbour, the Centre for Public Space Research–Realdania Research was chosen as an academic partner in the WCP in order to provide knowledge and data from many years of research in public space and public life.

'Bridging activities in harbour regeneration – linking the harbour and the city centre', was the overall theme for Odense's participation in the WCP. This focused on:

- breaking down barriers – connecting infrastructure: squares, bridges, pathways and streets;
- heritage – communicating the history: tours, homepage, a book and mobile phone information spots;
- temporary activities – events, communication: to open the harbour mentally for its citizens;
- industry and business – a task force to bridge the meeting between remaining industrial activity and new residential areas and city life;
- harbour forum – a bridge between stakeholders: dialogue, consensus and a shared vision.

Trying out new methods in planning the harbour's transformation provided the planners with new knowledge, and the municipality developed a Management of Transitions Model, which sums up the thesis and lessons from the bridging activities (Waterfront Communities Project, 2007, p.142). The project of transforming the harbour front is very diverse and includes many themes and methods. This chapter focuses only on how public space and temporary activities can be used as methods to initiate the development of new city areas.

The method of planning life before buildings

Odense Municipality tested two new and innovative planning methods in the harbour project:

- planning city life before buildings, using process instead of static plans;
- planning events and temporary activities to introduce a new city area to its stakeholders.

In the vision for the harbour, the municipality stated that the harbour will be used actively and be a living part of the city in the future. The methodological approach to developing the harbour therefore took as its starting point planning for city life instead of buildings and focusing on handling the process of change, inspired by the method developed by Jan Gehl at the Centre for Public Space Research–Realdania Research and Gehl Architects.[1]

This method inverts the usual planning process by following the steps listed below:

1   Define what city life is wanted in the new harbour area, including a definition of what users need to be invited, in order to ensure that type of city life.
2   Define what public spaces, elements and functions will support the desired type of city life and attract future users.
3   Finally, and only as the last step, the buildings can be planned and designed, creating the definition of space and supporting the planned city life and functions.

At Odense harbour, the starting point was the definition of the common vision around the living harbour for all citizens. Public spaces, streets, public promenades along the harbour front and a big harbour square were then laid out to welcome the further development of the area. Infrastructural projects that will link the harbour to the city centre, especially via a bridge over the railway tracks for pedestrians and bikes, were a part of the planning of the harbour development, with a longer-term view regarding implementation.

By the end of the WCP, the Harbour Square was not yet defined by the presence of buildings or supported by nearby functions; it was a vast concrete surface in a large-scale area which still had some industrial activity (see Figure 8.1). It might appear backwards to construct a large square when the users and

Figure 8.1 *Overview of Harbour Square, Odense*

Source: Solvejg Reigstad

functions to support the area's activities and life are not yet present; but the square has been successful from day one. The square is laid out on the roof of an underground car park for 210 cars and is part of the parking strategy for the whole area.

The Harbour Square is the biggest public space in Odense (6000 square metres) and offers many possibilities for staying in the area, taking part in sports and participating in events such as markets and concerts. From day one the municipality has used the square as a venue for big events for the city in order to fulfil the wish of introducing a new city area to its stakeholders. Concerts have especially brought people from the city and surrounding districts to the harbour area; but the annual harbour festival has also been a great success. The festival is advertised through different media, targeting as many stakeholders as possible, and the payoff has been that other activities are now being moved to, or held at, the square.

Concerts, sport and culture are the theme for many of the new city activities at the harbour. Its citizens saw new possibilities in the use of the area: a kayak-polo club asked for permission to use the harbour basin for training activities; event organizers choose the harbour area as a venue or location; flea-markets take place at the harbour during weekends; and festivals are held and planned.

The municipality summed up the experiences from the transformation of the harbour in eight guidelines for developing new city areas (Waterfront Communities Project, 2007, p.136). Some key guidelines and lessons based on these are as follows:

> *Make visions clear to everybody.* The city's vision for regeneration must be clear and widely accepted, both by stakeholders and ordinary citizens. The vision has to be specific regarding which city-wide goals are to be fulfilled, as well as the objectives for urban life in the area.

The Odense project process showed that it is very important that the vision is adopted by both the municipal organization and its users. A strong factor in getting everybody to become familiar with the vision and to support its realization was that the vision was ratified by politicians and communicated and distributed widely to officials, citizens and stakeholders. TV-spots, newspapers, advertising and big screen ads also drew attention to the development of the harbour, focusing on both the role of the new harbour in relation to the city and the possibilities in the area itself to ensure as many people as possible are interested in visiting and exploring the harbour in the future. The Harbour Forum workshop for invited stakeholders ensured that local groups feel ownership of the harbour, so that they now start up their own initiatives and activities in the area.

> *Use temporary activities as part of the process.* Harbour areas may be virtually unknown to the city's residents, who would have been discouraged or even forbidden in the past to access the area. In order to redress the situation, people need to be 'lured' to the waterfront via lively temporary activities, such as concerts, markets and fairs. This can help to establish more permanent activities.

In Odense, the municipality took on the role of event organizer – both constructing the 'scene' or 'stage' and illustrating the possibilities for using the harbour by financing and setting up temporary activities and arranging concerts and festivals. The wish was to transform the harbour into a destination instead of a 'non-existing' part of the city, and more and more events and activities are happening at the harbour. The municipality gradually intends to reduce their own events, letting other event organizers take over and take ownership of the use of the area and the harbour square.

However, harbour users today are not necessarily the same people who will ensure a living city in the long run. The process has to be followed up by cooperation with local users and new residents in order to ensure that they also gain ownership and use the area.

> *Make active use of evaluation.* Evaluation is essential, especially in long-term regeneration. The world is changing quickly, so strategies and plans have to be revised in order to secure objectives in a changing environment.

The extra time involved in developing strategies, visions and evaluations afforded by the municipality's participation in the Waterfront Communities Project proved to be very valuable. Vision and goals were brought forward, and methods and tools were evaluated during intervals. This ensured a good continuity in the process, putting the common goals upfront in all people's minds and ensuring that all stakeholders were working in the same direction. If Odense and other municipalities change their working process and include evaluation as a natural part of the planning process in the future, visions and goals will have a better chance of being realized and planners will get the chance to use their learning from the failures and successes in future planning.

The method of integrating the planning of a new city area with the planning of city life and public space needs a strong municipal organization or political unit which can define, formulate, control and regulate the vision and goals, seeing the process through to its implementation. It is also important that the method is evaluated step by step throughout the development process. This will give deeper knowledge about how the method works in each local context – knowledge that is valuable for the development of other areas.

Perspectives and cases from Scandinavia

In many cities, new city areas are being planned and built on brownfield sites, and central city areas have also grown due to economic development and growth in the housing market – often without considering the planning of attractive public space or sufficient time to evaluate the results. Copenhagen, in Denmark, and Oslo, in Norway, provide examples of different planning approaches. In this chapter, the cases from Copenhagen illustrate what happens if public life is not part of the planning process, and the Oslo case supports the learning from Odense: if you plan for public life you have a better chance of achieving a living city.

Copenhagen, Denmark

In Copenhagen, most of the harbour front was occupied by industry until the 1980s. Almost all industries have now closed or moved to other locations, giving space to new city activities, residential areas, business and recreation. The new accessibility of the harbour front to the public made the qualities of being a city with a long waterfront obvious to everybody. In order to secure the new recreational qualities and water access for all citizens, Copenhagen Municipality made a rule stating that the harbour front had to be publicly accessible, with a connecting promenade along the quay. Most of the quays are privately owned or have been sold to investors, so the municipality saves money for their maintenance.

However, the rule about public accessibility meets a contradicting private interest: landowners love their view over the water but do not want to invite the public to sit or stay just outside their buildings, and therefore they do not want to create nice places for the public to sit or stay. So even though the whole promenade is publicly accessible, nobody uses it because it looks private and dull. Not even the residents or users of the buildings feel invited to use the area along the harbour front.

A living environment depends upon how buildings relate to public spaces. It can be a big challenge for municipalities to hold back development until strategies and visions for public spaces are ready. Odense harbour already has one office building that has turned its back to the waterfront promenade – standing on pillars out into the basin with a closed façade, sending the signal that this part of the promenade is private – even though it is public. It will be essential for the future planning of the area that the vision of a living and varied city area is made concrete. Clear guidelines for the design of ground-floor façades and the harbour front areas have to be defined and followed to ensure that the promenades become inviting to public life (Gehl et al, 2004).

It has been an unwritten law for developers that the layout of public space is the least important part of constructing new buildings and is the responsibility of the municipality. During recent years, however, there has been more focus on user involvement, learning from the planning mistakes of the past and focusing on public space: the creation of living and liveable city areas. Today city life is considered an important factor in development creating value for the landowners, and Copenhagen is looking into new projects along the most deserted parts of the new harbour front, including Kalvebod Brygge (see Figure 8.2) – projects that will transform the areas into recreational parks for all citizens, such as Islands Brygge harbour front, which includes a harbour swimming pool.

In Ørestad, Copenhagen, the first component in the new city district was its infrastructure: the metro and streets. The income from selling the land financed the metro line, which connects Ørestad with the central and northern parts of Copenhagen. The presence of the metro as a modern and efficient public transport system raised the attractiveness and value of the building sites and helped the development to get going. The metro is the backbone of Ørestad and ensures easy access for pedestrians – a sustainable way of planning the modern city. But for this to be a success, the environment around the metro, including

Figure 8.2 *The deserted Kalvebod Brygge, Copenhagen*

Source: Solvejg Reigstad

its accessibility and connections to other means of public transport for pedestrians and bikes, has to support pedestrian and bike transport. Here the planning of inviting public space – streets and squares – is highly relevant. In Ørestad, the design of public spaces has not been integrated within the overall planning, and most squares are not inviting to pedestrians, city activities or recreation. The central square of Ørestad City (Kay Fiskers Square) is open to the wind, with no furniture to invite people to stay, and is designed on a scale, with very tall surrounding buildings, that seems suitable for highway traffic but not for the pedestrians who could offer the city life. The ground-floor façades that frame the square are blind and introverted, and there are no functions to support activity. A study of Kay Fiskers Square and Aker Brygge Torg in Oslo (Gehl, 2007) shows that even though there are two-fifths more people passing through Kay Fiskers Square, there is 39 times more activity at the Aker Brygge Torg because Aker Brygge Torg offers mixed functions, cafés and an environment that protects against wind, inviting people to stay (see also Chapter 9). This study shows a very clear lesson: if planners want a city area to be a living space, it is not enough to ensure that there are many people in the area and on the streets (e.g. through high density). The design of good and inviting public space is crucial.

In the northern part of Ørestad, the problem is that most of the planned squares had still not been constructed eight years after the first users and stakeholders moved into the district (see Figure 8.3). The reason for this is that all the squares were to be designed and built by individual developers, and most

Figure 8.3 *Ørestad North, with no squares to meet*

Source: Solvejg Reigstad

of the squares belonged to the later projects in the development. Until 2010, stakeholders and users, which include over 12,000 students from the Copenhagen University Faculty of Humanities and the IT-University, only had the streets as a possible location for events. After 2010, the first square was constructed and more residents, users and students moved in; but the use of the new squares (e.g. for events) will depend upon which layout and design of the square the landowner chooses to make and whether the landowner gives permission.

Because of the lack of public spaces in Ørestad North, the stakeholders' association (the Ørestad North Group), in cooperation with the landowners' association, decided to use construction sites temporarily as public spaces. These temporary spaces are employed as test laboratories for functions and activities that can be a part of the planning of future permanent spaces.

Oslo, Norway

Oslo has, like Odense, worked with different types of planning methods to open up the new harbour areas to the public. Oslo's TEMPO! Fjordbyen project used art to open people's eyes to the potential of new areas. One of the temporary projects was a 2.6km long red line that guided people through the harbour area where new city districts were to be built, including the new Opera House.[2] The line sent a signal of coherence within the area and introduced the qualities and potential of the area to new users, adding a twist of curiosity.

The Bjørvika architectural competition and the design of the opera are good examples of how public space is included in the planning process from the start. The Bjørvika competition focused on public space as the most important structural element for planning the new harbour area. Public spaces are used as links between town and sea and over infrastructural barriers, and the spaces

Figure 8.4 *The opera in Oslo: the roof is a public space*

Source: Gehl Architects

create a network of attractive places for pedestrians – different in scale and function – which also serve as links to the public transport system.[3] The opera is a part of the public space network; the whole roof of the Opera House is a public space that celebrates its central location on the edge of the sea and is open to the public, not only to paying visitors (see Figure 8.4). This is a strong signal to the public and other stakeholders that city life and public spaces for people are the main priority when planning new harbour areas.

As in Odense, Oslo's planning process has included many different elements, such as user dialogue and participation, an anthology/booklet to open people's minds to the harbour, the layout of public space as a kick-starter for city life in the new areas, a transport analysis of sustainable infrastructure focusing on pedestrians and bikes, and a new tramline to serve the harbour area.

How to plan living cities

Denmark has had a long tradition of innovative planning of public space. Particularly during the 1970s, Danish planners and architects created world-famous low-density housing areas with a focus on public and semi-public spaces for people in which to meet and stay. The transformation of Copenhagen from a car-city to a pedestrian-city started in 1971 when Strøget – the first pedestrian street in Copenhagen inner-city – opened. But since then the focus has changed to the design of buildings, creating spectacular landmarks; increasingly, areas are planned without looking into what will make them a living and attractive space for people's activities.

Many new residential areas are now planned without considering, or knowing, how the detailing of the public space will influence the use of the public area. Each flat has a balcony; cars are parked underground, with direct elevator access to the flats. The result of these new facilities and plans is that nobody needs to move through public spaces on foot. Nobody feels ownership of the external spaces, which are often designed so that they are nice for people to look at from their flats and balconies (Richter-Friis van Deurs, 2010). But if the intention of planners and architects is to develop living city areas with people on the streets – and most renderings shows us that this is the intention – then the planning of public space has to be taken seriously and prioritized.

It is important that architects and planners are aware of the fact that we build cities for human beings, and therefore need to have knowledge about human behaviour. What makes us feel welcome, sit down, initiate activities and set up meetings in a public space? Too many examples can be found where the focus is on the design of buildings and pavements, resulting in new city areas that are deserted, with no city life, even though the architects think that they have done their best, using expensive materials and good design. New city projects are being created, with project renderings that show people and city life, but end up with developments on the ground with no life and big disappointments from not getting what was expected.

However, during the last decade, the awareness of the need for greater focus on how people use public space has been influencing city planning in Denmark, and municipalities and developers now have stated agendas that include the creation of city life as an important factor in the visions and plans for new city areas.

But what really makes a living city?

In Denmark, since the 1970s, Jan Gehl has conducted research into what makes a living city and what elements and factors should be integrated within the planning process to ensure that public space attracts people, invites activities and is diverse and lively. Once public space is of good quality, city life can reach its full potential. The more inviting public space is, the better the chance that people will use it actively. But quality has many faces and meanings. Research by Jan Gehl has identified the 12 most essential quality criteria for planning public space (see Figure 8.5). The criteria can be divided into three categories: protection, comfort and enjoyment. All criteria influence the use and activity level in public spaces (Gehl et al, 2006).

By using the criteria to evaluate public space or public space projects, it is possible to see how spaces can be adjusted or planned to ensure that the appropriate conditions are provided for a diverse city life. Not all factors need to be present, and sometimes spaces will be planned with a focus on factors and aims other than city life. But it is important to be familiar with these criteria as a tool, and if the intention is to create a living space, it is important to optimize as many criteria as possible.

Research at the Centre for Public Space Research has also shown that city life can be divided into two categories: the necessary activities that will occur

THE 12 KEY QUALITY CRITERIA

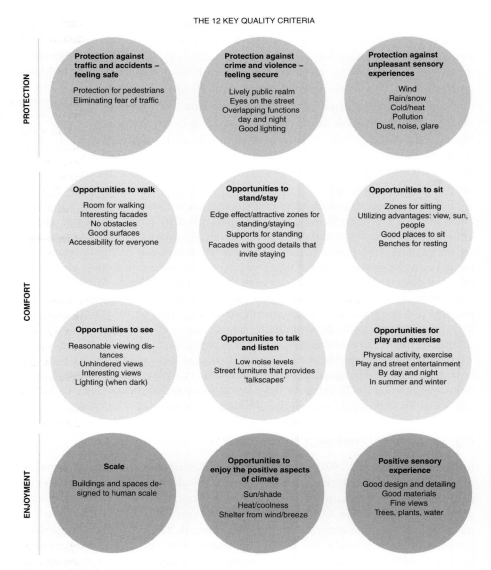

Figure 8.5 *Twelve quality criteria to evaluate city space*

Source: Gehl et al, 2006

regardless of the quality of space and the optional activities that will only occur by choice in people's spare time (see Figure 8.6).

If public space does not invite people to stay, people will go elsewhere in their spare time and only the minimum of activities will happen. If an event is arranged, visitors will come driven by interest; but the number of visitors will primarily be based on the character of the event and not on the quality of the public space. If planners want to create an active city 24/7, it is important to provide good-quality public spaces that invite optional activities on ordinary weekdays – and if everyday users use the public spaces actively, the area also has a better chance to become a destination for optional users.

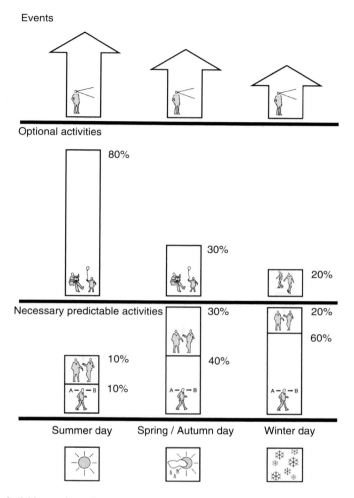

Figure 8.6 *Activities and weather*

Source: Gehl Architects

Learning from the development of Odense harbour front

In Odense, the municipality tested two new innovative methods to develop new city areas: planning life and public space before erecting buildings, and using events to introduce the area to citizens and stakeholders. These methods can be evaluated from different perspectives.

It is still too early to state whether the layout of public promenades and a square as an attractor and kick-starter for city life before buildings are built will ensure a living harbour front in Odense in the long run. The Harbour Square has been used from day one, giving room to a city life that did not have anywhere else to go, and introducing a new city area to the citizens through events and a positive atmosphere. One can expect that once the physical connections between the city and the harbour are made and the permanent functions have moved to the area, the harbour will be a city district like any other district in the city and a location in people's minds.

Holding back a development while a vision is being generated can be problematic, and planning is not static, but a process that should be able to meet changes in context and market. It takes visionary developers and a strong consensus and control within the municipal organization to hold back on development until the planning of the public space network is ready. And it takes power and will to stop projects that do not support vision and planning.

The process of starting with vision and strategy before building has, in some cases, at Odense harbour been set aside by market forces and economic interests. Unfortunately, the planners in Odense did not have enough power to keep development of the harbour back until the plan was ready. Office buildings have been built on very central locations along the waterfront, and their design does not support the vision's guideline that new buildings actively have to support city life. They have become mono-functional and introverted and have isolated themselves from public space.

It is a big challenge to implement visions and ideas in a planning process. Only by setting up specific conditions in the contract when selling the land can the municipality impose restrictions upon functions, rent and design; but then the quality of the public space depends upon contractual negotiations – and negotiations are all about making compromises at some levels to ensure optimal conditions on other levels. The municipality could try to train investors to work with it as a partner with key knowledge. By giving the investors an insight into the methods, visions and references to other feasible and visionary projects, the chance to reach consensus through dialogue instead of negotiations could be raised – and investors could then see the value in supporting the realization of the vision and planning for the area.

On the other hand, the first office buildings in Odense harbour kick-started development of the harbour, drawing the attention of other investors to the area, and showing the politicians that introverted buildings do not create the desired environment – that a life plan for the city is necessary.

But as this chapter has shown, the layout of a public space and promenades is not enough to ensure a living city – the design of the space itself is hugely important. Odense's Harbour Square can be evaluated using the 12 quality criteria presented earlier. Some of the criteria relate to the detailing and scale of the surrounding buildings; due to the absence of buildings near the square, these factors will not receive a positive evaluation. This does not mean that the factors are irrelevant; they still have to be considered once the buildings are being designed.

The square meets almost all of the quality criteria. It lacks protection against wind and crime prevention through natural surveillance, but this is expected to improve once the buildings are constructed. The greatest challenge when creating a big square is to combine the openness that can host thousands of people at events while providing protection against the elements and relating to the human scale. The harbour square in Odense has small-scale zones for 'sedentary' activities, as well as large open surfaces for sports – a good way to meet the challenge of the big scale and host the everyday living and optional activities that provide the basis for a naturally vibrant city.

Whether the use of temporary activities and events can kick-start the use of a former brownfield area depends very much upon levels of communication. The development of Odense harbour has been communicated to stakeholders through a variety of media in order to ensure that the target group is as broad as possible and that numerous people become interested in exploring the harbour in the future. The Harbour Forum workshop for stakeholders, which was held in Odense as a kick-off for the vision, provided local groups with a feeling of ownership so that they, in turn, could initiate projects and activities in the area.

When looking at the number of citizens who visited the harbour at the harbour festival, received a newspaper or saw the live broadcast of the summer concert, there is no doubt that the harbour development process in Odense transformed the area and created a new destination in the city in the minds of its citizens. There has been great interest in the webpage about the harbour, as well as tours and mobile phone information spots, all focusing on the history of, and plans for, the harbour development. By 2006, 10,000 copies of the book *Odense Docklands and Canal* had been sold in a Danish and English version. In the media, TV-spots, newspapers, advertising and big screen ads have drawn attention to the development of the harbour.

Odense's Harbour Square has proved very useful for events (see Figure 8.7); but it now needs to find a role for daily users because the area is still separate from the rest of the city. Supporting functions have not yet been established because the buildings that will frame the square still need to be constructed, as

Figure 8.7 *Odense harbour life*

Source: Lars Gemzøe

does the rest of the area. When local users move in, the harbour square will prove whether it is, indeed, a living part of the city.

A key lesson from the Odense case is that if you open a new area physically and mentally to its citizens and users, and develop inviting public spaces and places for activities, people will come. To start the planning of new areas with the planning and creation of public spaces is an efficient tool, but only if architects and planners know the tools and methods to create inviting public spaces. Hopefully, future planning will place the creation of good-quality public spaces at the beginning of the planning process so that all citizens have access to places where they would love to sit for another ten minutes before they have to go.

Notes

1   The working method is also introduced in Chapter 8 regarding the Harbourscape Aalborg workshop, where Gehl Architects were the team leader for one of the conceptual models. This working method is also described at www.gehlarchitects.com.

2   See www.prosjekt-fjordbyen.oslo.kommune.no/article50387{ndash}5716.html?articleID = 50387&categoryID = 5716&tip = 1.

3   See www.arkitektnytt.no/page/detail/article/10831/news{hyphen}4{hyphen}1963.html, Arkitektnyt 2007/07, Theme: Fjordbyen and www.bjorvikautvikling.no.

9

Successful Place-Making on the Waterfront

Maria Soledad Garcia Ferrari, Paul Jenkins and Harry Smith

Introduction

This chapter explores the meaning of, and ideas surrounding, the concepts of place and place-making, and focuses on the definition of a 'successful place' within the context of urban transformations in waterfront areas. In particular, it discusses the opportunities and conditions for a successful waterfront, looking into spatial, visual and social aspects of the 'place' created.

To set the scene, the first section discusses various approaches to understanding the concept of place, including analytical frameworks from political and economic perspectives, based on the understanding of global and local influences and power relations; from a physical and spatial point of view, in the context of understanding people's experiences of places from a perceptive or phenomenological approach; and from design and planning-oriented approaches to the notion of place, often of a more normative nature geared *a priori* towards the notion of successful place-making.

Following this brief review of relevant concepts and approaches, a series of case studies are introduced and analysed showing different levels of success with regards to place-making as 'test cases'. Each case explores the relationship between urban design quality, the processes of production of urban space, and the dynamics of social activity in modern cities. Therefore, different aspects of the processes of development are compared through the case studies analysis, with the objective of understanding the influences of varying levels of involvement, from planning departments and other stakeholders, in the creation of a 'successful place' on the waterfront.

The investigation presented in this chapter draws upon previous studies focused on place-making and urban design, and looks at some examples of regeneration among the partner cities in the Waterfront Communities Project (Garcia Ferrari et al, 2007). The analysis is focused on three North Sea waterfronts: Gateshead, Oslo and Malmö. The chapter demonstrates how some places are perceived as becoming successful in social and cultural terms, and how this relates to the spatial and visual environment. In this, the case studies analysis intends to be aspirational and not judgemental, focusing on the most successful aspects of the places analysed and aiming to understand the context in which the development took place and the different processes experienced.

The chapter then draws conclusions on key aspects for sustainable place-making at different geographical scales, including the importance of time in the creation of place, as well as providing some reflection on the physical characteristics of successful waterfront places.

Understanding what we mean by 'successful place'

Place can be defined as 'the predominantly socio-cultural perception and definition of space' (Jenkins, 2005, p.20) and is an important element of identity, whether individual or collective. The concept of place has been analysed within a variety of fields, ranging from those dealing with the collective (e.g. social and cultural geography) to the individual (e.g. environmental psychology), and from the analytical to the propositional (e.g. planning and design).

Cultural geographers and anthropologists tend to approach the question of place by adopting interpretive humanistic frameworks, enquiring into human experiences (Bachelard, 1964; Feld and Basso, 1996) and often blended with social theory (Walter, 1988). Another trend in cultural geography is framed within the neo-Marxist critique and associated globalization theory (Harvey, 1989; Soja, 2000), and is often focused on issues related to political action, institutional power and social control. Alongside these analytical trends, more recent approaches have focused on theorizing social identities. Within these different approaches, most work has looked at place as the result of both local and global power relations. Place in this context appears to be related to power struggles and resistance at different local, regional and global geographical scales (Feld and Basso, 1996), and to the formation of place-based forms of identity by socio-cultural groupings and institutions (Jenkins, 2005). These approaches tend to examine process rather than physical space and explain developments through the understanding of power relations, participation and different levels of institutional influence in development and management processes.

Within the field of environmental psychology, the concept of place is defined by the bonds and shared values created through perceptive experiences of places, linked to the notions of place attachment, sense of place and place identity, amongst others. Within this field there is general agreement that the generation of emotional connections with places is vital to achieving psychological equilibrium and encouraging local involvement and social interaction – linking this approach to the one above (Vorkin and Riese, 2001; Guardia and Pol, 2002; Brown et al, 2003). 'Place attachment'[1] is influenced by length of residence (Hernández et al, 2007), number and type of relationships within a community (Giuliani, 1991; Brown et al, 2003), and the physical attributes (and linked symbolic meanings) of a place (Stedman, 2003), among other factors. Place attachment is usually understood as a key component in the definition of place identity (Kaiser and Fuhrer, 1996);[2] however, the latter is seen by environmental psychology as an attribute of an individual rather than of a place. Nevertheless, the formation of a sense of place identity by an individual is inevitably influenced by the variety of people who live in a place and relies on the individual's position within a social network (Lewicka, 2008), and some explanations see traditions and cultural transmissions as being more influential than personal experiences.

While there has been much research in the field of environmental psychology into the perception and qualities of pre-existing settings and places, there has been less study of the significance of understanding the qualities of place as part of the architectural design process.[3] However, the qualities of place (and the concept of community, often related to values imbued within 'place') have been central to a series of critical writings on urban development and planning that emerged as a reaction to the results of modernist planning and urban design, particularly in the US. Jane Jacobs's (1961) writing on the negative impacts of urban renewal policies in the US and William Whyte's observation of how public spaces are actually used (Whyte, 1988) provided a basis for a move towards proactive 'place-making' within the field of urban planning and renewal. This professional area of activity has increasingly turned its attention to how to create 'successful places'.

The drive towards place-making in government and professional circles, and the resulting inclusion of this in planning and urban design policy and guidance have drawn only indirectly on the results of the research areas referred to above. Fields such as anthropology and environmental psychology may consider the notion of a 'successful place' as being linked to, for example, the extent to which it fulfils emotional needs (Korpela et al, 2001). But normative policy-making generally obviates such abstract explanations and focuses on praxis, with 'successful place-making' being addressed principally through two approaches: respectively focusing on the physical characteristics of place (with particular relevance to urban design) and the processes of social interaction (with particular relevance to planning process).

A classic example of the physical design approach is the Urban Design Compendium in the UK, which provides detailed guidance ranging from broad issues, such as the wider context of a development, through to more detailed topics such as plot size (Llewelyn-Davies, 2000). Its guidance is predicated on a notion of what is seen as the traditional city, offering 'places for people', and based on concepts such as connectivity, mixed use, mid to high densities, etc. This has provided a reference point for many detailed planning and urban design briefs throughout the UK. The approach relies on an assumption that the physical characteristics of a place influence how its users will interact with it and assumptions of certain collective social characteristics concerning cultural values embedded within places (whether public or private).

The approach that focuses on social interaction can engage with the actual process of planning and delivery of developments, or with the management of these. For example, guidance produced by the US Department of Housing and Urban Development (CONCERN Inc., 2002) sees design and decision-making tools as helping planners, policy-makers and citizens build consensus about the design and development of a place, and community participation in development processes and community-led activities as helping to achieve a 'successful place'. However, it highlights the complexity of the interrelated systems of values that define 'place' and, therefore, the importance of communication among participants in the process and analysis in successful 'place-making'. In another example of this procedural approach, Greenspace Scotland and Project for Public Spaces (2006) state that 80 per cent of the success of public spaces is due to their management rather than design – with management referring to 'programming' activities such as the provision of coffee shops, street markets, managing traffic, etc.

Focusing on waterfront areas, these have experienced significant urban regeneration processes during the beginning of the 21st century, as the examples presented in this book show. In the context of the discussion above, how can we analyse and define a successful waterfront place? The authors address this question by using three scales for assessing aspects of 'place' and 'place-making' in waterfronts: the macro-, meso- and micro-scale. The macro-scale refers to placing the waterfront in a wider regional, national and international context and is often linked to different approaches to 'marketing' the waterfront and locating the developed area on the map. This approach tends to be framed within the political-economy perspective described at the beginning of the analytical framework section above. The meso-scale refers to how the place fits into the overall area of the waterfront development and, in particular, how it connects to the surrounding city; hence, it tends to reflect physical design/planning guidance. The micro-scale refers to the sense of place at a human scale and the qualities of the physical, visual and social realm within this, and, hence, includes phenomenological aspects, although this also affects the meso-scales.

Case studies

As the Waterfront Communities Project (WCP) was coming to an end, the need to develop a research focus on the spatial, social and visual aspects of the waterfront areas undergoing regeneration emerged, with the aim of beginning to understand the conditions for place-making. In order to explore, in particular, the sense of place and nature of the socio-cultural use of waterfronts, the researchers asked the WCP partners to rate the participating waterfronts in terms of their success as places. This generated the initial steps towards the study presented in this chapter, which was based on information subsequently collected by the researchers during visits to the selected waterfronts, including interviews with key stakeholders involved in the process. The study initially focused on Gateshead Quays and Aker Brygge in Oslo. In writing this chapter, the case of Malmö, which was not a partner in the WCP, was added for further comparison. The following sections build upon some of the findings using case study analyses, with places being assessed using the three scales described above: the macro, meso and micro.

A place on the map: Gateshead Quays

The area known as Gateshead Quays was part of the industrial past of Gateshead City, which developed as part of a conurbation with Newcastle. As seen in Chapter 3, after several different forms of development during the centuries, ranging from the original urban settlement to dock activity, by the second half of the 20th century the area had become run down and disconnected from the nearby centre of Gateshead. During the 1990s, regeneration and economic revival began to reach Newcastle Quayside across the Tyne. The cleaning up of the river with the construction of the Tyne Interceptor Sewer also paved the way for regenerating the south bank, Gateshead Quays, as a result of the success of the urban transformations of the north bank. A number of landmark iconic buildings emerged, as part of the regeneration process: the Millennium Bridge and two cultural venues (the BALTIC Centre for Contemporary Art and the Sage Gateshead music centre) (see Figure 3.4). These flagship developments have been key to transforming the area (Garcia Ferrari et al, 2007).

The regeneration area is located on the northern edge of central Gateshead across the river from the centre of Newcastle. The urban regeneration strategy proposed by Gateshead Council extends along the River Tyne and includes the town centre, comprising approximately 16ha. Most of the land belongs to the city, with some notable exceptions (see Chapter 3). The development was not led by a comprehensive masterplan, but by the construction of separate flagship developments, which were aimed at generating the development of the surrounding areas. The area was divided into seven main large sites,[4] each of which was assigned a specific function or type of activity. When completed, the overall development will contain two cultural venues, two public squares linked to these, a residential development, a visitor centre located in the refurbished existing St Mary's church, and a mixed-use/leisure development. A proposal for the latter – containing restaurants, cafés and bars, a cinema, retail shops, a major hotel, a public car park and housing over a site of 2ha – was approved in 2006 but did not go ahead. This was subsequently developed in a masterplan for the whole of Gateshead Quays, produced in 2010, after completion of the flagship developments (RMJM, NG1 and Gateshead Council, 2010).

The Millennium Bridge is a key feature and the main initial landmark in the regeneration – a pedestrian link between Gateshead and Newcastle, allowing at the same time the passage of shipping traffic along the river through its unique tilting mechanism. A main physical characteristic in the overall area is the significant difference in the levels on both sides of the river and within the Gateshead waterfront area, with a drop of about 70m from the town centre to the riverside. Each of the large sites therefore presents a unique set of characteristics within the overall area, with little commonality. Interventions range in land use and type, from the refurbishment of an existing flour-mill, converted into the BALTIC Centre for Contemporary Art, to new developments on brownfield sites. Developments are sited topographically from a level on the actual riverbank (BALTIC and Exhibition Square) to development on steep slopes (the Sage, the housing development and the proposed mixed-use development). In spatial terms, the relationship between these sites and types of development also varies, ranging from the isolation of BALTIC and its large open public square to the adjacency of the housing and proposed mixed-use developments (Exhibition Square, see Figure 9.1).

Two public squares are provided in the overall development, with the main point of public encounter located between the two cultural icons, Sage and

Figure 9.1 *View of Exhibition Square, Gateshead Quays*

Source: authors

BALTIC (see Figure 9.2). However, there is no designated use for this space; it is designed as an open platform for pedestrians, although it could support temporary activities, such as theme fairs or open-air exhibitions. The other designed public area is Performance Square, associated with the Sage and providing an open terrace over the Quays, albeit with no sense of enclosure.

Access to Gateshead Quays occurs in various ways. Cars arrive at the highest level, with pedestrian access from a large car park provided through a

Figure 9.2 *View of iconic buildings along Gateshead Quays*

Source: Paul Jenkins

series of open concrete stairs, and additional car parking spaces behind the international Art Centre. The Quays can also be accessed by pedestrians across the Millennium Bridge from Newcastle (i.e. at the much lower river level). Public transport reaches the area and links the main buildings at the lower level of the riverbank.

The key buildings on the site present very different scales. The BALTIC Centre for Contemporary Art began its construction in 1998 and opened in 2002. This six-storey concrete and brick-clad building is scaled down to two storeys in the block that projects onto Baltic Square in order to provide a more inviting scale at the entrance. New internal platforms and three mezzanines are linked through a glass lift, which also serves as a moving viewing deck. Artist studios, cinema/lecture space, a library/archive and rooftop access are also provided. The south and north elevations were retained as in the original 1950s building. South of this, a 241-apartment residential development, Baltic Quay, comprises a series of linked blocks, ranging from 7 to 16 storeys, arranged along a curving plan and sitting on a three-storey base which fills the plot with a large car park. The Sage, opened in 2004, is the largest building in the area and is located at the upper side of the waterfront area, separated from BALTIC and its adjacent public square by a large sloping site still designated for future development. This iconic landmark building contains two performance spaces and one rehearsal space covered by a large independent steel and glass structure.

Rather than being a comprehensively masterplanned development with set phases, the regeneration of Gateshead Quays is an example of a process where council land ownership, strong leadership and the ability to seize opportunities while controlling risk were key drivers. Development proposals were based on the assessment of needs and activities that would change the profile of the site. The main objective of Gateshead Quays was to create a cultural hub – hence, the Sage and BALTIC developments. Funding was the result of successful bidding to the Millennium Commission (for the Millennium Bridge) and the Arts Lottery (for BALTIC and the Sage), mostly match-funded by Gateshead Council, followed by design competitions for the structures and buildings. Initiatives related to strategies for the public realm thus came later on in the process.[5] The result is that the public areas generated outside these iconic buildings were not the focus of design or in-depth treatment through the coordinated provision of street furniture, public art or landscaping. Intensity of use in these public areas therefore appears to be directly related to the activities that may be taking place within the flagship cultural buildings or the result of occasional large-scale public events.

The absence of relation between the sites results in the perception of a heterogeneous place lacking clarity of connections among its parts. Drawing on the analytical frameworks presented earlier in this chapter, a successful place should fulfil people's emotional needs and even influence mood. The lack of connection and meaningful open spaces between the flagship developments in Gateshead, however, seems to lead to a sense of dislocation and confusion in the human experience of place. It is perhaps the spectacular existing setting along the Tyne Gorge, with upstream views towards different generations of spanning bridges and views across the riverbanks to buildings of different ages climbing up Newcastle hillside, as well as the iconic images of the new flagship developments, which provide most of the sense of place.

However, from a wider regional perspective, development of this area has completely changed its public perception, and the regeneration has generated opportunities for the area to acquire regional significance with the provision of new cultural and tourism activities. Moreover, if we understand that place identity is defined by a sense of belonging to a place, the fact that Gateshead Quays are now widely visited and appear as an attraction on a much larger geographical scale could well have an influence on increasing people's level of attachment and emotional connections to the area – albeit transient. It is still early days in the regeneration process, and considering that the development strategies have achieved the initial success of 'putting the place on the cultural and tourist map', time may provide opportunities for the future to create attractive and successful places within the developed area.

In summary, Gateshead Quays seems to be succeeding at the macro-level, and belatedly stitching together the meso-level sense of place more actively. Its process has, however, affected the micro-level perceptions and success of place-making, although the macro-level success and on-going meso-level proactive activity may assist this development more in time.

A place in the city: Aker Brygge in Oslo

Aker Brygge is on the west side of one of Oslo's inner fjords – Pipervika – next to the 19th-century expansion of Oslo, where the city centre and the site of the town hall and its adjacent grand square are located, and close to the entertainment quarter of Vika and major central tourist attractions. It covers 5.8ha of flat land bounded on the south-east by the fjord, on the south-west by a former dry dock (now a water inlet), on the north-west by a main access road into central Oslo, and on the north-east by the site of a former railway station and a connection to the City Hall Square. At the northern end of the dockside is the terminal for the ferry linking Oslo city centre to the neighbouring municipality of Nesodden. Despite its central location, the area used to be largely cut off from the city centre by the main east–west motorway constructed during the 1960s, although this was spanned by a pedestrian bridge.

From 1854 the area developed as a shipyard, becoming a major employer in the city. Decline in the shipyard industry early in the 20th century led to the conversion of the area to engineering. At the end of the 1980s and due to shipbuilding moving to less valuable land elsewhere in the country, the company that owned the land decided to develop this in cooperation with financial institutions. The plan was to create a mixed-use urban area containing housing, offices, shopping and leisure facilities. This development was implemented in four phases between 1985 and 1998, which followed the layout of an overall masterplan. The construction of a tunnel for the main east–west traffic through Oslo, the pedestrianization and regeneration of adjacent Town Hall Square and the relocation of ferry landings to the Aker Brygge wharfs have all contributed to the success of the development (see Figure 9.3).

The masterplan for the development was based on a tight-knit street grid mainly following lines parallel and perpendicular to the south-east facing dockside. Within this regular basic grid, variety is introduced with other street orientations, different street and open space widths, and different types of

Figure 9.3 *Aerial view of Aker Brygge, Oslo*

Source: © City of Oslo

alignments of block edges. In addition, a series of internal streets are located through the commercial development. The development's urban blocks are similar in size to those found in Oslo city centre, with the largest being approximately 60m by 90m. Some are further subdivided by the narrow pedestrian lanes. Building heights vary from 6 to 12 storeys. Two pre-existing shipyard buildings have been refurbished, while the rest of the buildings are new, with considerable variety of design.

The street network is predominately pedestrian, with access provided for service vehicles. The main access points are on the north-east side of Aker Brygge, which is the most visible and better connected to the city centre via the western side of City Hall Square, where a tram stop and a taxi rank have been provided. Private vehicles can access the site from the north-west boundary road, leading to the entrance of the car park extending under most of the development area.

Aker Brygge is divided horizontally into layers. An underground layer contains parking, internal traffic and services. Above ground, many of the buildings are divided into three layers with a ground floor (and, in some cases, first floor) for public uses, cafés and shops; several floors above these providing offices; and the top few floors for housing, connected by pedestrian bridges high above street level.[6] The top layer also provides community facilities for their residents, who are mostly higher-income residents. This layering is linked to the high density of building, with 180,000 square metres of floor space built above ground, and a gross density of 3.1 square metres of floor space per square metre of development area.

Within the development, open space is entirely defined and enclosed by the surrounding buildings, with the exception of the spaces linked to the fjord: the dockside promenade, with its slight curving of the building line; and the main square at the western end of the development (Bryggetortet). The area has excellent views across the fjord and over water, along the edge promenade and from the streets connected to this, as well as from the main square of Bryggetortet. The different horizontal uses are visually expressed in changes of materials and fenestration, as well as with setbacks in some cases. The refurbished buildings and a preserved gate refer back to its earlier use as a shipyard and also contribute to the sense of place. The development shows a strong physical and visual connection to the water given by water sculptures, street furniture and a repeated theme of stepping down the water's edge of the promenade (see Figure 9.4).

Throughout the development there is hard landscaping based on simple but well-detailed stone and brick paving that is used to define areas and emphasize routes. Well-designed and abundant changes in levels are also featured. Public art is fully integrated with the landscaping scheme. Similar materials, textures and colours are used in the buildings in order to provide coherence and unity to quite different façade designs. Careful detail design contributes to the perception of a high-quality area. The high-density grain helps to shelter spaces from the wind. However, the high buildings block out sun from the main streets, with sunshine being enjoyed during long periods along the promenade and the main square (Gehl Architects, 1998).

The vertical layering of uses has resulted in a high density and diversity of activities. Public spaces are heavily used, particularly during the summer, and

Figure 9.4 *View along promenade overlooking the fjord, Aker Brygge, Oslo*

Source: Harry Smith

there is a variety of outdoor serving areas available which could potentially cater for nearly 4000 people. Two permanent venues (a theatre and two cinema screens) and the organization of specific events such as concerts in some of the public areas contribute to its success. Social facilities are concentrated mainly within the shared domain of the residential levels. The resulting lively environment, however, also generates some conflicts between users (e.g. regarding noise). Uses related to water have been retained in the area with the location of the ferry terminal at the head of the promenade and the provision of 250 small boat mooring berths along the dockside. The overall area provides a sense of security, with the variety of activities and number of people in the area contributing to this. There is a CCTV system in operation, run by the area's management company.

Aker Brygge development was initiated by the landowner, Aker Shipyards (Aker AS) and supported by urban changes that were taking place in the city as a whole. The development company Aker Brygge ANS was created as a subsidiary, in partnership with a Norwegian bank. The idea of creating a mixed-used area with high-quality public spaces was recognized in the land-use plan for the Oslo waterfront prepared by the local authorities, and the objective of creating a new living quarter informed the brief for an architectural competition for the area. Development phases covered different areas and suffered from financial crises and uncertainty involving various developers and the creation of new subsidiary companies.[7] However, all stages followed the direction of a strong masterplan, which provided cohesion to the overall area.

In addition to five large companies, property owners include small business and households. The development was divided into smaller units sold freehold and condominium law was applied to provide common facilities. Landownership was retained by the original landowner and leased. Each condominium has its own board of directors and manager. Responsibility for public space is shared by all property owners and managed through an overall management company, in which they all have shares. The company takes on tasks usually performed by local government, as well as providing an avenue for negotiation between the different users (i.e. conflicts over noise levels).

The initial masterplan was prepared by the architectural firm Telje-Trop-Aasen Arkitektkontor AS, with various other architects designing most of the buildings during phase 1. Phase 2 was designed by Niels Torp AS, who also redesigned the masterplan that was used for the following phases. The firm appointed different design teams for the buildings in order to achieve a variety of proposals, but retained some unity through the use of similar materials and finishes. Detailed design of subsequent phases was carried out by different architectural practices. The masterplan included a series of controls affecting the public realm, which were the result of negotiations with the municipality. Public space design was the responsibility of a single landscape architecture firm (13.3 Landskapsarkitekter AS), who was also responsible for the design of the public realm in the neighbouring Town Hall Square. This has enhanced visual and physical continuity throughout the area (see Figure 9.5).

Aker Brygge has been successful in attracting large numbers of visitors (5000 a day during the summer) due to the quality of its public spaces, the variety of activities, the views afforded by its location, the multitude of uses within the buildings, and its transport connections. The visionary masterplan, based on compact city ideals, closely coordinating design of built elements and landscape, together with complex development and management structures to implement these even during periods of economic uncertainty, have all contributed to this success.

In summary, the development has resulted in an area with a strong visual identity, and has become a place in the collective unconscious of Oslo citizens, who use it not only in passing to and from the city centre to other points around the fjord, but also as a lively and interesting destination. It thus succeeds at the micro- and meso-scales in terms of perceptions (individual, collective and in terms of external political economic values). Arguably, this is due to both a well-designed process and key coordination of detail design through the masterplan and other procedural aspects of design and development (including on-going management). It thus represents a designed and produced 'place' which has a range of successful attributes that were carefully considered in the process – and result from close collaboration between public and private action.

A place called home: Bo01 in Malmö

Malmö's Bo01 waterfront development area is located to the north-west of the city's historical centre. This Western Harbour area took shape during the 20th century and was constructed on land reclaimed from the sea until 1987, with the infilling of the dock for shipyard activity. After a brief period of use of the Western Harbour by SAAB as a production yard at the end of the 1980s, the SAAB factory

Figure 9.5 *Use of the public realm on the waterfront in Aker Brygge, Oslo*

Source: © City of Oslo

closed down and the land and buildings were bought by the City of Malmö in 1996. Subsequently, all SAAB's production buildings were transformed into trade fair space and conference facilities (City of Malmö, 2005).

To kick-start the waterfront development, the Municipality of Malmö proposed to relocate the Swedish International Housing Exhibition to the area, and in 2001 the city hosted the European Housing Expo, called 'The Ecological City of Tomorrow', supported by the Swedish government. The 25ha of housing exhibition were only part of the Western Harbour, which comprises a total of 140ha, and the development of the overall area is expected to continue for about 30 years.

With total ownership of the land and the possibility of a fully in-house planning process, the city's objective was to use the Bo01 site as the physical manifestation of new economic and social aims for Malmö, aiming to offer attractive housing for young professionals, reduce the levels of unemployment, and provide high standards of urban space and environmental sustainability.

As such, Malmö's municipality has been the main actor in the development of the Western Harbour area, establishing mechanisms to work in partnership with developers and professionals in order to ensure high standards of architectural and environmental quality. The Western Harbour masterplan was proposed and revised by the municipality, while the developers who bought the land undertook the design and construction according to the strict guidelines laid down by the masterplan (Quality Management Programme Bo01, 1999). Figure 9.6 shows the main landmark for the development, the Turning Torso.

Figure 9.6 *The Turning Torso, Malmö*

Source: Soledad Garcia Ferrari

With regards to management and implementation, since the municipality owned the land, it was in an advantageous position to implement experimental methods during the development process. A number of innovative processes for participation were thus implemented, such as quality management programmes, participatory project management tools, a planning forum and 'dialogues'.[8] In particular for Bo01, the main objective was sustainable urban development, and this was conducted through a comprehensive management programme comprising guidelines for architectural quality, building materials, use of energy, environmental issues, transport, etc. A unique aspect of the process of development in Bo01 was that this quality programme was put in practice before the sale of the land.

The Bo01 Expo company (Bo01 A/B) was wholly owned by Svenska Bostadsmessa (SBAB), a non-profit organization formed by the Ministry of Housing[9] to stimulate the housing market. The Bo01 Expo company acted as a coordinator of the developer's group, which was chaired by the director of the Malmö City Planning Office. Bo01 A/B comprised a staff of architects and coordinators and acted as a consultant. However, in 2001, following unfruitful attempts to recover from lack of private sponsorship, Bo01 declared bankruptcy. This economic turndown did not affect the overall development in the long term, but generated uncertainties surrounding the future of the area and negatively affected the public image of the project. Although the housing exhibition was not a financial success, the project appears to have been successful in terms of architecture, sustainability and urban environment (see Figure 9.7). By 2005, economic difficulties had been overcome and the development advanced towards completion.

Significant for the development of the Western Harbour has been a series of regional changes, which repositioned the city within its surrounding territory and provided the opportunity for proposing 'a new identity', as explained by Olsson and Rosberg (2005). The end of the shipbuilding industry during the 1980s coincided with the signing of the contract for building a link over Oresund connecting the city with Copenhagen. At the time, high levels of unemployment and economic difficulties had led to the loss of 30,000 jobs in the city between 1990 and 1993. In this context, the decision during the mid 1990s to establish Malmö University in the inner harbour was significant from a strategic planning point of view. The integration of the Malmö–Copenhagen region by the new bridge has also favoured conditions for housing, employment, education and the business sector; among these is the development of the Western Harbour.

The waterfront redevelopment is part of a wider regional strategy for better transport connections and services for the city of Malmö, and the Western Harbour project is part of a larger programme for regeneration, including the City Tunnel connecting the Oresund Bridge with the central areas of the city and the redevelopment of the southern areas, adjacent to the bridgehead. In this context, the Bo01 aimed to create a new neighbourhood by the sea that could attract highly skilled professionals in the framework of a change of perception of the city's identity, at a regional as well as local level, away from its industrial past and leading to a 'creative city' based on a new economically sustainable cultural, urban and social environment (i.e. helping the city to reinvent itself as a highly competitive location in a regional and global context) (Olsson and Rosberg, 2005).

Figure 9.7 *Domestic-scale environment with eco-houses, Malmö*

Source: Soledad Garcia Ferrari

The first stage of the Western Harbour development was focused on two areas: the Bo01 in the north-west and the university in the south-west. The university aimed to provide a long-term instrument for development and a new engine for city development. The masterplan for Bo01, prepared by Professor Klas Tham from Lund University, was based on a mixed-use development with 1000 residential units, and with offices and other services such as a school and leisure centre. There were three main design strategies in the masterplan: to create a surrounding area with high buildings in order to protect the inner areas from strong sea winds; the inner streets always leading to buildings for wind protection; and the proposal of a 180m high landmark tower, the Turning Torso, commissioned by the municipality from the Spanish architect Santiago Calatrava and completed in 2005 (see Figure 9.6). The architects who undertook the various parts of the project were chosen by the developers and this choice had to be confirmed by Professor Klas Tham and the Malmö Planning Department.

In addition to the guide on street grid, location of public spaces and development areas indicated in the masterplan, a detailed colouring programme for the façades was designed together with a green space programme. The development of each area was planned to be implemented in phases. A significant objective of the Western Harbour design has been the achievement of an environmentally sustainable environment. Among the requirements was the provision of green spaces, for which the masterplan indicated a need of 17 square metres of public green area and 12 square metres of private green area for every inhabitant (Quality Management Programme Bo01, 1999). In addition, 100 per cent renewable energy sources were to be incorporated. This was achieved by a combination of wind power (99 per cent of the needed electricity), solar energy (1 per cent of the needed electricity and 12 per cent of the heating power), heat pumps combined with aquifer reservoirs (85 per cent of the heating energy) and bio-gas (3 per cent of the heating energy), resulting in 0 per cent carbon dioxide emissions overall (Bo01 City of Tomorrow, 2001).

The waterfront boardwalk was designed as a public area and today includes restaurants, cafés and shops, creating a lively urban environment (see Figure 9.8). The area has been adopted not only by its residents, but also by the city's population at large. The high level of public participation can also be seen as

Figure 9.8 *Boardwalk at Bo01, with medium-rise perimeter buildings, Malmö*

Source: Harry Smith

an achievement of the project; however, the developers promoted the area as an exclusive neighbourhood and the owners of the apartments have raised complaints about the noise created by crowds along the sea front during the summer. In meeting these complaints, the municipality proposed to build alternative public spaces, further away from the housing, and a new island for swimmers. Housing provided in the area is mainly focused on higher income levels and there are future plans for incorporating social housing in order to secure a wider social mix.

In conclusion, a strong place identity has been created in Bo01, with the 'turning torso' acting as a beacon that has put the city on the map for cruise liners, the residential layout providing a distinctive living environment for residents, and the promenade providing a new open space and place for Malmö citizens – albeit contested in its use by neighbourhood residents and 'outsiders'. The success of place-making here has once again been the outcome of careful consideration of macro-level issues in political-economic terms, and the success has been linked to a city region development. In meso-level terms, the strong design control and participation processes have helped to provide well-designed spaces which residents and city dwellers enjoy, and at the micro-level there has been considerable success in environmental terms; however, the perception of users is perhaps more controversial.

Analysis: Who creates place? Why? For whom? How?

As explained in the introduction to this chapter, three scales can be used to assess aspects of place-making for waterfront developments: the macro-, meso- and micro-scale. These scales relate to the different aspects of place and place-making described in the literature review, from more perceptual approaches to place identity and place attachment, to managerial and implementation strategies interlinking different geographical scales in the development process.

In relation to the macro-scale, the waterfront cases presented here are the result of different sets of objectives. In the case of Gateshead Quays, the place-making policy led by the local authority was aimed at putting the place 'on the map' at a regional (North and England), national (UK) and even international level. Actions were focused on strategically assessing demands for certain functions across the UK and targeting certain funds that could be accessed. The outcome reflects a set of iconic built environment elements which are the main focus of the overall waterfront design and have influenced the rapid rise in land value, and subsequent flow of private investment in order to complete more recent phases of the development – business, retail, residential, etc. This process led to a development that lacked masterplanning and made evident the fact that the key building functions were the predominant nature of the whole 'Gateshead Quays place'.

On the other hand, Aker Brygge was primarily linked to the needs of this space within the city and its region, influencing, in particular, local migrations with the offer of an upmarket inner-city location for living, as well as for recreational use. Some larger-scale regional and national strategies also influenced the success of the development and intensified commercial and recreational use, such as the decision to move one of the busiest passenger ferry terminals in Norway to the entrance of the development area, together with other decisions related to linking local transport. The need to focus on the place itself was manifest in the process in Aker Brygge, which was the result of long-term masterplanning, including uses, building form and public spaces. Here the meso- and micro-level processes and products have been the main focus, although the development does also demonstrate success at a macro-level.

The case of Malmö can be identified as another example of place-making, with deliberate links between the micro-, meso- and macro-scales. Here, however, major urban structural changes taking place at a regional level had framed the way in which the city transformed itself, including the redefinition of its identity within the Oresund region. At the same time, significant social and spatial problems at the local scale influenced the development of new places in the city, which aimed to ensure social and physical sustainability with the provision of new public spaces and cultural hubs, as well as with the provision of zero-carbon emission zones. The local authority, the main actor leading the development of the Western Harbour, took the opportunity of national strategies linked to regional changes in order to bid for funding, as well as to create processes which ensured the quality of the places created. In addition, the success of the development relied on the level of trust from citizens and investors during times of economic uncertainty, and the various mechanisms for negotiation and participation here played a key role.

With regards to place-making, all three cases have been successful at the macro-scale, creating a destination for the city, the region and even the nation. At the meso-scale, however, there appears to be more disconnections in the case of Gateshead Quays, where the waterfront area appears to be better positioned in relation to Newcastle than to the centre of Gateshead. Whereas transport, pedestrian and visual barriers characterize the Gateshead Quays area, Aker Brygge is not only positioned in a key location in the centre of Oslo, but this has also been reinforced by decisions on new integrated transport routes (motorway tunnels, tramlines and ferry terminal). These links are enhanced by good visual connections across the city hall square, which in itself acts as an urban focal point.

In the case of Malmö's Western Harbour, the municipality put very influential transport strategies in place. Incorporating the university within the development of one of the most attractive areas in the city on the sea front, integrating this new function with the core of the city, and replacing the lost building and car industries by a new 'development engine' were strategies for positioning the city in the regional scene. These strategies show major achievements at the meso-scale, reinforcing significant macro-scale infrastructural changes in the whole city in relation to the Oresund link.

In the cases of Malmö and Gateshead, and due to the unique location of the waterfront developments within these cities, it is unlikely that internal changes in design and development process (i.e. at the meso-scale) could have influenced the overall success of development and levels of investment expected in the future. However, the case of Aker Brygge might be more vulnerable to other developments in the city, particularly along the waterfront, such as the area of the new Opera House, which has become an alternative urban focal point on the opposite site of Oslo city centre. The Oslo waterfront, is in fact, very extensive, due partly to the nature of the fjord, and achieving success at the level of Aker Brygge for the whole waterfront area will be a challenge in itself and may affect the outcome of this initial state of regeneration.

Within the micro-scale of place-making, this chapter refers to the aspects of waterfront spaces that make areas feel more 'comfortable', 'inviting', 'attractive' and potentially generate a sense of place attachment. Place-making at this scale is about the design of the buildings and the spaces in between these, including the public realm. The sense of place also depends upon other aspects, such as the way in which the existing heritage remains or is reinterpreted in the area, the sense of security of the waterfront, and the uses and activities given to different parts in the development. While this needs careful local input for a fuller analysis, an initial assessment has been made here by the authors.

In the case of Gateshead Quays, the spaces between the iconic buildings (the main focus for place-making at the macro-scale) were not treated as a whole in terms of urban design and landscape. As a result, these spaces are overshadowed by the main buildings. However, this is possibly a temporary condition as a more complex set of external and internal spaces is envisaged once other buildings are developed in the main site between the Sage and BALTIC, and the incorporation of other uses, such as housing, office and retail, is expected to provide a more dynamic urban space.

The introduction to this chapter states that place-making is also dependent upon communication and participatory mechanisms, and again it is not clear in Gateshead Quays to what extent the development included social, economic and cultural groups at local and city-region levels in the decision-making and implementation processes. However, in terms of the way in which the resulting place is perceived, transformations in the area represent an enormous improvement; hence, the waterfront is now recognized in the regional and even national scene.

Aker Brygge, on the other hand, experienced a more integrated design process with a strong masterplan and a limited number of key designers. The spaces between the buildings have been the focus of a much more complex design strategy, including more uses and activities, as well as more intricate connections between types of spaces and its use comprising public and communal areas. The overall quality and attention to design, including materials and form, are evident in the Aker Brygge area. In the case of the Bo01 in Malmö's Western Harbour, the quality of design is also carefully detailed on the masterplan beyond aspects related to the buildings, form and materials, to more specific technical requirements for creating a sustainable environment with zero carbon emissions. In this case, public spaces are also carefully located and designed, interlinking the different uses in the waterfront area. Here, much more explicit emphasis on wider participation in the process was built in from the start, although the main user population is again a rather privileged social group.

What can we learn from waterfront place-making?

Analysing these three waterfront case studies permits us to draw some general conclusions on successful place-making regarding waterfronts, which can have validity beyond such areas in other urban regeneration/design iniatives. First, in relation to the normative approach to place identity that is found in current place-making design guidance, it is clear that appropriate design strategies and processes are only part of the equation, with the social, political and economic contexts being a strong conditioner of success of both process and outcomes. The examples seen in this chapter show that resources, rules and ideas in any given context have a strong bearing on successful place-making predominantly at the meso-level; however, the most successful places also consider deliberate integrative strategies at the macro-level.

At the macro- and meso-levels, issues of power are seen to operate across all three scales. The reconfiguration of the identities of Gateshead (through culture and the arts) and Malmö (through its repositioning in the regional transport network and its waterfront redevelopment) is changing regional dynamics and the balance of economic and social power at the macro-level, with potential political consequences as well. All three, though perhaps most obviously in the case of Aker Brygge, created powerful attractors at the meso-level, with social and economic activity patterns across all three cities being consequently altered. Power issues are also evident at the micro-level (e.g. in the contested use and appropriation of the promenade in Bo01 by different groups).

Vision and leadership are key resources that have been essential to the success of the cases examined in this chapter. Continuity of objectives and intentions through overall strategies and physical masterplanning also play a positive influence on the creation of successful places, balanced with sufficient flexibility to grasp opportunities and to adapt to changing circumstances. Such overall strategies need to address the role that the new 'place' may have in the context of the city as a whole, or even the region (i.e. the meso- and macro-scales). This involves, among other factors, understanding the infrastructure connections, such as major transport routes and interchanges and how the new 'place' may link into these, as well as the function that the area may have within this wider context.

However, the functionality and success of the development as a place will ultimately depend upon how its users relate to it – also at the meso- and micro-levels. This requires identifying who these users are or will be, and creating the conditions for the creation of places which they will use and enjoy using – places to which they may grow attached in various ways. A key factor here can be the use of dialogue and participation processes that involve existing and potential 'communities' in decision-making. The way in which urban changes are communicated to such communities may also have an effect on the perceived identity of the places that result. The implementation of participatory processes in the regeneration of waterfront areas can, however, confront particular problems, such as the absence of an existing resident community – as illustrated in other chapters in this book. In this case, the creation of place includes the generation of a new identity which may draw on historic memory, on innovation or on a combination of both. Not all successful waterfronts, however, thus have, or can have, such processes – and here it is important that the development agencies reflect adequately on the potential user communities and what can be crucial to their engagement with the product. Learning from other waterfronts is a key action here, as long as this is adequately contextualized – something for which this book provides a unique resource.

Time is also a key ingredient in the creation of a successful place. Residential developments require time for new residents to develop their sense of 'place attachment', and success at micro-levels cannot be assessed in the short term. However, wider meso-scale place attachment can be stimulated successfully by flagship developments that turn a non-place into a place in the minds of the wider citizenry in a relatively short space of time, as seen in the arts- and culture-led regeneration in Gateshead. Thus, although the integrated approaches of Aker Brygge and Bo01 have 'created place' more fully than the approach at Gateshead, the meso-level can also be important for this aspect of place identity.

Finally, good design is a key ingredient in successful place-making on the waterfront in different ways. Design as a tool is perhaps most obvious in iconic buildings, and while good urban design may not be so obvious, it is essential in the creation of public spaces and mixes of uses that will contribute to the liveliness of new urban areas such as in Aker Brygge, or the residents' quality of life in places such as Bo01. Key here is deliberate design of the spaces between the buildings and ensuring that a sensitive and coordinated design approach reflects the wider ethos of the area and of user communities (dwellers and others). In this, available and realized design approaches and options depend upon a good understanding of the relevant sociocultural milieu and socio-economic conditions.

In conclusion, any waterfront development would benefit from developing a clear vision and strategy with regards to the various aspects of place-making – political, phenomenological and normative – and appropriate tactics and timing with regard to the scale at which each of these aspects is to be addressed. Ideas and discourses (of all kinds) have a key role to play in achieving this, not least through design strategies, which are discussed in the next chapter.

Notes

1   Hernández et al (2007, p.310) define 'place attachment' as 'the affective link that people establish with specific settings, where they tend to remain [or return to] and where they feel comfortable and safe'.
2   Proshansky (1978, p.147) describes 'place identity' as 'those dimensions of self that define the individual's personal identity in relation to the physical environment'.
3   Karlyn Sutherland is a Part II architect working on a design-based PhD in Architecture at Edinburgh College of Art. Her work focuses on translating theories of place attachment from environmental psychology into an architectural design methodology. Her thesis is expected to be published by March 2012.
4   This is within the core Gateshead Quays area in the Tyne Gorge. Other developments beyond the High Level Bridge (such as Tyne Bridge Hilton International Hotel) or not within the gorge (such as Baltic Business Park) are linked to Gateshead Quays' regeneration, but have not been considered within this study.

5   Gateshead Central Area: The Public Realm (2003) and a masterplan for Gateshead Quays (RMJM et al, 2010).

6   Offices provide 86,000 square metres of floor space, and shops and restaurants 24,000 square metres of floor space, which together provide around 5000 jobs. Residential use consists of 383 apartments ranging from 40 to 50 square metres in size (Gehl Architects, 1998).

7   Phase 1 (1985–1986) covered the blocks closest to the city centre and involved the refurbishment of two existing buildings and the erection of the 'gateway' building on the corner facing the Town Hall Square. During phase 2 (1989) the same company extended the development towards the south-west, along the dockside and incorporating the large central public space. This phase was affected by the market collapse and properties sold at a loss. Phase 3 (1991) comprised the large mixed-use block forming the southern corner of the development. This was developed by a subsidiary of DnB (Stranden AS) after Aker Brygge ANS had sold the development. This again was sold at a loss. Phase 4 (1998) filled in the western edge between the initial development and the route of the former east–west motorway through Oslo, completed by yet another developer (Storebrand).

8   Among these is Q-books, which is a quality management programme to establish a platform for discussions between all stakeholders. The Q-books programme not only focuses on strategic decisions, but is also concerned with building issues such as parks, streets, quays, etc. LOTS project management is also a mechanism based on participation and discussion among stakeholders on specific issues, but organized through parallel focused working groups and within a more informal framework. The Urban Planning Forum West Harbour is also a neutral meeting place for landowners, developers, business owners and city officials, where issues regarding the development are proposed and discussed, including specific workshops and exhibitions. The Build-Live Dialogue focuses on the continuation of sustainability, also based upon discussion opportunities among companies, municipality and the national government.

9   National Board of Housing, Building and Planning.

10

Design Strategies for Urban Waterfronts

The Case of Sluseholmen in Copenhagen's Southern Harbour

Maria Soledad Garcia Ferrari and Derek Fraser

Introduction

As presented earlier in this book, economic changes created the conditions for significant spatial transformations in waterfronts and port areas, where large portions of land have been left derelict, bringing about new opportunities for regeneration and redevelopment. Local, regional, national and occasionally transnational authorities and organizations play an important role in these complex processes, which require vision, negotiation, participation, public and private investment, consensus on design strategies, etc. Building on the cases discussed in this book, this chapter discusses the relationship between the processes of waterfront development and the design strategies adopted in the case of Sluseholmen in Copenhagen.

Copenhagen's waterfront[1] presents an interesting case study in the sense that the design strategies and development process are closely linked to recent strategic changes in the approach to development along the waterfront taken by the City of Copenhagen authorities. These changes were in response to controversies and public criticism over waterfront development in the central area of the city at the end of the 1990s. The resulting debate increased awareness of the solutions proposed, as well as recognition of the need for a more carefully considered approach to the design proposals and masterplan strategies for waterfront development. In particular, and following discussions over the high-profile central harbour site south of the Royal Library, with its much acclaimed new extension (the 'Black Diamond, 1995'), the city realized the importance of achieving better-quality design solutions, extending strategic masterplanning into a wider region, generating debate over design for specific areas and widening involvement to international contributors.

In both the northern and southern harbours, two Dutch consultants were invited to contribute to the discussions. This was a brave approach and also slightly controversial within the Danish architecture community. Both Dutch architect/masterplanners were known internationally for their pioneering work in the Java Island and the Borneo developments in the Amsterdam Eastern Docklands: Adrian Geuze of West 8 for Borneo/Sporenburg and Sjoerd Soeters of Soeters Van Eldonk Ponec for Java Island. Although both architects initially looked at both locations, Geuze became responsible for the northern harbour and Soeters for the southern. The final design solution for Sluseholmen takes some of the initial ideas tested in Amsterdam and develops a specific design answer for Copenhagen. The proposal deals head on with a number of key issues facing contemporary urban design and place-making, not least of which is how to create a new neighbourhood offering a rich variety of building façades in a street-style frontage, within the fast timescale of modern construction. Given that the final design implemented has been met with very positive reactions from professionals and public alike, and has been recognized with awards,[2] it deserves to be analysed in detail.

This chapter discusses how the design strategies adopted were the result of productive interactions among all parties involved and how the positive result in terms of successful place-making is related to significant changes in development and implementation processes. However, regarding the design solution, the Sluseholmen development has also met with some criticism from the architecture community concerning a lack of integrity or ethics because the variety of façades proposed does not express the repetition of apartment layouts. It is interesting to note that in many cases of Baroque or Georgian city designs, the emphasis was often put on the design of façades or unified 'palace' street frontages, which served a 'civic' function, above and beyond that of the function behind the façade. It could be argued that although Sluseholmen inverts this concept by having uniform residential form fronted by a variety of different façades, it clearly regards the art of 'place-making' as more important than creating a collection of individual buildings. This debate brings into focus differences of opinion between the 'modernists' and 'traditionalists' in theories of architecture and urban design. Sluseholmen, however, deals with the polemic by blending together aspects of both the modern and the traditional. It is also apparent in the case of Sluseholmen that the new residents have chosen to live there because of its unique connection with the water. Surprisingly for such a water-based city, Copenhagen offers very few opportunities for real interaction with it, and perhaps it took the eye of an outsider such as Soeters – from a country with substantial experience in creating areas for living along waterfronts – to realize this and help to deliver such an innovative and successful design solution.

The analysis of the Sluseholmen case presented below will focus on the design strategies, which – grounded in the theory explained earlier in this book – are contextualized in this particular development processes. The intention is then to understand these processes by looking at the different types of relations between resources, regulations and ideologies. The investigation questions the connections, interactions and influences between design solutions and development processes. Furthermore, it asks: can we reflect on the perceived achievements of the design strategies set up by the different sectors involved in the process?

A number of semi-structured interviews were undertaken during the research process upon which this chapter is based, where three key areas of questions were formulated in relation to vision, process and post-completion reflection. These aimed to canvas views from all sectors involved, such as designers, planners and developers. Some users were contacted informally during the visit to the site; however, the objective is to follow on this research with a second stage when the same set of questions will be proposed to users in order to gain knowledge on what their vision and objectives are, and how these are perceived to have been achieved.

The following section focuses on the initial stages of redevelopment along the city's waterfront and reflects upon some case studies and debates over their quality in terms of both design and place-making.

The redevelopment of the Copenhagen waterfront since the late 1970s

In order to provide a context to the specific area of study, this section presents an overview of development in Copenhagen's waterfront and, in more detail, the masterplan strategies for the southern part of the waterfront area. The aim is to explain how a change of attitude in the development process for waterfront areas has contributed to the level of success of some recent sectors in Copenhagen's waterfront.

Copenhagen[3] city is bisected by its harbour, creating a complex waterfront area and presenting various areas with different types of relationships with the water and the rest of the city. The port itself assumed most of its current form during the 1900 to 1920 period, when the Free Port was extended and the south harbour added. The functioning of the port has undergone significant changes during the last 30 years, resulting in the abandonment of large areas of port activities due to industrial transformations and the increase in the use of shipping containers. At the end of the 1970s, national and local authorities began to consider these large disused areas to be significant opportunities for urban redevelopment.

During the 1970s, a period of economic decline in Copenhagen, together with significant changes in the industrial harbour areas, led the Danish government and the Municipality of Copenhagen to undertake a number of initiatives in order to identify waterfront problems and to seek possible solutions. In 1972, Denmark's adviser on aesthetic and architectural matters (*Akademirådet*) organized an architectural competition for the development of the docks, which by the end of the 1970s generated a public debate concerning the future of the port areas and the waterfront (Hansen et al, 2001). This debate raised an issue that has been central to discussions ever since: whether port areas should be developed according to a comprehensive plan or left to the discretion of individual landowners (Desfor and Jorgensen, 2004). Although the recommendation from the *Akademirådet* was very much for the development of a comprehensive plan, the actual process followed a different path.

During the 1980s, the need for government intervention in Copenhagen in order to overcome the economic crisis increased, and national authorities began to discuss the future of the city. A report presented by the Danish Parliament entitled *The Capital: What Should We Do About It?*[4] is evidence of this, describing 20 key points for the future development of the city in becoming an international centre able to attract new investments. Amongst these key points were the improvement of higher education and cultural institutions, the establishment of a fixed link to Sweden, the expansion of the airport, the planning of the Ørestad area, and the development of harbour areas. These new policies were justified by the need to compete successfully on an international stage – an approach to urban development that differs from previous strategies – which were more oriented towards the national scene (Desfor and Jorgensen, 2004).

National involvement on Copenhagen waterfront can be observed with the creation of a specific committee (Copenhagen Harbour Committee)[5] set up by the Danish Parliament in 1987, with the objectives of studying alternative frameworks for the port areas by identifying port boundaries and considering financing models for possible development schemes. The City of Copenhagen declined to have a representative on this committee, expressing doubts about the use of its findings for the city's forthcoming 1989 plan (Desfor and Jorgensen, 2004). There were political and ideological differences between the city and the national government, with the city under the control of the 'New Left', while a liberal–conservative coalition ruled the country.

The Copenhagen Harbour Committee published its report in April 1989 with the recommendation that port activities should be concentrated in the northern harbour, while housing, office, commercial, cultural, entertainment and recreational activities were to be located in the inner and southern harbours. In addition, this report suggested the establishment of a new organization to manage waterfront developments that would be based on a partnership between the Danish government, the Municipality of Copenhagen and the Port Authority. Finally, in May 1989 the government announced that the navy would be moving its facilities from the inner harbour on Holmen, vacating 70ha of prime waterfront land and creating the possibility of a range of alternative uses.

In 1992 the government proposed the creation of an administration with responsibility for both the management and conversion of port areas. A specific law established that, initially, the Port Authority of Copenhagen, besides running the port, should also direct and run the redevelopment of the harbour areas no longer used for port activities. It also defined the composition of the organization's board of directors[6] and determined that the port had to remain a self-governing institution.[7]

Although the 1990s were characterized by renewed economic growth, there were high levels of unemployment, particularly in Copenhagen.[8] In order to overcome this, the actions undertaken by the city tended to be based on selling the land that it owned, leaving powerful economic forces to come into play and opening up opportunities for privately funded developments. These uncoordinated actions were possible because of the lack of agreement on a unified masterplan for the harbour, as well as economic pressures on the city. The solutions adopted often lacked an agreed design strategy and could be seen as isolated developments with little connection to the urban dynamics of the city (Garcia Ferrari, 2006).

In 2000, by Act of Parliament, the government finally transformed the Port Authority of Copenhagen into a publicly owned limited liability corporation – the Port of Copenhagen Company (Københavns Havn A/S). At this point the

Copenhagen Harbour Committee ceased to operate. The government subsequently transferred the port's assets to Københavns Havn A/S. In 2001, another new organization was established, Copenhagen Malmø Port AB (CMP), to operate the port and terminal activities of both Malmø and Copenhagen. This company is a Danish/Swedish harbour enterprise, the central harbour operator in the Øresund region. Since 2007, the Danish part of CMP has been owned by CPH City and Port Development (By & Havn). The latter was founded in 2007 when Københavns Havn A/S and the Ørestad Development Corporation I/S merged. CPH City and Port Development (By & Havn) are now owned by the City of Copenhagen (55 per cent) and the state (45 per cent).[9]

The role of the Port of Copenhagen Company (Københavns Havn A/S) has been very significant for the initial stages of development of the city's waterfront. The company owned approximately 4000ha of land. This organization – supported by its board of directors, a combination of local politicians, state representatives and prominent industrialists – acted as a private sector establishment following the needs and fluctuations of the market. Under this perspective the company was not initially interested in the development of a comprehensive municipal plan since that plan could go against its freedom to develop sites for purchase and sale, which was a very profitable activity (Garcia Ferrari, 2006).

The Municipality of Copenhagen, on the other hand, had originally not managed to adopt a unified position regarding the creation of a comprehensive waterfront plan, and had supported a number of individual private initiatives, which led to largely fragmented developments usually initiated by the private sector. Desfor and Jorgensen (2004) link this lack of unanimity to a fractured process of planning in Danish local government during the 1990s. With regard to the waterfront, there are three major departments with responsibility for urban planning: Financial Directorate, Building and Construction Administration and the Department of the Environment. Each has its own bureaucratic procedures and political aims. More fundamentally, the municipality did not have a clear incentive to exercise its waterfront planning powers because of the perceived exceptional status of the Port of Copenhagen Company (Desfor and Jorgensen, 2004).

The municipality stated that it had encouraged the initiatives for the development of the waterfront in a response to more recent industrial changes with the emergence of new enterprises, such as in the information technology (IT) sector (Garcia Ferrari, 2006). However, early in the 2000s a zoning plan for the harbour area was presented by the municipality promoting the development of new housing projects, and expressing the need to build 2000, 900 and 5000 units, respectively, in the northern, inner and southern harbours (*Københavns Havn Blue Plan*, 2005).[10]

An example of development process during this initial stage of waterfront regeneration in Copenhagen is the Kalvebod Brygge development, on land owned by the City of Copenhagen. This scheme was widely perceived by both the general public and leading politicians as having been flawed and sparked an intense debate. The predominance of large office buildings prevented easy pedestrian access to the waterfront and blocked views of the water that city dwellers had come to expect. It was specifically this public outcry over the Kalvebod Brygge development that led politicians to realize that discussions needed to take place for the future redevelopment of the harbour, which included the concerns of all actors involved and considered the aims and expectations of both the private sector and civil society.

In this context, major criticism was directed at the lack of long-term planning and strategies for transforming large-scale areas. As a response to the extreme fragmentation in the initial stages of development of the waterfront areas (such as Kalvebod Brygge), together with the absence of a unified plan for the harbour, an *ad hoc* organization – Vision Group (Steering Committee for Harbour Development) – was created in 1999, bringing together politicians and bureaucrats from the state and the municipality.[11] The objective of this committee was to oversee the waterfront developments with the specific task of ensuring that the experience of Kalvebod Brygge development would not reoccur, while at the same time bringing stability to a turbulent political and fractured economic situation (Desfor and Jorgensen, 2004). The overall aim of this organization was to ensure 'high-quality development' in the waterfront area, searching for coherency in urban public policy. High-quality development involved aspects of design, place-making and community-building (*Københavns Havn Plan-Vision 2010*, 1999).

Contrary to the idea of designing a comprehensive plan, 'focus areas' were identified by the Port of Copenhagen and the Vision Group, with the aim of providing flexibility to the planning and design process and to include the strategic objectives and needs of developers, investors, architects and planners in a more 'developer-friendly' process. This process, however, appeared to be focused mainly on participation from the different groups of political institutions involved and on developers, rather than on the residents or existing small businesses.

The Vision Group actions therefore show the beginning of a planning strategy taking place in tandem with the regular planning process, which by law is the responsibility of local government. The spatial objectives initiated by the Vision Group can be observed in the most recent developments. In particular, development is to promote 'spatial quality', which is expected to better attract investment and people. In this sense, the Copenhagen waterfront developments are presented as an alternative for those leaving the city's central areas for quieter suburbs. The slogan 'quality developments' presented in the *Plan-Vision* document reflects the aim of an emerging model for property-based capital accumulation (*Københavns Havn Plan-Vision 2010*, 1999).

Along with the disagreements and debate, during the process of developing Copenhagen's waterfront since the 1990s symbolic buildings such as the new Museum of Modern Art (The Ark, 1996), the annex to the Royal Library (the Black Diamond, 1995) and the new Opera House (2004) have emerged along the waterfront as isolated icons. With regards to land use, at the end of the 1990s one of the aims that began to emerge was to promote a mix of office buildings and housing. However, this also caused controversy. While, at the end of the 1990s, office building construction was more profitable than housing in Copenhagen, the municipality considered that its housing stock needed to be improved. The need for housing, however, also reflects the overall aim of economic growth, since the units provided are expected to compete in an international market and to attract key workers and young professionals (Københavns Havn, 2001). This is particularly reflected by the new typologies proposed for the Sluseholmen area, with the provision of 'water dwellings' (Københavns Havn, 2001).

The case of Sluseholmen, explained in the next section, is the result of a more integrated approach to developing the waterfront and closer negotiation between the city, the port and the developers. This case is also significant in understanding the design strategies promoted by these sectors. Sluseholmen is also a good example to analyse the links between these strategies and the development process, which in this case appear to be woven into the priorities of all stakeholders.

The case of the Sluseholmen development

The Port of Copenhagen stretches 12km from north to south and includes almost 40km of quays. The waterfront area is divided into four zones: the north harbour (Nordhavnen), including Southern Freeport (Sondre Frihavnen – southern part of the north harbour), the East Harbour (Østhavnen/Provestenen), the central harbour (Inderhavnen, including Kalvebod Brygge) and the south harbour (Sydhavnen) (see Figure 10.1). Since the mid 1980s, commercial traffic has been concentrated in the north and east harbours. In these areas new operating techniques have been available and old quays and warehouses restored. The new port, in the north and east harbours, has over 700 leaseholds and extends over 4 million square metres (Københavns Havn, 2001).

In the North Harbour Freeport, the area around Amerika Plads was masterplanned by Adrian Geuze for a new district holding 500 housing units, 50,000 square metres of commercial properties and a new ferry passenger terminal. A landmark of this area is the 16-storey high Copper Tower (2004 by Arkitema). The north harbour around Århusgade is still being developed and the area plan includes 2000 homes and 200,000 square metres of commercial buildings.

South of the Black Diamond, in the central harbour area, development followed a more commercial and business approach. This waterfront site, consisting of a narrow strip of land between the harbour and the highway called Kalvebod Brygge, was judged not suited for housing because of the traffic noise. Originally owned by the municipality, it was sold to a Swedish development/construction company, which constructed a row of office buildings and a shopping mall (Fisketorvet) during the 1990s. The scheme generated negative criticism about the architectural quality of the new buildings and of absence of 'life' on the promenades. Debates concluded that the requirements in the local plan of 1990 had not been adequate enough to secure a high-quality development. In 2004, during the second phase of development for the area around the shopping mall, the same developers adopted a masterplan by the Swedish architect Gert Wingårdh, which includes a pedestrian bridge across the harbour, an outdoor swimming pool and high-quality residential buildings. This has proved to be more successful.

Figure 10.1 *Plan of Copenhagen showing four main harbour areas*

Source: Copenhagen Planning Department, 2010

Further south from this is the southern harbour and the redevelopment of the old industrial area where Sluseholmen is located. Due to the move of the port activities to the north harbour, the remaining functions in the southern area consist of scrap yards, empty factories and derelict industrial land, which presented the city with a tough challenge and took longer to be phased into the city's programme of expansion and redevelopment.

Copenhagen city planners initially sketched a series of objectives for the area, mostly based on increasing the provision of housing (primarily low cost). Later the city introduced a masterplanning stage into the planning approvals process, demanding a more detailed series of requirements, which resulted in a series of revised plans in consultation with the firm of architects Souters Van

Eldonk Ponec. The later masterplan created a vision for dense, urban waterfront/canal-side living with high-quality housing, as well as schools, workplaces, shops, public transport, roads and services. The southern harbour masterplan predominantly uses perimeter blocks surrounded by canals linked to a new north–south route connecting the disparate parts of the area (see Figure 10.2). Given the apparent success of the Sluseholmen project and others, it could be argued, therefore, that the southern harbour has benefited from the experience gained and the mistakes made in the areas developed earlier without a clear vision or agreed masterplan.

From the city planners' point of view, within the south harbour, the Sluseholmen area became the exemplar or ideal urban design model, demonstrating what can be done to create an attractive place to overcome Copenhageners' prejudice against this unattractive industrial area. The city's investment in this project illustrates how high-quality design can have a positive influence on a challenging area from the perception of quality of life and liveability.

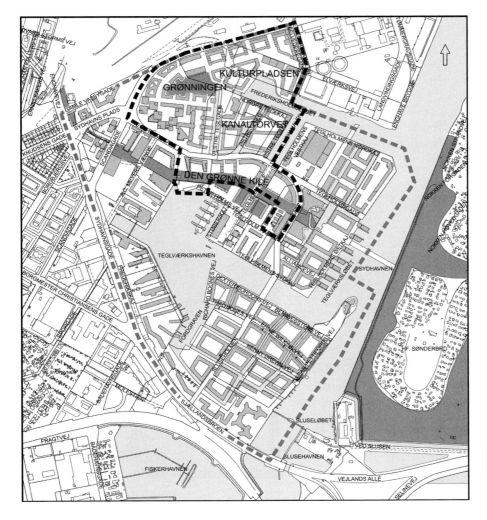

Figure 10.2 *South Harbour masterplan*

Source: Copenhagen Planning Department, 2010

The vision for Sluseholmen[12]

The interviews with the various stakeholders revealed that the development of a vision for Sluseholmen evolved as the main expectations were revisited and refined after the initial start. Since the existing south industrial harbour operations were declining during the 1990s and businesses began to withdraw, the city planners' original development framework for the wider region, set out in 1999, was for 9000 residential units and 20,000 workplaces. The Sluseholmen development was then intended to be predominantly residential, covering 133,000 square metres and with 20,000 square metres of commercial area consisting of a supermarket and two small shops (a café and convenience store) located along the main access road adjacent to the new harbour link bridge (completed in 2011) (see Figure 10.3). However, Sluseholmen should be understood in the wider context, where other uses and services are provided. The overall masterplan for the wider south harbour area proposes a mix of commercial areas (workplaces and shops), schools (kindergarten and lower school) and leisure facilities.

Following a process of discussion with potential developers and designers, it became clear that the particular problems with the Sluseholmen area, linked to its industrial past, required more careful consideration if the expectations of creating residential areas were to be met. Only after the involvement of the consultant Sjoerd Soeters and the approval of a more detailed comprehensive masterplan for the entire south harbour were the expectations for the area agreed upon. It is important to highlight that the development company involved at this stage, Sjælsø, was also involved in the building of the new business park in the south-western edge of the south harbour (Teglværkshaven, 2005–2008), and for that reason it was invited to participate from the discussions.

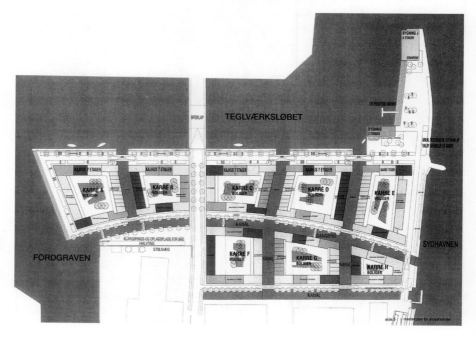

Figure 10.3
Sluseholmen masterplan

Source: Project
development director of
Sjælsø Danmark A/S, 2010

Initially, it was felt by the developers that the site of Sluseholmen would only be suitable for low-cost housing as it was part of a large derelict industrial harbour with very poor connections to the city centre. Expectations changed after a year or so when the city adopted a new strategy of 'high-quality design'. The final masterplan enabled a more upmarket private ownership to become feasible.

A leading principle in the design strategy was to create the image of a coherent district, but also to give the individual houses an identity of their own. However, the final tactics adopted to meet such aims took a while to emerge. After the early period (1999 to 2000), and following many discussions and debates about the varying quality of the central harbour developments, it was agreed that an improved strategic approach was required for the northern and southern harbours. Since the city was keen to get the best results for all of their new harbour developments, they invited a number of experts from abroad for consultations before appointing the two Dutch architect/masterplanners, Adrian Geuze (West 8) and Sjoerd Soeters (Soeters Van Eldonk Ponec).

For this exercise in masterplanning, various partnerships were formed with city planners, architects, developers and the newly formed Harbour Authority (By & Havn). Visits were made to various locations around the world to seek good examples, as well as not so successful examples, to learn from. However, all of the parties involved in this study made it clear that the intention was not just to lift and transport an existing solution, but to help the team find an appropriate one for Copenhagen. The final designs adopted for the north harbour by Geuze were based on high-density mixed use, and those for the south harbour (and Sluseholmen) by Soeters on canal-side living.

The emerging main aims of the city were to allow a southern expansion of the city centre into a redundant industrial harbour. From the developers' point of view, one of the main objectives was to achieve a design strategy, which would overcome the reality that 'nobody wanted to live there'. For the design of Sluseholmen, two important influences from the Amsterdam Eastern Docklands were Java Island (by Soeters) and Borneo Sporenburg (by West 8).

Achieving a high-quality design solution was seen by the city as a possible strategy to repopulate the area. From the developers' and designers' perspective, this could be achieved by maximizing access to the water and taking advantage of proposing other possible uses and activities in the emerging neighbourhood. In addition, the perimeter block typology, with streets, courtyards and basement parking, provided an answer to the strategic aim of the design team to seek a dense urban solution. This typology has the bonus of enabling the introduction of a network of canals running through the development, which provide direct access to water to a large number of dwellings.

The Danish architects Arkitema, chosen by the developers to work with Soeters on Sluseholmen, carried out initial feasibility studies to see how many units could be realized on the site in order to achieve commercial viability. This showed that a built floor area of 135,000 square metres over the 7.16ha of the site would provide around 1310 residential units. Apartments were initially based on a total floor area of between 80 to 90 square metres, but grew by an additional 5 to 10 square metres towards the later phases of the development when confidence in the market increased. This density plus the canal concept was then adopted as part of the city's local development plan for Sluseholmen. Given the radical nature of the design development process, Arkitema believes that tactically it was a good move by the city to invite a foreign lead architect consultant as it meant that more people in authority were inclined to listen and agree.

The overall plan layout for Sluseholmen consists of eight perimeter block islands separated by a network of canals and access roads. In addition, a standalone tower is proposed as the southern harbour landmark and treated as a separate project, with different architects and developers. The urban layout employs a curved main route promenade running east–west, with both the canal and canal-side roads cutting across the orthogonal plan. This concept successfully results in a plan layout where variety is ensured: no two blocks have the same footprint, each courtyard is different and the perspective views on the ground have closed vistas (as with the central Amsterdam ring canals). Open-stepped passages in the corner of each block provide glimpses down onto the canal and across to the courtyard of the neighbouring block (what Jorgen Bach of the architects Arkitema describes as the 'Venice views'). Bridges, quays and waterside steps allow residents to access the water for sport, leisure or just enjoying the view (see Figure 10.4). Channelling the harbour water between the blocks through canals maximizes the water-edge effect and provides more residents with closer proximity to the water. However, it is the building façades' variety of colour and material that give the design its special identity.

Figure 10.4 *Cross-canal image showing corner apartments and flanking double duplexes*

Source: Derek Fraser

With regards to housing typologies, a mix of apartments and two-storey or duplex houses exists. In the solution employed, the ground floor corners of each perimeter block have been designed in order to allow for commercial use or to combine live–work. To reach the required density, the north and south sides of each perimeter block contain linked apartment buildings of five to seven storeys, while the east and west sides consist of linked duplex houses stacked one above the other, reaching four storeys. Initially, the architects had reservations about the design concept of placing one duplex on top of another; but early design concepts using four-storey houses proved to be commercially unattractive and did not help to achieve the required density. It is interesting to note, however, that it was these double duplexes which sold first on completion of every block. The strategy of apartment blocks with surface parking employed in the early developments of the south harbour was abandoned in favour of a more 'urban' solution in the case of Sluseholmen, with its perimeter blocks, basement parking, communal courtyards and canal houses. Although the majority of blocks are predominately residential, there is a small commercial edge along the side of a block fronting onto the main through road to the new harbour link bridge.

During the design collaboration between Soeters and the Danish architects, much time was spent in establishing a set of rules or dogmas as design guidelines and housing density. For example, building heights could vary from four to seven storeys, with the four-storey building to the narrow side canals; the five-storey building to the wider canal-side road; and the six- or seven-storey building overlooking the wider harbour. This variety in height optimizes solar penetration into the blocks and, although adding a limited variety to the skyline, could have offered more tall landmarks from a townscape point of view. A site area of 7.16ha (including canals) is developed with a 135,000 square metre floor area on a footprint of 24,420 square metres, giving 183 units per hectare, which is a very high density for a contemporary scheme. Access roads are shared surface for pedestrians, bicycles and vehicles. Canal widths vary from 16m alongside the four-storey building and 20m alongside the five-storey building. Bridges have a 1:20 incline with heights of 2.5m above water and a minimum of 1.6m boat clearance.

The construction of the bridges linking various parts of the southern harbour and the link bridge to Sluseholmen are key to enabling residents to access various functions and uses in the area. Initially, the absence of these bridges has caused problems, with residents having to make long journeys to access facilities such as the primary school.

The Danish architects, in particular, regarded it important that each apartment building should have a 'social' dimension, where neighbours could share spaces and get to know each other, perhaps reflecting upon the Danish social democratic tradition. Each perimeter block should have a central social recreational space, shared by the residents and accessible to visitors. These internal courtyards contain children's playgrounds, bike stores, barbecue areas, landscaping with a variety of surfaces and small trees (see Figure 10.5). Following Danish law, these shared private spaces are managed and maintained by an obligatory residents' association, with rules and regulations normally found throughout the country.

(a)

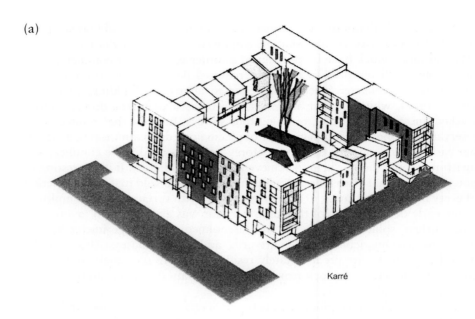

Karré

(b)

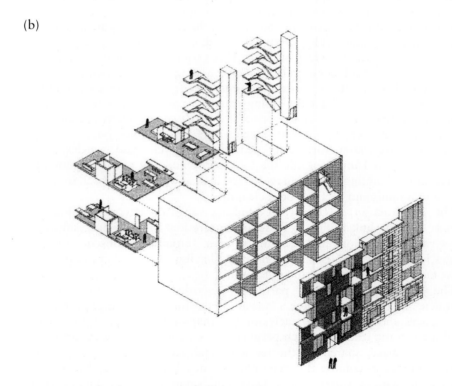

Figure 10.5a and 10.5b *Perimeter block with apartment buildings and duplex town houses. The sketch on the bottom shows standardized construction with a variety of individually designed façades*

Source: Project development director of Sjælsø Danmark A/S, 2010

On the eastern edge of the site there was an existing row of small boathouses traditionally rented out to residents of Copenhagen, which has been kept. This traditional and colourful activity brings in a different community and adds a vibrant edge to the site.

In summary, had the initial idea of low-cost housing and surface parking been realized, it would have no doubt brought an improvement to the area. However, the more ambitious vision set by the city authorities has resulted in the creation of a high-quality living environment with a forward-looking design solution successfully offering a new vibrant district for which the city is justifiably proud.

The planning and development process

During the first year, the city planners formed a regeneration development company for the southern harbour and worked with private developers who were interested in getting involved due to the building boom. It was this company that started to invest in the infrastructure and the clearing of grounds for the first developments. It was quickly realized, however, that this 'piecemeal' approach was not the best, and following the creation of the south harbour masterplan, various sites were identified and phases planned. With the Sluseholmen site, architects were given commissions from developers (Arkitema by Sjælsø), and in other cases in the south harbour, architects won competitions (Vandkusten at Teglværkshavnen). Four development companies were originally involved with the Slusholmen project, reduced to three by the end of the project. Two construction companies won the tenders and were given a timescale in which the work was to be completed.

The major stakeholders involved were the Copenhagen city planners, the Port Authority (By & Havn), development companies, architects, technicians and engineers. The main developers were invited to be involved in initial discussions about the southern harbour redevelopment by the City of Copenhagen because of their performance record on other projects in the city. In particular, the city invited the developer, and suggested that this company select two or three other development companies with whom to work in order to widen involvement and overcome the tight timescale. The lead architects, Arkitema, also invited other architects to become involved in the design of the façades of both apartment buildings and canal duplexes as part of the design strategy. Most welcomed the opportunity, but a few were unhappy to produce only 'façade' designs.

With regards to consultation mechanisms, no direct consultations with existing residents took place because the site is remote from other inhabitants. However, on the eastern water's edge of Sluseholmen sits the old Valby Boat Club, with a series of rented red-painted boathouses with a communal clubhouse. This was originally owned by the Port Authority (later part of By & Havn), which had allowed Copenhageners to rent and use the facility. Initially, this was thought to be in the way of the new development: the area was sold to developers and plans were made for its removal. However, and following a protest by the users, it was bought back by the Port Authority when its social importance was realized. The old clubhouse was demolished and replaced by a new floating one, funded by the developers. The club is self-administered and continues with a long tradition in the city. It serves the nearby residential area and adds a delightfully colourful and active edge to the east of the site.

Regular design development meetings took place as required between the city planners, the developers and the architects. The design process followed the usual processes in the city and included the normal two or three general public consultations.

The changes in the administration of the regeneration company for Copenhagen's waterfront areas in 2007, when the initial Københavns Havn A/S was dissolved and the new Harbour Authority was created – CPH City and Port Development (By & Havn)[13] – contributed to the change in attitude towards the development of the waterfront and the renewed expectations for the places created.

In many cases, it is not unusual for complex development plans such as Sluseholmen to encounter difficulties and constraints in the process of design and implementation. However, in this case, the working relationship between developers and architects was very positive. Initially, developers expressed some difficulty with the first meetings when they had to deal with a different architect within the firm each time. However, from the time that a dedicated project partner was allocated to the project, the rapport was very good.

Although there were many discussions within the planning process, these revolved more around the details of design than with the overall design strategy. The choice of materials was open; but this did not create any problems. The water level can rise or fall by 1.6m, which created design problems for connections to the canals and the design of the bridges, as it needs to allow a minimum head clearance. The basement parking proved expensive and, although similar in cost to other Copenhagen locations, it has been anticipated that some of the next phases of waterfront development in the southern harbour will not feature this.

The three developers also had to carry the cost of removing the pollution from the site, and there was an informal agreement that the developers would pay for the construction of the link bridge. This essential link from north to south is key to completing the main route for vehicles and pedestrians to access the different functions of the south harbour redevelopments.

Given the unattractive appearance and disconnected location of the redundant harbour, the area was slow to attract development under the initial planning strategy. It took until 2004 with the creation of the new vision and revised masterplan before confidence grew and the market was strong enough for the development to be commercially feasible. Responding to commercial strategies, Soeters advised that each building within each perimeter block should not be sold to individual developers, as in the Java Island case in Amsterdam, as this had led to problems when some developers delayed construction or sold their buildings on, leading to the loss of control over the timescale and generating variable construction quality. This advice, together with good project management, enabled the Sluseholmen development to be completed on time and within budget, with planning approvals scheduled for 2004 and construction completed in 2008.

Overall, the process went well mainly due to the involvement of all the key stakeholders from the outset; developers, city authorities and lead architects expressed this during the interviews. Given the complexities of the design with so many stakeholders working together, the big challenge was to ensure that the developers could deliver within the required timescale and according to budget. Complex project management was required and a team of specialists from the architects firm Arkitema also acted as project managers, executing this management task with military precision. However, it is important to highlight that some of the difficulties emerged when the contractors became involved as they were not used to such design complexity and variation, and some may have lost out financially as they had not all anticipated the sophisticated refinement of the design.

Selling the apartments and duplexes was initially a challenge for the agents, who found it difficult to attract buyers to visit a noisy, windy construction site in an old redundant harbour. A full-size floating duplex was constructed which could provide prospective buyers with a first-hand experience of waterside living. This proved successful, especially during the first stages of construction, as it could be located at more attractive locations nearby. The added value of a connection to the water was always a factor in carrying the extra costs of constructing canals. In this case, the developers were very happy that this extra cost was more than covered by the additional value added to the canal duplexes. As confidence grew over the construction, apartment floor areas were increased by 5 to 10 per cent, and sales were going well until the recession that began in 2008. Occupation by April 2010 was around 70 per cent, rising to approximately 80 per cent by March 2011, but with many of the original owners having to rent out to tenants due to the current economic recession.

Construction costs on the first block had to be very tightly controlled, resulting in much repetition of core elements and materials. The group of architects involved in the façade designs were first proposed by Arkitema and vetted or approved by the Port Authority (By & Havn), city planners and developers. The choice of façade materials was slightly constrained initially and no plastic or smooth render was allowed. This was later relaxed and a wider variety of materials and finishes were permitted. However, a vertical emphasis on façade proportions was required. Although each invited architect was allocated a specific apartment building, it later proved desirable to move some around to suit the overall composition within the block (i.e. not have two white buildings together). The design sessions in 'orchestrating' the composition of the amalgamated façades involved Arkitema, Soeters and city planners (who would normally grant approvals). A wide variety of well-known established architects and some younger less-recognized architects were invited to participate. Some of the well-known refused (questioning the ethics), while the younger architects involved took to the exercise with more enthusiasm, especially with the small duplex façades (see Figure 10.6).

Most unusually for such a major urban project, the scheme was completed as envisaged and planned. No major changes were made to the initial design proposals during the process and no significant changes were made to the design during implementation and construction. Clearly, the method of construction using prefabricated modular building elements was necessary to meet the timescale and budget. This allowed for both speed of construction and

Figure 10.6 *Vista along the central curved roadside canal showing the variety of apartment buildings*

Source: Derek Fraser

variety. Moreover, it was the design approach of introducing colour and material variations to the façades that not only widened the availability and supply of materials, but avoided monotony and repetition, providing the scheme with its successful image.

The stakeholders' views of the results

Remarkably, all of the stakeholders involved in the development of Sluseholmen agree that the final design achieved the original strategic objectives by using high-quality design solutions to provide an opportunity for new residents to experience a new quality of life by living close to the water. They also agree that the project not only succeeded in reflecting the initial expectations, once these were fixed and in agreement, but also that Sluseholmen was completed within the timeframe and budget allocated. All of the interviewed stakeholders concurred that the final result exceeded expectations with regards to design and urban quality, as well as economic success, achieving the change of public perception of an area from a derelict ex-industrial location to a new, attractive and desirable quarter of the city. Each of the various teams was very proud of the project and the acclaim that it has received.

Overall, the residential and commercial units have been occupied reasonably quickly. All properties have been sold by the developers to private owners and property companies. The earlier blocks were a little slow; but this speeded up later on as confidence in the success of the area grew. By March 2011, some of the units were still unoccupied, particularly in the latest completed block, with individuals and property companies feeling the pressures of the recession.

Originally, there was no social housing planned for the Sluseholmen development (usually delivered in Denmark by different development companies). In the completed project, only 100 of the 1130 units are designated as social housing. However, with the recession, many units became rented instead of owner occupied, bringing an unplanned social mix to the area.

In retrospect, some would have liked to see Sluseholmen contain more of a mixed use, with places for people to work in the area. The kindergarten was completed during construction; but the planned harbour link bridge connection to other parts of the southern harbour, including the primary school, came later. This caused controversy with residents who claimed that these were intended to be completed following the construction of the first two blocks. Overall, by comparison, the south harbour has 90 per cent residential areas compared to the north harbour's 60 per cent (masterplanned by Adrian Gauze). However, it could be argued that this difference is related to the original visions of 'waterside living' by Soeters and 'dense urban living' by Gauze.

In general, the design is considered a success with its design and planning awards and its popularity with residents. The little criticism received seems to emanate from some architects who question the ethics of separating the façade designs from the building behind. It sparks debate between those who follow the principles of 20th-century modernism and those who see value in learning from the successful place-making of historic cities. Positive reviews highlight the atmosphere, created by a series of imaginative, lively and varied street and canal frontages – in strong contrast to the uniformity of many other contemporary blocks. Involving up to 20 architects designing façades in each block brings a rich variety, both at the scale of the apartment blocks aligning the canal-side roads and the smaller narrower double duplex town houses on the cross canals. This orchestrated medley picks up on the scale and character found in many other harbours and previously employed by Soeters in his design for Java Island development in the Amsterdam Eastern Docklands. Inspiration for this 'variation on a theme' with street façades can be found in cities such as Amsterdam, Venice and Copenhagen's Nyhavn and Chistianshavn districts, where historically the individual buildings developed more accretively.

Reflections and conclusions on the design strategies and development process adopted for Sluseholmen

The interest of this investigation was to understand the relations between the design strategies adopted and the development process. As a result, this concluding section first summarizes the specific design strategies applied in the Sluseholmen development and their results, and then focuses on the process of development.

The large scale of the harbour with an open body of water north of the Sluseholmen site provides the biggest open space and the main genius loci. This aspect is recognized in the design by placing the tallest apartment blocks along the northern edge and adopting a mainly orthogonal grid-iron plan where tangential views are also possible from the side canals (see Figure 10.7). The smaller scale of these side canals provides a spatial contrast from

(a)

(b)

Figure 10.7a and 10.7b
*Courtyard view of double
duplexes and 'Venice' view
from the courtyard across
the canal*

Source: Derek Fraser

Overall, the process went well mainly due to the involvement of all the key stakeholders from the outset; developers, city authorities and lead architects expressed this during the interviews. Given the complexities of the design with so many stakeholders working together, the big challenge was to ensure that the developers could deliver within the required timescale and according to budget. Complex project management was required and a team of specialists from the architects firm Arkitema also acted as project managers, executing this management task with military precision. However, it is important to highlight that some of the difficulties emerged when the contractors became involved as they were not used to such design complexity and variation, and some may have lost out financially as they had not all anticipated the sophisticated refinement of the design.

Selling the apartments and duplexes was initially a challenge for the agents, who found it difficult to attract buyers to visit a noisy, windy construction site in an old redundant harbour. A full-size floating duplex was constructed which could provide prospective buyers with a first-hand experience of waterside living. This proved successful, especially during the first stages of construction, as it could be located at more attractive locations nearby. The added value of a connection to the water was always a factor in carrying the extra costs of constructing canals. In this case, the developers were very happy that this extra cost was more than covered by the additional value added to the canal duplexes. As confidence grew over the construction, apartment floor areas were increased by 5 to 10 per cent, and sales were going well until the recession that began in 2008. Occupation by April 2010 was around 70 per cent, rising to approximately 80 per cent by March 2011, but with many of the original owners having to rent out to tenants due to the current economic recession.

Construction costs on the first block had to be very tightly controlled, resulting in much repetition of core elements and materials. The group of architects involved in the façade designs were first proposed by Arkitema and vetted or approved by the Port Authority (By & Havn), city planners and developers. The choice of façade materials was slightly constrained initially and no plastic or smooth render was allowed. This was later relaxed and a wider variety of materials and finishes were permitted. However, a vertical emphasis on façade proportions was required. Although each invited architect was allocated a specific apartment building, it later proved desirable to move some around to suit the overall composition within the block (i.e. not have two white buildings together). The design sessions in 'orchestrating' the composition of the amalgamated façades involved Arkitema, Soeters and city planners (who would normally grant approvals). A wide variety of well-known established architects and some younger less-recognized architects were invited to participate. Some of the well-known refused (questioning the ethics), while the younger architects involved took to the exercise with more enthusiasm, especially with the small duplex façades (see Figure 10.6).

Most unusually for such a major urban project, the scheme was completed as envisaged and planned. No major changes were made to the initial design proposals during the process and no significant changes were made to the design during implementation and construction. Clearly, the method of construction using prefabricated modular building elements was necessary to meet the timescale and budget. This allowed for both speed of construction and

Figure 10.6 *Vista along the central curved roadside canal showing the variety of apartment buildings*

Source: Derek Fraser

variety. Moreover, it was the design approach of introducing colour and material variations to the façades that not only widened the availability and supply of materials, but avoided monotony and repetition, providing the scheme with its successful image.

The stakeholders' views of the results

Remarkably, all of the stakeholders involved in the development of Sluseholmen agree that the final design achieved the original strategic objectives by using high-quality design solutions to provide an opportunity for new residents to experience a new quality of life by living close to the water. They also agree that the project not only succeeded in reflecting the initial expectations, once these were fixed and in agreement, but also that Sluseholmen was completed within the timeframe and budget allocated. All of the interviewed stakeholders concurred that the final result exceeded expectations with regards to design and urban quality, as well as economic success, achieving the change of public perception of an area from a derelict ex-industrial location to a new, attractive and desirable quarter of the city. Each of the various teams was very proud of the project and the acclaim that it has received.

Overall, the residential and commercial units have been occupied reasonably quickly. All properties have been sold by the developers to private owners and property companies. The earlier blocks were a little slow; but this speeded up later on as confidence in the success of the area grew. By March 2011, some of

On the eastern edge of the site there was an existing row of small boathouses traditionally rented out to residents of Copenhagen, which has been kept. This traditional and colourful activity brings in a different community and adds a vibrant edge to the site.

In summary, had the initial idea of low-cost housing and surface parking been realized, it would have no doubt brought an improvement to the area. However, the more ambitious vision set by the city authorities has resulted in the creation of a high-quality living environment with a forward-looking design solution successfully offering a new vibrant district for which the city is justifiably proud.

The planning and development process

During the first year, the city planners formed a regeneration development company for the southern harbour and worked with private developers who were interested in getting involved due to the building boom. It was this company that started to invest in the infrastructure and the clearing of grounds for the first developments. It was quickly realized, however, that this 'piecemeal' approach was not the best, and following the creation of the south harbour masterplan, various sites were identified and phases planned. With the Sluseholmen site, architects were given commissions from developers (Arkitema by Sjælsø), and in other cases in the south harbour, architects won competitions (Vandkusten at Teglværkshavnen). Four development companies were originally involved with the Slusholmen project, reduced to three by the end of the project. Two construction companies won the tenders and were given a timescale in which the work was to be completed.

The major stakeholders involved were the Copenhagen city planners, the Port Authority (By & Havn), development companies, architects, technicians and engineers. The main developers were invited to be involved in initial discussions about the southern harbour redevelopment by the City of Copenhagen because of their performance record on other projects in the city. In particular, the city invited the developer, and suggested that this company select two or three other development companies with whom to work in order to widen involvement and overcome the tight timescale. The lead architects, Arkitema, also invited other architects to become involved in the design of the façades of both apartment buildings and canal duplexes as part of the design strategy. Most welcomed the opportunity, but a few were unhappy to produce only 'façade' designs.

With regards to consultation mechanisms, no direct consultations with existing residents took place because the site is remote from other inhabitants. However, on the eastern water's edge of Sluseholmen sits the old Valby Boat Club, with a series of rented red-painted boathouses with a communal clubhouse. This was originally owned by the Port Authority (later part of By & Havn), which had allowed Copenhageners to rent and use the facility. Initially, this was thought to be in the way of the new development: the area was sold to developers and plans were made for its removal. However, and following a protest by the users, it was bought back by the Port Authority when its social importance was realized. The old clubhouse was demolished and replaced by a new floating one, funded by the developers. The club is self-administered and continues with a long tradition in the city. It serves the nearby residential area and adds a delightfully colourful and active edge to the east of the site.

Regular design development meetings took place as required between the city planners, the developers and the architects. The design process followed the usual processes in the city and included the normal two or three general public consultations.

The changes in the administration of the regeneration company for Copenhagen's waterfront areas in 2007, when the initial Københavns Havn A/S was dissolved and the new Harbour Authority was created – CPH City and Port Development (By & Havn)[13] – contributed to the change in attitude towards the development of the waterfront and the renewed expectations for the places created.

In many cases, it is not unusual for complex development plans such as Sluseholmen to encounter difficulties and constraints in the process of design and implementation. However, in this case, the working relationship between developers and architects was very positive. Initially, developers expressed some difficulty with the first meetings when they had to deal with a different architect within the firm each time. However, from the time that a dedicated project partner was allocated to the project, the rapport was very good.

Although there were many discussions within the planning process, these revolved more around the details of design than with the overall design strategy. The choice of materials was open; but this did not create any problems. The water level can rise or fall by 1.6m, which created design problems for connections to the canals and the design of the bridges, as it needs to allow a minimum head clearance. The basement parking proved expensive and, although similar in cost to other Copenhagen locations, it has been anticipated that some of the next phases of waterfront development in the southern harbour will not feature this.

The three developers also had to carry the cost of removing the pollution from the site, and there was an informal agreement that the developers would pay for the construction of the link bridge. This essential link from north to south is key to completing the main route for vehicles and pedestrians to access the different functions of the south harbour redevelopments.

Given the unattractive appearance and disconnected location of the redundant harbour, the area was slow to attract development under the initial planning strategy. It took until 2004 with the creation of the new vision and revised masterplan before confidence grew and the market was strong enough for the development to be commercially feasible. Responding to commercial strategies, Soeters advised that each building within each perimeter block should not be sold to individual developers, as in the Java Island case in Amsterdam, as this had led to problems when some developers delayed construction or sold their buildings on, leading to the loss of control over the timescale and generating variable construction quality. This advice, together with good project management, enabled the Sluseholmen development to be completed on time and within budget, with planning approvals scheduled for 2004 and construction completed in 2008.

the open harbour and creates a visual variety from a series of narrow townhouses directly fronting the water without a roadway – accessed from the courtyard. An intermediate scale is provided by the central east–west access road running alongside a canal and curving in such a way as to provide a series of closed vistas. Although there is an access road along the north edge with surface parking and the south for basement parking access, this central route with its shared surface and timber-humped bridges successfully mixes pedestrians, bicycles and vehicles without roadside markings or obtrusive road signs.

The courtyards of each perimeter block vary in size, shape and landscape character, and provide more sheltered semi-private open spaces for residents' communal activities of relaxation and play. In addition, each ground-floor apartment and duplex is given its own terrace, which, although small in size, is still able to accommodate the *al fresco* meal or plant pot collection while serving as a tactical buffer zone. In addition to having a small terrace to the court, the lower duplexes also have direct access to their own canal platform, while the upper duplexes lead to their own private roof garden. Each of the apartment buildings also provides the facility of a roof garden shared by the residents of the building.

Such a clear strategic use of spatial hierarchy succeeds in bringing together various building heights, external spaces, access routes and functions in a solution that provides a balance between order and legibility – variety and surprise.

Employing design refinements, such as bringing water to the edges of the blocks with canals, underground parking and a variety of typologies, succeeds in creating a strong sense of place with a special atmosphere of its own contrasting intimate canal-side locations with framed vistas and open views over the harbour. Many other schemes in such locations adopt the simpler finger block strategy by placing lineal apartment buildings at right angles to the water to enable everyone to have a tangential view. This solution usually involves lower density, and the surrounding windswept space is often given over to car parking.

At the north-eastern corner of the masterplan of the southern harbour, a high-rise residential tower, Metropolis, designed by the English architectural firm Future Systems is located at the head of the Sluseholmen jetty (see Figure 10.8). As part of the design strategy to provide a vertical landmark and a point of reference, it serves this purpose best when approached on the waterbus from the north where its narrow width and 11 storeys make it appear sufficiently taller than the 7-storey heights of the Sluseholmen blocks. Otherwise, the tower remains invisible from other parts of the site due to its dense urban form. Perhaps, on reflection, the design could have benefitted from the addition of some taller structures within the blocks to add more variety and landmarks to the skyline. Arguably, a more successful landmark, which interestingly was not part of the original masterplan, sits horizontally along the eastern water's edge of Sluseholmen. The decision to retain the row of small rented boathouses has created a vibrant activity along the water's edge. A group of local fishermen and boat owners self-manage this community and, with the provision of a clubhouse, attract visitors.

Figure 10.8 *Sluseholmen eastern edge showing existing boathouses and the new landmark 'Metropolis' tower*

Source: Derek Fraser

With regards to understanding the development process, the Sluseholmen case can be analysed from different perspectives. Concerning vision and expectations, part of the success that Sluseholmen achieved in the local sphere is due directly to policy changes made by the city as a result of earlier mistakes along the waterfront in the central harbour. Another contributing factor to its success is the clear vision and strategic approach shared among the stakeholders. This vision satisfied municipal and professional goals, while providing a high-quality design solution, creating a new district for the community and the city. High-quality design also contributed to the economic success of the development, responding to the aims of the investors and developers.

The establishment of the design and development team early in the process also proved important in maintaining the agreed expectations, aims and objectives of the early stages. The design strategies and solutions also responded to the pragmatic criteria of the construction and the required timescale, ensuring the quality of spaces created, such as street canals and courtyards.

Within the process, it is also important to consider that the control achieved by the municipality in generating the masterplan, even if relying on consultants, is related to the fact that the land was owned by the city and there were no major pressures for development due to the public perception of the area as derelict and lacking a neighbourhood identity.

As with any urban projects of this scale, the design strategy can be analysed on several levels, each relating in some way to the three criteria of built form, open space and function. On a pragmatic level in Sluseholmen, this amounts to the adoption of the residential perimeter block with streets, canals and courtyards. It is only through a more detailed analysis and evaluation of the design decisions and final construction that the quality of the overall design can be assessed.

Notes

1   Both authors have specific knowledge and expertise in this area as a result of former and current research work. Since early in his career, Derek Fraser has continued teaching and research connections with the Royal Danish Academy of Fine Arts. His knowledge of design developments in Danish contemporary housing across a number of contexts recently extended into the harbour areas. The Oresund region between Copenhagen and Malmö was one of the focus areas in Dr Soledad Garcia Ferrari's PhD and following research work. Particular focus of this research has been on cases of waterfront development in both cities.

2   Sluseholmen has won three awards: Foreningen til Hovedstadens forskønnelse (Association for Copenhagen's Beautification), first prize to Sluseholmen, in 2007; Københavns Kommunes arkitekturpris (Copenhagen Municipality Architecture Prize) for Sluseholmen, in 2009; and Foreningen af Byplanlæggere (Danish Association of Planners), Byplanprisen, in 2009.

3   The population of Copenhagen Municipality in 2005 was 502,362 inhabitants, while the city and its metropolitan area had a total population of 1,212,485 inhabitants.

4   This report was published by the Danish Ministry of the Interior in January 1989. It was the result of an investigation carried out by an 'initiative group' created by the prime minister. It is established in the report that the main objective of this group was to analyse and evaluate the situation of Copenhagen and to propose initiatives in order to increase the competitiveness of the city in light of the European Union internal market. This report also stated that the government's objective was not to move activities from the rest of the country to Copenhagen, but to seek, develop and attract new activities in the capital city since this would benefit the whole country (Danish Ministry of the Interior in January, 1989).

5   The Harbour Committee was integrated by the Greater Copenhagen Authority, the Port Authority of Copenhagen, the Ministry of Transportation, the Ministry of Environment, academics, private-sector businesses and union officials.

6   The 1992 law established that the board of directors for the Port of Copenhagen should consist of 12 members; 6, including the chairman, were elected by the Danish state, 3 by the Municipality of Copenhagen, 1 by the Chamber of Commerce and 2 by the union of the workers in the harbour.

7   Law 209, 29 April 1913, established this.

8   In 1994 the level of unemployment peaked, reaching 13 per cent in the Municipality of Copenhagen and Vestegnen (west of Copenhagen). Unemployment was particularly high among immigrants (in 1994 it was 25 per cent, while that of Danes was 4 per cent), unskilled labour, the young and the elderly (Hansen et al, 2001).

9   See www.byoghavn.dk/en/OmByoghavn.aspx.

10   Blue Plan (proposed in June 2003 and approved in April 2005) was a debate proposal or a political statement made by the Municipality of Copenhagen, focusing on the need to define the use of the water in the city. This debate was an invitation to discuss ideas and views of physical and administrative changes, as well as activities and events that may take place in the waterfront areas. This plan was an addition to the municipal plan approved in 2001. It is important to highlight that use of the water is the only component of the waterfront that the municipality has absolute control over.

11   Plan-Vision 2010: Studies and Visions of Copenhagen Harbour was released in November 1999 (Københavns Havn, 1999). Following the publication of this plan, the Vision Group

was created, including the Municipality of Copenhagen, the Port of Copenhagen, the Ministry of Environment's Spatial Planning Department and Freja Ejendomme (the state-owned real-estate corporation with a mandate to develop and sell state land).

12   The three following sections present the findings from the interviews. In order to gain a clear understanding of the development process and the priorities in terms of design strategies from each sector, a number of stakeholders involved in the process were interviewed between March and July 2010, representing Copenhagen city officials, developers and design consultants. The interviewees were representatives from the City of Copenhagen Planning Department; the lead development company, Sjælsø; the Copenhagen City and Harbour Authority (By & Havn, City and Harbour Authority); and Arkitema, the lead architectural firm. The semi-structured interviews all followed the same procedure, with a sequence of questions based on three main categories: vision, process and reflection.

13   As explained earlier in the chapter, the newly created By & Havn was the result of merging the original Københavns Havn A/S company and the Ørestad Development Corporation I/S, and it shares ownership between the city and the state.

Part 3

Conclusions

11

Lessons from Shared Experiences in Sustainable Waterfront Regeneration around the North Sea

Harry Smith and Maria Soledad Garcia Ferrari

Introduction

The preceding chapters present in-depth studies of key waterfront regeneration initiatives around the North Sea during the first decade in the 21st century. These experiences vary in size, in the relative strength and powers of stakeholders and in their legal and institutional frameworks, but have been developed within a region which, at the global level, is fairly homogeneous with similar institutional structures and economic and social goals.

The case studies have been written from a range of disciplinary perspectives, providing a wealth of ways of understanding the phenomenon of waterfront regeneration. Instead of mechanistically applying the analytical framework presented in Chapter 2, they focus on specific aspects of this, allowing in-depth exploration of the relevant issues. Collectively, however, they do provide a useful basis to build an overview of waterfront regeneration trends in the region during the last decade, which can serve as a basis for comparisons with other regions in the world, as well as a source of lessons that can be used for reflection in relation to waterfront regeneration elsewhere.

This chapter therefore first presents an overview of key characteristics of recent waterfront regeneration around the North Sea, focusing, in turn, on the three elements used here to analyse urban development: allocative structures, authoritative structures and systems of meaning. This is complemented with a brief analysis from a political economy perspective. Following this, a reflection on the analytical framework proposed and used in this book is provided, looking at potential refinements of the framework and at its applicability as a tool for analysing waterfront regeneration at various scales, from that of the locality up to the regional and even national scales. The chapter ends by considering the key challenges ahead for waterfront developments in the North Sea and around the world.

Lessons from the case studies of waterfront regeneration around the North Sea

The impact of allocative structures

Chapter 3 explored allocative structures around a key resource for urban development – *land* – with a strong focus on the experience in the UK, but also drawing on relevant examples elsewhere around the North Sea. Most examples of major waterfront regeneration projects around the North Sea take place near or relatively near city cores. Examples abound of developments on land that was reclaimed during the port expansion (or creation) period, and reclamation continues to be used during regeneration (e.g. in Edinburgh and Oslo).

Although major port areas tend to be under the ownership of a single landholder, or in some cases a limited number of owners, some of the major waterfront regeneration projects around the North Sea extend beyond the harbour areas and into a range of adjacent land uses, including industrial, residential and mixed use (the latter sometimes being long-established or 'historic' parts of the city). This makes the landownership picture in the region rather complex, and highlights the importance of land-use control systems at the interface between allocative structures and authoritative structures. The cases discussed in this book highlight how control over land-use and land development is key to the success of waterfront regeneration. In cases where land was not all under the control of the authority initiating the regeneration, due to land belonging to either a few large landowners or a multiplicity of smaller landowners (the cases of Edinburgh and Gothenburg's Östra Kvillebäcken, respectively), regeneration has faltered or been slow and complex. Where either most land was under the control of the regeneration authority, or the land that was under such control was used strategically, regeneration proceeded at a good pace and had an impact upon the surrounding area (the cases of HafenCity Hamburg and Gateshead Quays, respectively).

With regards to *funding and finance structures*, the experience observed around the North Sea confirms the growing worldwide trend for private-sector involvement and adoption of market-based mechanisms and organizational forms. However, the cases presented here also highlight the continuing importance of the state in this region – whether local, regional or national – as the initial investor and creator of favourable conditions for the regeneration. The state continues to be the source of any strategic approach and initiator of any long-term vision or visioning process, and through its permanency is in a position to give some continuity to long-term planning and implementation (i.e. allocation of resources to the generation of strategies and visions and to their implementation is crucial, though this does not guarantee the realization of such visions; see, for example, the case of *Dialog Södra Älvstranden* in Chapter 5). This can contribute to the resilience of a project, as is evidenced when contrasting the case of Edinburgh (where the regeneration of the waterfront, very reliant on the private sector, was badly hit by the economic crisis of 2008) with the case of HafenCity Hamburg, where the public development company-driven regeneration has continued – though the crisis affected Germany to a much lesser extent than the UK.

Although the state has continued its strong role around the North Sea (less so in the UK), it has become more entrepreneurial, developing ways of managing its assets in order to help finance and create appropriate conditions to encourage waterfront regeneration. In many cases it has focused its resources on the creation or renewal of appropriate physical infrastructure. In some cases, it has creatively used its control over land (through transferring this to a publicly owned development company, as in Edinburgh or Hamburg, or through land assembly, as in Hull) to use this as a generator of funds to finance such infrastructures. The state has also adopted strong branding and marketing approaches (evident across most of the cases presented here) to attract investment, as well as developing strategic and opportunistic approaches to tapping into sources of public money (as in the case of Gateshead Quays).

Regarding *labour*, the cases of waterfront regeneration around the North Sea follow the general trend of resident (or nearby) port- and industry-related workforces, often unionized, being replaced in the new developments and conversions by a combination of multi-skilled and 'foot-loose' knowledge workers and employees in the service sector. The new 'pieces of city', with their offer of variety and quality in places for living, work and leisure, are being created with a view to attracting such types of workforce. In addition, new jobs are emerging as part of the regeneration process itself, such as the 'social supervisor' and 'floor manager' in the case of Schiedam (see Chapter 4), and as part of the on-going management of regenerated areas, such as the *Wegewart* in HafenCity Hamburg (see Chapter 6) – both of which require appropriate allocation of resources from the agencies responsible for regeneration and urban management.

The cases presented here do not look specifically at *materials* and other construction resources, and this is an area that merits more research. Examples of the impact of globalization upon the 'materiality' of regenerated waterfronts are found around the North Sea, a particularly illustrative one being the use of granite from India to repave the City Hall Square next to Aker Brygge in Oslo, the capital of a country that is rich in granite. This kind of practice is generated by the impact of the allocative structure of the global market. However, as foreseen in Chapter 2, this is increasingly being addressed by building standards stemming from the relevant regulatory authorities (i.e. authoritative structures) mostly at a national level, though there are some examples of waterfront regeneration projects leading the way. Chapter 9 analysed Bo01 in Malmö, which was developed as a model of sustainable urban development. Here the project specified the avoidance of hazardous materials in the construction process, and the use only of materials that could be recycled when the buildings are demolished. HafenCity, presented in Chapter 6, developed its own eco-label certification scheme for individual projects within the waterfront area, two years before a national certification system for sustainable building was approved across Germany. However, besides these two pioneering examples, most of the waterfront regeneration projects included in this book have been subject to national standards, which are becoming increasingly stringent.

With regards to *energy*, the regeneration initiatives covered in this book have been designed and/or implemented at a time (the first decade of the 21st century) during which the mental model of the zero carbon economy has gained wide acceptance in the countries around the North Sea, and has become recognized in legislation towards lowering greenhouse gas emissions. The response to the relatively fast-changing regulatory environment in these regeneration projects has therefore evolved during the decade, with many significant initiatives in this area having been developed after the Waterfront Communities Project closed. Again, Bo01 in Malmö stands out as a pioneering project that specifically addressed this issue from the outset. Here the aim was to achieve all electricity supply locally through harnessing renewable sources, by means of solar panels built on top of some of the buildings, and one of Sweden's largest wind turbines. It was a pilot project which showed an underestimation of energy consumption in the houses once occupied, and as such helped to refine the methods used for such calculations in subsequent developments. HafenCity has also pioneered responses to lowering carbon emissions by developing a system of combined remote and local district heating systems, which use a range of renewable sources of energy. Heating supply for western and eastern HafenCity, respectively, has been contracted out to companies that had to meet strict conditions regarding maximum levels of emissions. In the Port of Leith, during 2011, the feasibility of a biomass combined heat and power plant was being considered, which would not only provide electricity to Edinburgh, but also feed a district heating system in the waterfront. In all of these cases, proposed and implemented local but centralized systems have been facilitated by the concentration of the development initiative within the hands of a single large landowner or developer: there is less experience of more decentralized approaches in these waterfronts.

One element that might have increasingly been expected to feature prominently in the skyline of waterfront developments is wind turbines. There are limited examples of these directly in the waterfronts included in this book (e.g. Malmö); but what has become evident during the last few years is that the harnessing of wind power has become a major priority around the North Sea, and that this is being approached on an industrial scale rather than at a decentralized local scale. Waterfronts in the region are therefore becoming the arena for competition over their use, as they are now being sought after as platforms for construction, assembly and shipping of wind turbines destined for large offshore windfarms, as well as to provide the infrastructure for land-based connections to energy grids once the windfarms are operational. We return to this point in 'Challenges ahead' at the end of this chapter.

Finally, all of the above are linked to changes in *institutional resources*, which have been evidenced in the cases of waterfront regeneration studied here. In most cases, implementation of the regeneration has required, first and foremost, investment in organizational restructuring (e.g. creation of dedicated waterfront departments and offices within the local authorities, including information and dissemination centres, as well as creation of new types of post) and the creation of new organizations (such as publicly owned development companies). These substantial changes in allocative structures evidence the significance attached to the regeneration of waterfronts in these cities. These changes have been possible through the intervention of the authoritative structures, as we see next.

Evolving authoritative structures

The case study chapters in this book illustrate two fundamental shifts which are taking place in authoritative structures that have a bearing on waterfront regeneration: the increasing engagement of the private sector in regeneration activities, and the widening and diversification of forms of public involvement, engagement and participation.

Although waterfront regeneration around the North Sea is primarily driven by public-sector initiatives, it is increasingly using private-sector approaches to this activity through:

- changing the operational mode of what were previously public-sector agencies, such as port authorities (e.g. Aalborg, Edinburgh, Oslo);
- establishing new companies to manage what were previously public-sector assets (e.g. Edinburgh, Hamburg, Hull); and/or
- engaging with the private sector as a partner in developing the waterfront.

There is a diversity of approaches, depending upon specific contexts and waterfront histories; indeed, some of the case studies combine all of these approaches. The common thread is the increasing adoption of private-sector and market-driven approaches in regeneration processes. This appears to be in keeping with worldwide trends.

What may be more distinctive about the North Sea experience in waterfront regeneration, in terms of authoritative structures, is the widening of civic engagement. The form that this takes again is very much influenced by the specific context. The cases of Hamburg and Gothenburg, for example, illustrate the differences in approach that can occur depending upon the existing stakeholders – including residents. These also depend upon how such stakeholders are defined, as 'local' (i.e. on or adjacent to the land affected by regeneration) or more widely at city or even regional level. National trajectories in civic engagement in planning and in governance, in general, have a strong influence on how civil society is engaged in the planning, implementation and long-term management of waterfront regeneration. Chapter 4 reflects the tradition of consensual governance that has been long established in The Netherlands. Experimentation with the role of a 'social supervisor' to connect the authoritative structures with citizens during planning and implementation must be seen in this context. Other figures are being tested elsewhere for the long-term management and maintenance of spaces created through waterfront regeneration, such as that of a designated person who is in charge of overseeing the maintenance of quality and amenity of public space, and is a point of contact in this regard for the public at HafenCity and the first pilot neighbourhood improvement district (NID) (Steilshoop), both in Hamburg. In the UK, growing community activism and the legal basis for this can be seen not only in the state-supported community-based organizations which are increasingly common in urban regeneration projects, but also in active citizen groups that contest developments and propose alternatives.

Underpinning this wealth of experience in civic engagement, mostly channelled through state-regulated and initiated mechanisms, is the social democratic polity which emerged and became consolidated in Northern and

Western Europe, largely during the 20th century. This socio-economic model, with its various manifestations in the different countries in the region, is fairly unique in global terms. The implications of this model in terms of the goals of waterfront regeneration and the means whereby these are achieved are key distinctive features of this activity around the North Sea, in comparison with other parts of the world. This is manifested in locally specific ways in the region, based on the historic trajectory of nations and territories, and on the various legal and institutional frameworks. As seen in Chapter 3, these frameworks divide European countries into several 'legal families' with their respective approaches to land-use planning – and therefore to urban development and regeneration – and importantly linked to particular 'mental models'.

In the development of approaches to wider participation in waterfront regeneration in this region, the mental models of representative democracy and the state as guarantor of the public good are still very strong. In this context, the mostly state-initiated participatory processes seen in the case study chapters show a high degree of experimentation in ways of achieving communication between different stakeholders and generating ideas, which can be a rich vein for future waterfront regeneration processes. However, there is very limited empowerment of other stakeholders outside the state, other than the companies set up by the state. Strategic decisions are still kept very much within the control of the elected government bodies and their officials, with more local and lower-scale areas of decision-making being opened up more to community involvement. Even at this level, the amount of delegated power or control (in Arnstein's and Davidson's terms, respectively) is limited. In this regard, experiences from elsewhere, such as Brazil's participatory budgeting, can offer ideas for further restructuring of authoritative (and allocative) structures in waterfront regeneration around the North Sea.

Shared and context-specific systems of meaning

The underlying socio-economic model seen above also underpins the discourses that accompany waterfront regeneration around the North Sea. The preceding chapters show how places such as Aalborg, Copenhagen, Edinburgh, Hamburg, Odense and Schiedam are striving to create extensions to the city (thus, the focus on the mixed use, medium-density physical model), including a mix of affordable housing. 'Integration' with the surrounding urban areas, particularly where these are seen as deprived and therefore with the potential to benefit from the new development, is a core element in the prevailing official discourse in some of the case study cities. Although there are apparent exceptions to this, such as that of Gateshead Quays, even here the focus on culture-led development and the strategy of attracting real-estate investment at the higher end of the market is part of a larger city-wide regeneration strategy that seeks the improvement of quality of life across all social sectors. Potentially in tension with this goal of integration is the aim to create areas with their own identity. This is sometimes for the waterfront development as a whole, and in other cases, where these developments are particularly large, for smaller neighbourhoods within the overall scheme which are designed to have their own character – as in the 'quarters' that HafenCity Hamburg is divided into, the 'character areas' used in the masterplan for Granton Harbour, Edinburgh, or the case of Sluseholmen area in Copenhagen's waterfront.

This discourse is related to that of the recovery of civic life, now linked to provision for amenity and leisure activities, which form an increasing part of the economy in North Sea countries. A physical or design manifestation of this is the increasing importance attached to the amount, quality, diversity and use of public space, expanding our understanding of this to include 'blue space', as is illustrated in the case of Aalborg. Connections with this 'blue space' are explored at three different levels in the case study cities:

1   at the macro-level, reconnecting city and water (e.g. Edinburgh, Gateshead and Odense);
2   at the meso-level, connecting public spaces with the water (e.g. Aalborg, Hamburg and Oslo); and
3   at the micro-level, connecting buildings with the water (e.g. Aalborg and Copenhagen).

The importance attached to 'connections' and to 'civic life' has led to public space being central to most waterfront developments in the North Sea region, though notably less so in the examples from the UK. However, the approach to public space varies greatly across the case studies. In Odense, this was defined first, with blocks and buildings coming later. In HafenCity Hamburg, the approach was to invest heavily in key 'flagship' public spaces provided by the development company to help draw in people from elsewhere in the city. In Edinburgh, an overall framework for distribution and general form of public space was provided by means of the initial masterplan in Granton (and development framework in Leith); but the detailed design and development of such spaces have been left to the individual landowners – subject to the statutory planning process. In Gateshead Quays, investment focused initially on the buildings, with public spaces coming later, the opposite of the experience in Odense. Finally, the balance between public and private space also varies, with interesting examples being the approach taken in HafenCity to blur the boundaries between the two, making many privately owned spaces generally accessible and to the same standard as public space, and that taken in Copenhagen's Sluseholmen, where small private gardens flow into a larger communal space, with privacy being marked more by personalization than by actual physical or visual barriers.

As a result of all this, it can be argued that distinctive features of the discourse in relation to waterfront regeneration around the North Sea and the physical manifestations of these are a focus on creating 'pieces of city' which are accessible to all sectors of society, and which include a range of spaces, often connected to the water, from civic to domestic. This can, perhaps, be contrasted with notable examples of waterfront regeneration elsewhere in the world, ranging from that of Shanghai's waterfront (where world-class business and high end of the market real estate are the focus) to that of Guayaquil in Ecuador (where regeneration of the promenade has resulted in the semi-privatization of public space, according to its critics).

Finally, another distinctive strand shared across all these waterfronts, though not unique to the region, is the recovery of the port identity of cities through the regeneration of these areas, which in many cases had been unused or increasingly rundown for decades. This is being achieved through the use of heritage and the (re)construction of narratives that link the city, or its waterfront, to past histories of trading and port-related industries. This is manifested physically in the re-use of old buildings – often as information centres, venues for events or cultural hubs – and integration of industrial and port heritage within the new designs, such as the almost ubiquitous cranes. And it is also expressed in the publications and other media produced as part of the marketing and awareness-raising campaigns. In some cases, this is being used to try to change the perception of the city's identity as a whole (though effecting this change depends largely upon the actual physical success of the waterfront development on the ground), and in others it is reinforcing the already existing strong mental model of the city as a port, as is the case in Hamburg.

A political economy perspective

As alluded to above, the socio-democratic polity around the North Sea appears to be a highly influential 'structure' in the way in which waterfront regeneration is being approached in this part of the world. The institutional structure that developed in Western and Northern Europe during its centuries of world hegemony set the context, and this structure continues to develop, partly responding to pressures from globalization (largely underpinning the increasing role of the private sector) and partly reacting to social demands (largely pushing for wider civic engagement).

Although these processes are taking place, comparatively in world terms the state continues to be a strong player around the North Sea, supported by well-established taxation systems and a citizenry that expects and demands some form of welfare state to be in place. The strong position in the world economy achieved by this part of the world through centuries of worldwide trading, colonial and post-colonial expansion, as well as through its early industrialization, continues today through its strong role in world trade, finance and the knowledge economy. This provides the possibility – both material and institutional – for the type of waterfront regeneration that has been discussed here. This, however, is changing in the context of shifts in trading patterns and the balance of economic power across the world, as is seen in the final section of this chapter.

One of the things that the waterfront regeneration cases studied here shows is that global economic processes, such as the changing patterns in the flow of goods and capital around the world, encounter local histories, political and institutional structures, and physical infrastructures, which mediate the impact of such flows upon local development. The worldwide changes in waterborne trade, which have brought about the obsolescence of old port facilities, as well as industrial decline through migration of production elsewhere, have had different consequences at the local level, depending upon the local political economy as well as national and regional contexts. Indeed, such changes have not always led to overall decline of port activity as a whole, but in some cases have been linked to actual increase in port activity, fuelled by increasing concentration of transoceanic shipping routes in fewer strategic ports.

The cities studied here have initiated the regeneration of their waterfronts from very different starting points. With the risk of simplifying somewhat, it can be said that some have started from a position of strength, where the challenge has been to harness their healthy economy to channel resources and vision into their waterfronts. Such are the cases of Hamburg, with its continuing strong port activity; Edinburgh, with its strong position as an international financial centre; and Oslo, with the revenues generated by North Sea oil. Others have used the regeneration of their waterfront as an opportunity to change the perception of the city and to attract investment, as is exemplified by Gateshead.

The role of national and regional political and economic priorities and strategies has also been important in some cases. The regeneration of Malmö's waterfront was possible as part of the wider regional (and transnational) strategy of developing the Oresund region, with major investment in infrastructure, such as the bridge linking Denmark and Sweden, being key to its success. The conditions for the regeneration of HafenCity were established when the reunification of Germany and the resuming of economic links between Western and Eastern Europe put Hamburg in a strategically advantageous position as gateway to a large hinterland. In summary, these cases clearly show that an understanding of the political economy at various geographic levels, linked to the institutional approach used here, helps to explain the drivers for, potential of and levels of success of waterfront regeneration and development initiatives.

The relevance of the analytical framework in understanding waterfront regeneration around the world

As was explained in Chapter 2, the analytical framework proposed in this book has not been applied in a mechanistic fashion throughout the case study chapters, which each provided a focus on some of the issues addressed by the framework. It has, however, been useful to provide insights at the detailed level explored within the case studies, as well as to articulate an overview, as presented above. Application of the framework repeatedly showed how there are close connections between allocative structures, authoritative structures and systems of meaning, the understanding of which can be as helpful as the explanatory power of each of these types of relations alone.

On reflection, one of these types of relations – systems of meaning – has the potential to be developed further to become a more precise and structured heuristic tool. As defined in Chapter 2, its application to the case studies was, in practice, more fluid and perhaps more difficult to focus than that of the concepts of allocative and authoritative structures. Part of the difficulty derives from its links to the other two types of relations, which paradoxically contribute to its usefulness as a line of enquiry. Another part of the difficulty lies in the nature of planning, urban design and architecture as activities and as products. Here systems of meaning (e.g. frames of reference, ideology, rationalities and discourses, as seen in Chapter 2) are not limited to their verbalization in documents, marketing material, debates and so on, but become embedded in the actual urban developments and buildings, which can to some extent then be 'read'. A case in point is that of public space, which in the cases analysed in this book has been shown to reflect different rationalities that not only appertain to the authoritative structures which have created the legal and procedural conditions for their shaping, but also respond to deeply embedded socio-cultural norms that are context specific, as well as to innovative discourses proposed by designers.

A clear lesson emerging from the application of this framework to our understanding of waterfront regeneration around the North Sea is that, although global forces provide drivers for such regeneration (here as elsewhere), there is a layer of institutional density that moderates the direction, pace and form of change. An important part of the learning experience during the Waterfront Communities Project was about how the different political economy conditions, allocative and authoritative structures, and systems of meaning among the various project partners posed different sets of challenges and possible solutions. It became clear that there was scope to learn from each other through exposure to the different systems and questioning of each other's own systems, but limited scope for direct transfer of mechanisms and processes. It was necessary to understand the context of each partner's experiences, de-contextualize these to extract key principles and lessons, and re-contextualize in each partner's own situation. The analytical framework proposed in this book is seen as a tool to aid such context-aware and sensitive learning processes.

Despite the differences between these case studies, the analytical framework has enabled the exploration of similar waterfront regeneration experiences across the North Sea, as set out earlier in this chapter. The 'identity' of North Sea waterfront regeneration could be more clearly defined by comparison with that of similar experiences elsewhere; but at the time of writing there is a dearth of studies of waterfront regeneration at the scale of world regions. Publications on waterfront regeneration tend to focus on single cases, either as monographic papers and books or as edited collections of cases from across the world. An exception are the volumes edited by Carmona (2003a, 2003b) on globalization and city ports, rather than on waterfront regeneration, focusing, in turn, on the Northern and Southern Hemispheres; but these do not provide a characterization of waterfront regeneration at the scale of regions (such as, for example, Western Europe or Latin America). The analytical framework used in this book could provide a platform for comparative studies of waterfront regeneration experiences across different regions of the world.

Challenges ahead

Having presented key experiences in waterfront regeneration around the North Sea during the first decade of this century, we conclude by looking at the challenges ahead for continuing and future urban development in these locations, many of which are relevant to developments elsewhere.

Progress in the development of the North Sea waterfronts analysed in this book was affected by the global economic crisis of 2008. The effects of this crisis varied, however, largely depending upon the exposure of national economies to the slowdown. In the UK, for example, development of the Edinburgh waterfront slowed down dramatically, with completions dwindling. This had a negative impact upon the valuation of the landholdings in the areas marked for regeneration. The City of Edinburgh Council had to explore innovative ways of funding infrastructure, based on expected future business rates. In contrast, development in HafenCity Hamburg, within a strong national German economy that continued to create employment, carried on unabated. This continued to underpin the strong position of the development company in imposing strict conditions upon developers.

The bigger challenge for North Sea waterfronts, however, may be the long-term change in the global economy production and trading patterns. During the initial decades of displacement of port activity away from central harbour areas, which freed up land for regeneration, the North Sea continued to be a major hub in world shipping trade. However, during the first decade of the 21st century, the number of North Sea ports among the ten busiest in the world dropped from three to one.[1] This is related not only to growth in ports and port activity in Asia, but also to the increasing concentration of trade in strategic ports. Although the economies underpinning waterfront regeneration around the North Sea have diversified, it remains to be seen to what extent a reduction in the world standing of shipping to and from this area may affect its overall economy and, therefore, continuing regeneration.

Decarbonizing the economy is another major challenge affecting waterfront regeneration. Some of the countries around the North Sea are at the forefront of exploring ways of producing more sustainable built environments through policy, regulation and fiscal incentives. As seen earlier in this chapter, Bo01 in Malmö is a cutting edge example of low-energy settlement planning, specifically designed for the North Sea climate. This level of experimentation is, however, not yet the norm, and there is scope for much more innovation in the production of zero-carbon waterfront settlements, for which increasingly stringent regulations are already setting the scene.

A factor that has emerged during recent years is that large-scale generation of renewable energy may become a competitor for land around North Sea waterfronts. The European Union has very ambitious goals for offshore wind energy generation, and windfarms are now being planned and built at further distances and in deeper waters, posing new challenges in terms of logistics. There are two approaches to the production of such facilities, one based on the assembly of wind turbines on land, the other based on partial or full assembly of wind turbines at sea. Germany's massive programme of offshore windfarm construction has led to four of its North Sea and Baltic ports having been transformed into key logistical and supply centres. The case of Bremerhaven, by the North Sea, shows an old port economy that was in decline being regenerated by a concentration of different windfarm production-related activities (research, manufacture and assembly), which has been given access to land and municipal support. The UK's even larger drive to increase its offshore wind energy production is requiring the provision of onshore facilities for the assembly and 'shipping' of turbines, as well as for the connection and distribution of the power generated by these to the mainland. In Hull, a large site adjacent to those regenerated through mixed-use developments (see Chapter 3) has been allocated for this kind of use, thus retaining it for industrial use rather than offering scope for further expansion of the city.

A major aim of such decarbonizing of the economy, of course, is the mitigation of climate change and sea-level rise. Most waterfront cities around the North Sea are heavily exposed to sea-level rise, and responding to this is a key challenge. Responses are already being put forward at different scales, ranging from planning to urban and architectural design. As seen in Chapter 3, the potential of scenarios such as retreating from sea-level rise, defending existing settlements and advancing into the sea using a variety of design approaches has been explored in Hull and elsewhere. Waterfront regeneration is increasingly being seen within a wider context of coastal management; but this has not generally affected the production of more responsive and resilient urban waterfront layouts.

HafenCity Hamburg does provide examples of solutions being tested at the urban design and architectural scales due to the fact that it is located in a stretch of the River Elbe which is prone to flooding, and this new neighbourhood is not within the area protected by the city's flood defences. These solutions include the use of floating pontoons for public spaces, stepped cross-sections at ground level raising all buildings above the maximum expected level of floods and sacrificing part of the public space to the river during flooding episodes, and the use of panels that seal off commercial premises on the promenades in such events. These measures had already been put to the test by flooding episodes on more than one occasion by the end of the decade.

A challenge that is increasingly being acknowledged in cities where ports are still very active is that of achieving fuller integration between city and port in a variety of ways. This includes strengthening institutional links and achieving synergies in transport, energy and waste. Highly relevant to this striving for 'symbiosis' is the concept of industrial ecology, which sees industrial processes as closed-loop systems, where waste from one process can become an input for another.

Linked to this concept is the idea of port development which is integrated with local, national, regional and international economic and development policies, seeking a large-scale approach to port regionalization. Although the local economic impact of port activities in most European port cities is decreasing – commonly through deindustrialization, containerization and increased use of automated port handling technologies – regional impacts, however, appear to have gained in importance, with increasing development of port networks, regional calculation of economic impact and nodal gateways (Dooms and Verbeke, 2007). In this context, port regionalization is seen as an approach to defining logistic sites, multimodal transhipment centres, primary and secondary logistics zones, and logistics poles (Notteboom and Rodrigue, 2005). These changes at regional level may also have an effect on each specific waterfront area in the near future, generating new pressures and dynamics for development.

Finally, returning to Shaw's (2001) suggestion that a fourth generation of post-industrial waterfront development may be emerging at the beginning of the 21st century (see Chapter 1), the cases we have seen around the North Sea do not necessarily constitute a generation of ideas that radically break from the past in terms of allocative and authoritative structures, but rather continue an evolution already begun in previous generations towards higher use of market mechanisms and partnerships. Perhaps the most innovative aspects demonstrated by some of the case studies have been in experimenting with forms of visioning and engaging different stakeholders, though there is scope for further development of these, particularly in relation to carrying through to implementation and ensuring continuing engagement of stakeholders in a meaningful way. The aim of achieving a strong identity is also evident in these experiences, sometimes drawing on the 'local' through heritage, other times through innovation. And key to achieving this identity, as well as to achieving a 'liveable' urban development, has been the role of public space, as seen above. But Shaw may be right in suggesting that rethinking resource use may be a key focus for innovation in new generations of waterfront developments. The practice emerging during the latter years of the experiences analysed in this book suggest that what characterizes a new generation of waterfront regeneration projects may be precisely how they deal with the challenges that have just been described, including developing low carbon solutions, dealing with sea-level rise and striving for integration. These are not purely technical matters, however, and they will require creativity in the design of appropriate allocative and authoritative structures, as well as the development of radical ideas.

Note

1   Port activity data from www.bts.gov/publications/americas{lowbar}container{lowbar}ports/ 2009/html/table{lowbar}05.html (accessed 20 July 2011).

References

Aalborg Kommune (1999) *Fjordkataloget: Aalborg Kommunes Fjordkyster,* www.aalborgkommune.dk/images/teknisk/B&M/PDF/PlanVis/stadark/fjord.kat/Fjordk99.pdf

Aalborg Kommune (2004) *Visioner for Aalborg Havnefront,* Aalborg, Denmark

Aalborg Kommune (2005) *Forslag til Hovedstruktur 2005,* Aalborg, Denmark

Andersson, L. and Kiib, H. (2007) 'Multifaceted programming and hybrid urban domain', in H. Kiib (ed) *Harbourscape,* Aalborg University Press, Aalborg, Denmark

Arnstein, S. (1969) 'A ladder of citizen participation', *Journal of the American Institute of Planners,* vol 35, pp. 216–44

Bachelard, G. (1964) *The Poetics of Space,* Orion Press, New York, NY

Bader, M., Obermeyer, K., and Rick, M. (2009) 'Aalborg catalyst' in H. Kiib (ed) *Architecture and Spaces of the Experience City,* Aalborg University, Aalborg, Denmark

Baggesen Klitgaard, M. (2002) *Policy-Convergence in Scandinavian Welfare States,* Aalborg University, Denmark

Barke, M. and Harrop, K. (1994) 'Selling the industrial town: Identity, image and illusion', in J. R. Gold and S. V. Ward (eds) *Place Promotion: The Use of Publicity and Marketing to Sell Towns and Regions,* John Wiley & Sons, Chichester, UK

Bialecka, E., Rehal, S. and Strömberg, K. (2006) 'Dialog Södra Älvstranden: Analys av dialogprocessen, bilaga 3, utvärdering av Dialog Södra Älvstranden', Stadsbyggnadskontoret (City Planning Office), Gothenburg, Sweden

Bo01 City of Tomorrow (2001) *European Housing Expo and Exhibition Main Report,* City of Malmö, Malmö, Sweden

Bohme, K. (2002) *Nordic Echoes of European Spatial Planning,* Nordregio, Sweden

Breen, A. and Rigby, D. (1996) *The New Waterfront: A Worldwide Urban Success Story,* Thames & Hudson, London and McGraw-Hill, New York, NY

Breen, A. and Rigby, D. (1997) *Waterfronts: Cities Reclaim Their Edge,* second edition, The Waterfront Press, Washington, DC

Brown, B., Perkin, D. and Brown, G. (2003) 'Place attachment in a revitalizing neighbourhood: Individual and block levels of analysis', *Journal of Environmental Psychology,* vol 23, pp. 259–71

Bruttomesso, R. (1993) *Waterfronts: A New Frontier for Cities on Water,* International Centre Cities on Water, Venice, Italy

Bruttomesso, R. (ed) (1995) *Cities on Water and Transport,* International Centre Cities on Water, Venice, Italy

Bruttomesso, R. (2001) 'Complexity on the urban waterfront', in R. Marshall (ed) *Waterfronts in Post-Industrial Cities,* Spon Press, London and New York, NY

Building Futures RIBA and ICE (Institution of Civil Engineers) (2009) *Facing up to Rising Sea Levels: Retreat? Defend? Attack?,* Building Futures RIBA and Institution of Civil Engineers, London

Carlberg, N. and Christensen, S. M. (2005) *Byliv og Havnefront,* Museum Tusculanums Forlag, Copenhagen, Denmark

Carley, M. and Garcia Ferrari, S. (eds) (2007) *The Cool Sea: The Waterfront Communities Project Toolkit,* Edinburgh, UK, www.waterfrontcommunitiesproject.org/toolkit.html

Carley, M., Jenkins, P. and Smith, H. (eds) (2001) *Urban Development and Civil Society: The Role of Communities in Sustainable Cities,* Earthscan, London and Sterling, VA

Carmona, M. (ed) (2003a) *Globalization and City Ports: The Response of City Ports in the Northern Hemisphere (Globalization, Urban Form and Governance 9),* Delft University Press, Delft, The Netherlands

Carmona, M. (ed) (2003b) *Globalization and City Ports: The Response of City Ports in the Southern Hemisphere (Globalization, Urban Form and Governance 10)*, Delft University Press, Delft, The Netherlands

Carr, D. (1985) 'Phenomenology and relativism', in W. S. Hamrick (ed) *Phenomenology in Practice and Theory*, Martinus Nijhoff Publishers, Dordrecht, Boston and Lancaster

Cars, G. and Strömberg, K., (2005) 'Spelet om staden: Att göra sin röst hörd', in F. Gun (ed) *Spelet om Staden*, Swedish Research Council Formas, Stockholm, Sweden

Castells, M. (1996) *The Rise of the Network Society,* Blackwell, Oxford, UK

Chung, C., Koolhaas, R. and Cha, T.W. (2001) *Harvard Design School Guide to Shopping*, Taschen, Köln, Germany

Città d'Acqua (2007) *Città Portuali e Waterfront Urbani. Ricerca Bibliografica*, Centro Internazionale Città d'Acqua, Venice, Italy

City of Edinburgh Council (2011) *Waterfront and Leith Area Development Framework (Draft)*, City of Edinburgh Council, Edinburgh

City of Malmö (2005) 'Welfare provision for all – the twin obligation', City of Malmö, Malmö, Sweden

CONCERN Inc. (2002) *Placemaking: Tools for Community Action*, CONCERN Inc., Environment Simulation Center, Washington, DC

Couch, C., Fraser, C. and Percy, S. (2003) *Urban Regeneration in Europe*, Blackwell Science Ltd, Oxford, UK

Cuthbert, A. R. (2007) 'Urban design: Requiem for an era – review and critique of the last 50 years', *Urban Design International*, vol 12, pp. 177–223

Czarniawska, B. (2000) *A City Reframed: Managing Warsaw in the 1990s*, Harwood Academic, Amsterdam, The Netherlands

Czarniawska, B. (2004) *On Time, Space and Action-Nets*, Göteborg Research Institute, Gothenburg, Sweden

Danish Ministry of the Interior (1989) *The Capital: What Should We Do about It?*, Danish Ministry of the Interior, Copenhagen, Denmark

Danish Royal Ministry of Foreign Affairs (2002) *Denmark*, Danish Government, Denmark

Davidson, S. (1998) 'Spinning the wheel of empowerment', *Planning*, 3 April, pp. 14–15

de Haan, H. (2003) 'The Port of Amsterdam', in M. Carmona (ed) *Globalization and City Ports: The Response of City Ports in the Northern Hemisphere*, Delft University Press, Delft, The Netherlands

de Vries, J. (1984) *European Urbanization 1500–1800*, Methuen & Co Ltd, London

Desfor, G. (2008) 'The city walks on water: The social production of Toronto's Port Industrial District', Paper presented at the Conference on *Fixity and Flow of Urban Waterfronts*, Hamburg, 10–11 October 2008

Desfor, G. and Jorgensen, J. (2004) 'Flexible urban governance: The case of Copenhagen's recent waterfront development', *European Planning Studies*, vol 12, no 4, pp. 479–96

Desfor, G. and Laidley, J. (2011) 'Introduction: Fixity and flow of urban waterfront change', in G. Desfor, J. Laidley, Q. Stevens and D. Schubert (eds) *Transforming Urban Waterfronts: Fixity and Flow*, Routledge, New York and London

Desfor, G., Jennefer, L., Stevens, Q. and Schubert, D. (eds) (2010) *Transforming Urban Waterfronts: Fixity and Flow*, Routledge, New York, NY, and Abingdon, UK

Dooms, M. and Verbeke, A. (2007) 'Stakeholder management in ports: A conceptual framework integrating insights from research in strategy, corporate social responsibility and port management', Paper presented at the Annual Conference of the International Association of Maritime Economists (IAME), Athens, Greece, 2007

Dovey, K. (2005) *Fluid City: Transforming Melbourne's Urban Waterfront*, Routledge, London

Eckstut, S. (1986) 'Solving complex urban design problems' in A. R. Fitzgerald (ed) *Waterfront Planning and Development*, American Society of Civil Engineers, New York, NY, pp54–57, cited in Gordon, D. L. A. (1996) 'Planning, design and managing change in urban waterfront redevelopment', *Town Planning Review*, vol 67, no 3, pp. 261–90

EIB (European Investment Bank) (2009) *Joint European Support for Sustainable Investment in City Areas: Hamburg, Evaluation Study, Final Report*, EIB, Luxemburg

Ellin, N. (1996) *Postmodern Urbanism*, Blackwell Publishers Ltd, Cambridge, MA, and Oxford

European Commission (1997) *The EU Compendium of Spatial Planning Systems and Policies*, Office for the Official Publications of the European Communities, Luxembourg

European Commission (1999) *The EU Compendium of Spatial Planning Systems and Policies; The Netherlands*, Office for the Official Publications of the European Communities, Luxembourg

Falk, N. (undated) *Turning the Tide*, www.urbed.com/cgi-bin/get_binary_doc_object. cgi?doc_id=215&fname=extra_pdf_1.pdf, accessed 28 May 2008

Feld, S. and Basso, K. (1996) *Senses of Place*, School of American Research Press, Santa Fe, NM

Findlay, A. and Sparks, L. (2008) *The Retail Knowledge Base Planning Briefing Paper 10: Business Improvement Districts (BIDs)*, Institute for Retail Studies, University of Stirling, Stirling, UK

Fjordbykontoret (2004) *Oslo Sjøfront 2030: Program for 3 Fremtidsbilder-Oslo-Charrette, 1–5 November 2004*, Oslo, Norway

Florida, R. (2002) *The Rise of the Creative Class: And How It's Transforming Work, Leisure, Community & Everyday Life*, Basic Books, New York, NY

Florida, R. (2004) 'Cities and the creative class', *B and M*, vol 31, pp. 98–112

Flyvbjerg, B. (1988) 'Empowering civil society: Habermas, Foucault and the question of conflict', in M. Douglass and J. Friedmann (eds) *Cities for Citizens: Planning and the Rise of Civil Society in a Global Age*, John Wiley & Sons, Chichester, UK

Forsemalm, J. (2007) *Bodies, Bricks and Black Boxes: Power Practices in City Conversion*, Digressiv Produktion, Gothenburg, Sweden

Fortuin, K. and de Meere, F. (2004) *Advies Sociaal Supervisorschap Inverdan* [*Advice on Inverdan Social Supervision*], Verwey-Jonker Institute, Utrecht, The Netherlands

Freien und Hansestadt Hamburg (2003) *Sprung über die Elbe/Leap Across the Elbe*, Documentation of the International Design Workshop, Hamburg

Garcia Ferrari, M. S. (2006) *What Mediates the Impacts of Globalization on Urban Form and Physical Infrastructure in Specific Contexts? Case Studies of the River Plate and Oresund*, PhD thesis, Heriot-Watt University, Edinburgh

Garcia Ferrari, S., Jenkins, P. and Smith, H. (2007) *On the Waterfront: Making Successful Places within Waterfronts*, Waterfront Communities Project, Edinburgh, UK

Gateshead Council (2003) *Gateshead Central Area: The Public Realm*, Gateshead Council, Gateshead, UK

Gehl Architects (1998) *Byrum and Byliv – Aker Brygge* [*Public Space and Public Life in Aker Brygge*], Oslo

Gehl, J. (2007) 'Public spaces for a changing public life', *Topos*, vol 61, pp. 16–22

Gehl, J. and Gemzøe, L. (2000) *New Public Spaces*, Danish Architectural Press, Copenhagen, Denmark

Gehl, J., Reigstad, S. and Johansen Kaefer, L. (2004) 'Nærkontakt med huse' *Arkitekten*, vol 9, Arkitektens Forlag (translated to English as 'Close encounters with buildings')

Gehl, J., Gemzøe, L., Kirknaes, S. and Soendergaard, B. (2006) *New City Life*, The Danish Architectural Press, Copenhagen, Denmark

GENECON (2008) *Hull Citybuild. Interim Evaluation: Executive Summary*, GENECON, Leeds, UK

Giddens, A. (1984) *The Constitution of Society: Outline of the Theory of Structuration*, Polity Press, Cambridge, UK

Giuliani, M. V. (1991) 'Towards an analysis of mental representations of attachment to the home', *Journal of Architectural and Planning Research*, vol 8, pp. 133–46

Gonzalez, S. and Healey, P. (2005) 'A sociological institutionalist approach to the study of innovation in governance capacity', *Urban Studies*, vol 42, pp. 2055–70

Goodwin, C. (1994) 'Professional vision', *American Anthropologist*, vol 96, no 3, pp. 606–33

Gordon, D. L. A. (1998) 'Different views from the water's edge', *Town Planning Review*, vol 69, no 1, pp. 91–7

Gospodini, A. (2002) 'European cities in competition and the new "uses" of urban design', *Journal of Urban Design*, vol 7, no 1, pp. 59–73

Greenspace Scotland and Project for Public Spaces (2006) *Placemaking Scotland: How to turn a place around – Scottish seminar series notes*, Greenspace Scotland and Project for Public Spaces, Stirling, UK

Guardia, J., and Pol, E. (2002) 'A critical study of theoretical models of sustainability through structural equation systems', *Environment and Behavior*, vol 34, pp. 137–49

HafenCity Hamburg (2008) *HafenCity Hamburg: Projects – Insights Into Current Developments*, HafenCity Hamburg GmbH, Hamburg

HafenCity Hamburg (2010) *HafenCity Hamburg: Projects – Insights Into Current Developments*, October, HafenCity Hamburg GmbH, Hamburg

Hague, C. and Jenkins, P. (2005) 'Background to place identity, participation and planning in Europe', in C. Hague and P. Jenkins (eds) *Place Identity, Participation and Planning*, Routledge, London and New York, NY

Hall, P. (2002) 'The creativity of cities. An idea whose time has come', in Ministry of Housing, Spatial Planning and the Environment (ed) *Generating Culture: Roots and Fruits*, Ministry of Housing, Spatial Planning and the Environment, The Hague, The Netherlands

Hall, P. A. and Taylor, R. C. R. (1996) 'Political science and the three new institutionalisms', *Political Studies*, vol XLIV, pp. 936–57

Hansen, A., Andersen, H. and Clark, E. (2001) 'Creative Copenhagen: Globalization, urban governance and social change', *European Planning Studies*, vol 9, no 7, pp. 851–69

Harms, H. (2003) 'Long term economic cycles and the relationship between port and city: The case of Hamburg', in M. Carmona (ed) *Globalization and City Ports: The Response of City Ports in the Northern Hemisphere*, Delft University Press, Delft, The Netherlands

Harnow, H. (2004) *Odense Docklands and Canal: The City's Gateway to the World*, Odense City Museums, Odense, Denmark

Harvey, D. (1989) *Condition of Postmodernity: An Enquiry into the Origins of Cultural Change*, Blackwell Publishers, Oxford, UK

Healey, P. (1996) 'The communicative turn in spatial planning theory and its implications for spatial strategy formulation', *Environment and Planning B: Planning and Design*, vol 23, pp. 217–34

Healey, P. (1997) *Collaborative Planning: Shaping Places in Fragmented Societies*, Macmillan, London

Healey, P. (1999) 'Institutionalist analysis, communicative planning and shaping places', *Journal of Planning Education and Research*, vol 19, pp. 111–22

Healey, P. (2007) *Urban Complexity and Spatial Strategies: Towards a Relational Planning for Our Times*, Routledge, Abingdon, UK, and New York, NY

Hernández, B., Hidalgo, M. C., Salazar-Laplace, M. E. and Hess, S. (2007) 'Place attachment and place identity in natives and non-natives', *Journal of Environmental Psychology*, vol 27, pp. 310–19

Histon, V. (2006) *Unlocking the Quayside: Newcastle Gateshead's Historic Waterfront Explored*, Tyne Bridge Publishing, Newcastle upon Tyne, UK

Home, R. (2009) 'Land ownership in the United Kingdom: Trends, preferences and future challenges', *Land Use Policy*, vol 26S, pp. 103–08

Hoyle, B. S. (ed) (1996) *Cityports, Coastal Zones and Regional Change*, Wiley, Chichester, UK

Hoyle, B. S., Pinder, D. A. and Husain, M. S. (1988) *Revitalising the Waterfront: International Dimensions of Dockland Development*, Belhaven, London

Hoyman, M. and Faricy, C. (2009) 'It takes a village: A test of the creative class, social capital, and human capital theories', *Urban Affairs Review*, vol 44, pp. 311–34

Huygen, A., Fortuin, K. and Wentink, M. (2003) *Betekenisprofiel Stationsplein Zuidzijde Station Schiedam Centrum [Significance Profile for Station Forecourt South, Schiedam Centrum Station]*, Verwey-Jonker Institute, Utrecht, The Netherlands

Jacobs, J. (1961) *The Death and Life of Great American Cities*, Random House, New York, NY

Jenkins, P. (2005) 'Space, place and territory: an analytical framework', in C. Hague and P. Jenkins (eds) *Place Identity, Participation and Planning*, Routledge, London and New York

Jenkins, P. and Smith, H. (2001) 'The state, the market and community: An analytical framework for community self-development', in M. Carley, P. Jenkins and H. Smith (eds) *Urban Development and Civil Society: The Role of Communities in Sustainable Cities*, Earthscan, London and Sterling, VA

Jenkins, P., Smith, H. and Wang, Y. P. (2007) *Planning and Housing in the Rapidly Urbanising World*, Routledge, London and New York, NY

Jensen, O. B. and Hovgensen, H. H. (2004) *Broerne i vore hoveder: Om forestillede og reelle broer mellem Aalborg og Nørresundby*, Department of Development and Planning, Department Working Paper Series no 296, Aalborg University, Aalborg, Denmark

Johnson, J. and Curran, P. (2003) 'Gateshead Millennium Bridge – an eye-opener for engineering', *Proceedings of ICE, Civil Engineering*, vol 156, pp. 16–24

Kaiser, F. G. and Fuhrer, U. (1996) 'Dwelling: Speaking of an unnoticed universal language', *New Ideas in Psychology*, vol 14, pp. 225–36

Karyotis, S., Tudjman, T., Masson, K. and de Jong, W. (2005) *Jeugd en Buitenruimte in Rotterdam: Het Thuis op Straat Project [Youth and Outdoor Space in Rotterdam: At Home on the Street Project]*, RISBO, Rotterdam, The Netherlands

Keenleyside, C., Baldock, D., Hjerp, P. and Swales, V. (2009) 'International perspectives on future land use', *Land Use Policy*, vol 26S, pp. 14–29

Kiib, H. (2004) 'The consumption landscape of the welfare city/Velfærdsbyens Konsumlandskaber', in H. Kiib, G. Marling, O. M. Jensen, and C. Beck-Danielsen (eds) *Urban Lifescape: Space, Lifestyle, Consumption*, Aalborg University Press, Aalborg, Denmark

Kiib, H. (2007) *Harbourscape*, Aalborg University Press, Aalborg, Denmark

Kiib, H. (2009) *Architecture and Spaces of the Experience City*, Aalborg University, Aalborg, Denmark

Københavns Havn (1999) *Vision-Plan 2010: Studies and Visions of Copenhagen Harbour*, City of Copenhagen, Copenhagen, Denmark

Københavns Havn (2001) *Water City*, City of Copenhagen and the Port of Copenhagen, Copenhagen, Denmark

Københavns Havn (2005) *Blue Plan 2005*, City of Copenhagen, Copenhagen, Denmark

Korpela, K. M. (1989) 'Place-identity as a product of environment self-regulation', *Journal of Environmental Psychology*, vol 9, pp. 241–56

Korpela, K. M., Hartig, T., Kaiser, F. G. and Fuhrer, U. (2001) 'Restorative experience and self-regulation in favorite places', *Environment and Behavior*, vol 33, pp. 572–89

Kreutz, S. (2007) 'The model of neighbourhood improvement districts in Hamburg: New strategies for private sector involvement in area development', *10th Conference of the European Urban Research Association 'The Vital City'*, 12–14 September, Glasgow, Scotland

Kreutz, S. (2009) 'Urban improvement districts in Germany: New legal instruments for joint proprietor activities in area development', *Journal of Urban Regeneration and Renewal*, vol 2, no 4, pp. 304–17

Kreutz, S. (2010) *Case Study Report: NID Steilshoop*, Unpublished paper for the Transnational Assessment of Practice, Interreg IVB Project 'Making Places Profitable: Public and Private Open Spaces (MP4)', HafenCity Universität, Hamburg (www.mp4-interreg.eu/cmsFiles/Neighbourhood%20Improvement%20DistrictSteilshoop%20Hamburg.pdf)

Kreutz, S. (2011) 'BID experience Hamburg', Unpublished paper for the Peer Review of Model Agreements for Place-Keeping, Interreg IVB Project 'Making Places Profitable: Public and Private Open Spaces (MP4)', HafenCity Universität, Hamburg

Kreutz, S. (undated) *Case Study Report: HafenCity Hamburg*, Unpublished paper for the Transnational Assessment of Practice, Interreg IVB Project 'Making Places Profitable: Public and Private Open Spaces (MP4)', HafenCity Universität, Hamburg (http://mp4-interreg.eu/cmsFiles/Reinventing%20HafenCity%20Hamburg.pdf)

Krüger, T. (2009) 'HafenCity Hamburg – ein Modell für moderne Stadtentwicklung?', *RaumPlanung*, vol 146, pp. 193–98 (www.hcu-hamburg.de/fileadmin/documents/Professoren_und_Mitarbeiter/Projektentwicklung–management/Publikationen/Krueger_2009_HafenCity_Hamburg–ein_Modell_monitor_RAUMPLANUNG_146.pdf)

Landry, C. (2000) *The Creative City: A Toolkit for Urban Innovators*, Earthscan, London

Landry, C. (2006) *The Art of City-Making*, Earthscan, London

Latour, B. (2005) *Reassembling the Social: An Introduction to Actor-Network Theory*, Oxford University Press, New York, NY

Lewicka, M. (2005) 'Ways to make people active: Role of place attachment, cultural capital and neighborhood ties', *Journal of Environmental Psychology*, vol 4, pp. 381–95

Lewicka, M. (2008) 'Place attachment, place identity, and place memory: Restoring the forgotten city past', *Journal of Environmental Psychology*, vol 28, pp. 209–31

Llewelyn-Davies (2000) *Urban Design Compendium*, English Partnerships and The Housing Corporation, London

Madanipour, A. (1996) *Design of Urban Space: An Inquiry into a Socio-Spatial Process*, Wiley, Chichester, UK

Malmö Municipality (1999) *Quality Management Programme for Bo01*, Malmö Municipality, Malmö, Sweden

Malone, P. (ed) (1996) *City, Capital and Water*, Routledge, London

Marling, G. and Kiib, M. (2007) 'Designing public domain in the multicultural experience city', in H. Kiib (ed) *Harbourscape*, Aalborg University Press, Aalborg, Denmark

Marshall, R. (ed) (2001) *Waterfronts in Post-Industrial Cities*, E & FN Spon Press, London and New York, NY

McLoughlin, B. J. (1994) 'Centre or periphery? Town planning and spatial political economy', *Environment and Planning A*, vol 26, pp. 1111–22

Millspaugh, M. L. (2001) 'Waterfronts as catalysts for city renewal', in R. Marshall (ed) *Waterfronts in Post-Industrial Cities*, Spon Press, London and New York, NY

Minton, A. (2003) *Northern Soul: Culture, Creativity and Quality of Place in Newcastle and Gateshead*, RICS/Demos, London

Minton, A. (2009) *Ground Control: Fear and Happiness in the Twenty-First-Century City*, Penguin Books, London

Moulaert, F., Swyngedouw, E. and Rodriguez, A. (2003) *The Globalised City,* Oxford University Press, Oxford, UK

Muxi, Z. (2004) *La Arquitectura de la Ciudad Global*, Barcelona, Gustavo Gili, Barcelona, Spain

Newman, P. and Thornley, A. (2006) *Urban Planning in Europe*, Routledge, London

Notteboom, T. and Rodrigue, J.P. (2005) 'Port regionalization: Towards a new phase in port development', *Maritime Policy and Management*, vol 32, no 3, pp. 297–313

Novy, J. and Colomb, C. (2011) 'Struggling for the right to the (creative) city in Berlin and Hamburg: New urban social movements, new "spaces of hope"?', Paper presented at the International RC21 conference 2011, *The Struggle to Belong: Dealing with Diversity in 21st Century Urban Settings*, Amsterdam 7–9 July (extended abstract available at www.rc21.org/conferences/amsterdam2011/edocs2/ Session%2018/18{ndash}2-Novy.pdf, accessed 18 July 2011)

Odense Municipality (2006) *Vision for Odense: Havnen i Odense – ny levende bydel ved vandet*, Leaflet, Odense Municipality, Odense, Denmark

Öhrström, B. (2005) *Urban Processes and Global Competition: Enabling Factors for Mutual Urban Economic Development at Norra Älvstranden in Göteborg*, Chalmers University of Technology, Gothenburg, Sweden

Olshammar, G. (2002) *Det permanenta provisoriet: Ett återanvänt industriområde i väntan på rivning eller erkännande*, Chalmers Tekniska Högskola, Gothenburg, Sweden

Olsson, M. and Rosberg, G. (2005) 'Malmø', *Arkitektur DK Magazine*, Denmark

Peck, J. (2005) 'Struggling with the creative class', *International Journal of Urban and Regional Research,* vol 29, no 4, pp. 740–70

Pine, B. J. II and Gilmore, J. H. (1999) *The Experience Economy: Work Is Theatre and Every Business a Stage*, Harvard Business School Press, Boston, MA

Proshansky, H. M. (1978) 'The city and self-identity', *Environment and Behavior*, vol 10, pp. 147–69

Richter-Friis van Deurs, C. (2010) *Uderum Udeliv: Udformning og brug af udearealer i nyere dansk boligbyggeri*, PhD thesis, Kunstakademiets Arkitektskole (The Royal Danish Academy of Fine Arts, School of Architecture), Copenhagen, Denmark

Ristilammi, P. M. (1994) *Rosengård och den svarta poesin: En studie av modern annorlundahet*, Symposium, Lund, Sweden

RMJM, NG1 and Gateshead Council (2010) *Gateshead Quays: Masterplan Summary*, Gateshead Council, Gateshead, UK

Robertson, R. (2003) *The Three Waves of Globalisation: A History of a Developing Global Consciousness*, Zed Books, London

Rykwert, J. (2000) *The Seduction of Place: The History and Future of the City*, Oxford University Press, Oxford, UK

Sandercock, L. (1988) 'The death of modernist planning: Radical praxis for a postmodern age', in M. Douglass and J. Friedmann (eds) *Cities for Citizens: Planning and the Rise of Civil Society in a Global Age*, John Wiley and Sons, Chichester, UK

Sandercock, L. (2003) 'Out of the closet: The importance of stories and storytelling in planning practice', *Planning Theory and Practice*, vol 4, no 1, pp. 11–28

Schmid, C. U. and Hertel, C. (2005) *Real Property Law and Procedure in the European Union: General Report*, European University Institute (EUI), Florence/European Private Law Forum and Deutsches Notarinstitut (DNotI), Würzburg

Schön, D. and Rhein, M. (1994) *Frame Reflection: Towards the Resolution of Intractable Policy Controversies*, Basic Books, New York, NY

Schubert, D. (2011) 'Waterfront revitalizations: From a local to a regional perspective in London, Barcelona, Rotterdam and Hamburg', in G. Desfor, J. Laidley, Q. Stevens and D. Schubert (eds) *Transforming Urban Waterfronts: Fixity and Flow*, Routledge, New York and London

Shaw, B. (2001) 'History at the water's edge', in R. Marshall (ed) *Waterfronts in Post-Industrial Cities*, Spon Press, London

Sica, P. (1980) *Historia del Urbanismo. El Siglo XIX*, second edition, Instituto de Estudios de Administración Local, Madrid, Spain

Sklair, L. (2006) 'Iconic architecture and capitalist globalization', *City*, vol 10, no 1, pp. 21–47

Smith, H. (2005) 'Place identity and participation', in C. Hague and P. Jenkins (eds) *Place Identity, Participation and Planning*, Routledge, London and New York

Soja, E. (2000) *Postmetropolis: Critical Studies of Cities and Regions*, Blackwell Publishers, Malden, MA, Oxford, UK, and Carlton, Australia

Stadsbyggnadskontoret (2006) *Utvärdering av Dialog Södra Älvstranden*, Stadsbyggnadskontoret (City Planning Office), Gothenburg, Sweden

Stedman, R. (2002) 'Toward a social psychology of place: Predicting behavior from place-based cognitions, attitude, and identity', *Environment and Behavior*, vol 34, no 5, pp. 561–81

Stedman, R. C. (2003) 'Is it really just a social construction? The contribution of the physical environment to sense of place', *Society and Natural Resources*, vol 16, no 8, pp. 671–85

Stock, K. and Tummers, L. (2010) 'Contemporary tools of urban development – oriented on equity?', in M. Schrenk, V. V. Popovich and P. Zeile (eds) *REAL CORP 2010 Proceedings: Cities for Everyone: Liveable, healthy, Prosperous*, Vienna, 18–20 May, pp. 141–54

Strömberg, K. (2001) 'Facilitating collaborative decision development in urban planning', Themed issue on 'Tools for interaction in urban planning', *Scandinavian Journal of Architectural Research*, vol 4, pp. 61–74

Strömberg, K. (2008) 'Urban design and development in the Swedish tradition', in T. Haas (ed) *New Urbanism and Beyond*, Rizzoli, New York, NY

Strömberg, K. and Kain, J. H. (2005) 'Communicative learning, democracy and effectiveness: Facilitating private–public decision-making in Sweden', in J. K. Friend and A. Hickling (eds) *Planning under Pressure: The Strategic Choice Approach*, Elsevier, Oxford, UK

Stuart-Murray, J. (2005) 'Landscape, topography and hydrology', in B. Edwards and P. Jenkins (eds) *Edinburgh: The Making of a Capital City*, Edinburgh University Press, Edinburgh

United Nations (2004) *World Urbanization Prospects: 2003 Revision*, United Nations, New York, NY

Urry, J. (1995) *Consuming Places*, Routledge, London

Verma, N. (ed) (2006) *Planning and Institutions*, Elsevier, Oxford, UK

Vorkinn, M. and Riese, H. (2001) 'Environmental concern in a local context: The significance of place attachment', *Environment and Behavior*, vol 33, no 2, pp. 249–63

Walter, E. V. (1988) *Placeways: A Theory of the Human Environment*, University of North Carolina Press, Chapel Hill, NC

Whyte, W. (1988) *City: Rediscovering the Center*, University of Pennsylvania Press, Philadelphia, PA

Whyte, W. F. (ed) (1991) *Participatory Action Research*, Sage, Newsbury Park, CA

WRR (2005) *Vertrouwen in de Buurt* [*Trust in the Neighbourhood*], WRR, Amsterdam University Press, The Hague and Amsterdam

Youngson, A. J. (1966) *The Making of Classical Edinburgh*, Edinburgh University Press, Edinburgh

Zandbelt & vandenBerg, (2005) *Big and Beautiful: Comparing Stadshavens in Europe*, Stadshavens Rotterdam and Zandbelt & vandenBerg, Rotterdam

Zukin, S. (1991) 'Post-modern landscapes: Mapping culture and power', in S. Lash and J. Friedman (eds) *Modernity and Identity,* Blackwell Publishers, Oxford, UK

Index

Note: Page numbers in **bold** indicate figures; Page numbers in *italics* indicate tables.